More praise for *The Terr*

Named one of *Slate*'s best books of 2007

"Disturbing and persuasive—it is based upon a thoroughly considered view, one that has taken into account not only historical precedent but the actual circumstances in which the Bush administration was making its decisions. . . . a subtle and judicious appraisal."
                                                    —*Commentary*

"Goldsmith . . . makes a strong case that our national security apparatus is overlawyered."
                        —Michael Barone, *U.S. News & World Report*

"The record of Bush and his lawyers on torture is grippingly examined . . . one of the most interesting and most insightful books yet to come out of the Bush White House."
                                                    —*Chicago Tribune*

"Goldsmith is one of those rare legal scholars who write with unforced clarity. . . . His arguments are clear, formidable and authoritative. . . . . On the long shelf of books written from inside President George W. Bush's administration, none is more fundamentally significant, nor as challenging to the preconceptions of left and right, as Jack Goldsmith's *The Terror Presidency*."
                                                    —*Los Angeles Times*

"The record of Bush and his lawyers on torture—is grippingly examined by Jack Goldsmith. . . . Goldsmith's arguments are the more convincing because they are not premised on traditional liberal or civil libertarian views." —*New York Times Book Review*

"Goldsmith ... provides ... a welcome insider's analysis of policy discussions and legal interpretations after the attacks of Sept. 11, 2001." ⋅ —*National Law Journal*

"*The Terror Presidency* is the most gripping and revealing book about the pathology of this White House I have read."
—*Financial Times*

"Illuminating. . . . valuable account . . . a compelling case . . . Goldsmith argues convincingly that the administration could have cured its legal problems and simultaneously met its security needs if it had worked more cooperatively and openly with the Congress and with others right from the start."
—David Gergen, Director of the Center for
Public Leadership at the Kennedy School
of Government at Harvard, *Boston Sunday Globe*

"[*The Terror Presidency*] details an extraordinary story—that of a conservative lawyer who found himself saying no to the president of the United States on some of the nation's key intelligence programs in the midst of a war."
—Benjamin Wittes, member of the Hoover Institution
Task Force on National Security and Law, *New Republic*

"A careful and thoughtful book." —*American Spectator*

"[*The Terror Presidency*] is superb—deceptively casual and eminently readable, yet profoundly considered and argued. . . . [It] reaches beyond personal memoir to offer a historical comparison of the legal powers available to Presidents in time of war and emergency." —*Times Literary Supplement* (UK)

"This is not the only book about the inner workings of the Bush administration. . . . But for lawyers, it surely will be the most fascinating. . . . A sobering revelation of how Bush lawyers stretched and bent the law in an effort to aggrandize presidential power." —*New York Law Journal*

"Goldsmith's book is more interesting . . . because of what it reveals, at times unintentionally, about the inner workings of the administration." —*American Prospect*

"*The Terror Presidency* . . . will prove valuable beyond the Bush administration." —*Federal Lawyer*

"[This] book is a brisk, well-written, and earnest attempt to deal with some of the knottiest legal problems confronting modern presidents during war-time. . . . No thoughtful reader can come away from [*The Terror Presidency*] uninstructed." —*Claremont Review of Books*

The
Terror
Presidency

ALSO BY JACK GOLDSMITH

Who Controls the Internet? Illusions of a Borderless World (with Tim Wu)

The Limits of International Law (with Eric Posner)

The
Terror
Presidency

LAW AND JUDGMENT INSIDE THE
BUSH ADMINISTRATION

Jack Goldsmith

W. W. NORTON & COMPANY

New York London

For information about permission to reproduce selections from this book,
write to Permissions, W. W. Norton & Company, Inc.,
500 Fifth Avenue, New York, NY 10110

For information about special discounts for bulk purchases, please contact
W. W. Norton Special Sales at specialsales@wwnorton.com or 800-233-4830

Manufacturing by RR Donnelley, Bloomsburg
Book design by Chris Welch Design
Production managers: Andrew Marasia and Sue Carlson

Library of Congress Cataloging-in-Publication Data

Goldsmith, Jack L.
The terror presidency : law and judgment inside the Bush
administration / Jack Goldsmith.
p. cm.
Includes bibliographical references and index.
ISBN 978-0-393-06550-3 (hardcover)
1. War and emergency powers—United States.
2. Rule of law—United States. 3. Bush, George W.
(George Walker), 1946– 4. Misconduct in office—United States.
5. United States. Dept. of Justice. Office of Legal Counsel
6. Executive power—United States. 7. War on Terrorism, 2001–
8. Human rights—United States. I. Title.
KF5060.G65 2007
342.73'062—dc22

2007034337

ISBN 978-0-393-33533-0 pbk.

W. W. Norton & Company, Inc.
500 Fifth Avenue, New York, N.Y. 10110
www.wwnorton.com

W. W. Norton & Company Ltd.
Castle House, 75/76 Wells Street, London W1T 3QT

1 2 3 4 5 6 7 8 9 0

TO MY PERSON

That comprehensive and undefined presidential
powers hold both practical advantages and grave dangers for
the country will impress anyone who has served as
legal adviser to a President in time of transition
and public anxiety.

—*Associate Justice and former Attorney General Robert Jackson, concurring
in* Youngstown Sheet & Tube Co. v. Sawyer, *343 U.S. 579 (1952).*

CONTENTS

PREFACE

I t is customary for senior officials in the Department of Justice to hang portraits of former Attorneys General in their office. I qualified for the portrait privilege as the head of the Justice Department's Office of Legal Counsel (OLC), a job I held from the fall of 2003 until I resigned, less than ten months later, in July of 2004. Though little known outside the government, OLC holds an exalted status within it as the chief advisor to the President and the Attorney General about the legality of presidential actions. This small office of twenty-two lawyers determines whether the government's most important and sensitive plans are lawful, and thus whether they can be implemented.

When I came to OLC three years into President Bush's first term, the most popular Attorney General portraits had been taken. On the wall across from my desk in my OLC office hung a painting that no one else wanted: that of Elliot Richardson, Richard Nixon's third Attorney General. Richardson was a distinguished lawyer who served as Attorney General for five months before resigning as part of Watergate's "Saturday Night Massacre." On Saturday, October 20, 1973, Nixon ordered Richardson to fire Watergate Special Prosecutor Archibald Cox, who had subpoenaed Nixon for tapes of conversations made in the Oval Office. But Richardson had promised the Senate during his confirmation hearings that he would "not countermand, nor interfere with the special prosecutor's decisions." So he told Nixon that he would quit rather than carry out his order. "I'm sorry that you insist on putting your personal commitments ahead of the public interest," Nixon angrily told Richardson in the Oval Office. "I can only say that I believe my resignation *is* in the public interest," Richardson responded, during his last meeting ever with Nixon.[1]

At first, I paid little attention to the beady stare from behind the oversized eyeglasses in Richardson's portrait. Two months into my job, however, I had thought a lot about the sixty-ninth Attorney General. During those eight weeks, I was briefed on some of the most sensitive counterterrorism operations in the government. Each of these operations was supported by OLC opinions written by my predecessors. As I absorbed the opinions, I concluded that some were deeply flawed: sloppily reasoned, overbroad, and incautious in asserting extraordinary constitutional authorities on behalf of the President. I was astonished, and immensely worried, to discover that some of our most important counterterrorism policies rested on severely damaged legal foundations. It began to dawn on me that I could not—as I thought I would eventually be asked to do—stand by or reaffirm these opinions.

My first reaction to the opinions was to draft a resignation letter—the first of three such letters I would draft during my nine and a half months of service. I did so mainly because I didn't think the

White House or the Attorney General would appreciate the new OLC boss questioning the legal framework for their important counterterrorism work of the past two years. I also worried, more selfishly, that dirtying my hands with this mess would stain my professional reputation no matter how I acted. But I soon realized I could not quit. We were in the midst of a war in which many had lost their lives and scores had risked professional reputations by making thorny wartime decisions. I had knowingly taken a difficult job at a difficult time, and had promised to uphold the laws of the United States. I couldn't just run away at the first sign of trouble. So I decided to try to fix the opinions to save as many of the policies that a sound legal analysis would support. I was pretty sure, in December 2003, that this decision would put me on a collision course with my superiors. But I figured it was more consistent with my oath of office and professional responsibilities, and that my superiors would let me know when I should leave.

Seven months and many confrontations later, I was gone. This book is about what I learned in my short time as the head of OLC, what I wish I had known when I began the job, and what my reflections have taught me since I resigned in the summer of 2004. It is also about the unprecedented and still-unappreciated challenges that Islamist terrorists pose to the institution of the presidency. Everyone in the administration with access to highly classified intelligence on threats to the homeland was scared of another deadly attack, and of not knowing how to prevent it. This fear created enormous pressure to stretch the law to its limits in order to give the President the powers he thought necessary to prevent a second 9/11. Such pressures are not new. Some of our greatest presidents—including Thomas Jefferson, Abraham Lincoln, and

Franklin D. Roosevelt—bent the law in times of crisis. But unlike these other presidents, President Bush acted in an era in which many aspects of presidential war power had become encumbered by elaborate criminal restrictions, and in which government officials seriously worried that their heat-of-battle judgment calls would result in prosecution by independent counsels, Justice Departments of future administrations, or foreign or international courts.

These twin pressures—fear of not doing enough to stop the next attack, and an equally present fear of doing too much and ending up before a court or grand jury—lie behind the Bush administration's controversial legal policy decisions about the Terrorist Surveillance Program, the Geneva Conventions, military commissions, interrogation techniques, Guantanamo Bay, and more. In defending some of these decisions and criticizing others, this book examines the surprisingly central and sometimes unfortunate role that lawyers played in determining counterterrorism policy. It also tries to give a sympathetic account of the unusual psychological pressures on executive branch officials who are personally responsible for preventing hard-to-fathom terrorist attacks that could kill thousands. And it seeks to put the Bush administration's responses to these pressures in historical perspective, comparing the first presidency in the post-9/11 era with other crisis presidencies, especially those of Franklin D. Roosevelt and Abraham Lincoln.

I cannot speak about many of my experiences in government. Much of what I learned must remain hidden behind thick walls of classified information, and cannot be written about for years, if ever. Despite this limitation, I believe I can illuminate important themes, debates, and pathologies that have dominated the executive branch since 9/11 and that will continue to dominate it for the foreseeable future. In doing so, this book follows in a long tra-. dition of Justice Department officials and other executive branch lawyers who have felt it important for the American people to understand how and why critical decisions were made during their service in government.[2]

The
Terror
Presidency

CHAPTER 1

The New Job

The Robert F. Kennedy Department of Justice Building occupies the entire block between Pennsylvania and Constitution avenues, about halfway between the White House and Congress. If you enter through one of the ornate twenty-foot aluminum doors to the six-story, million-square-foot limestone building and take one of its twenty-five elevators to the fifth floor, you will reach the power center of the Justice Department, home of the Attorney General, the Solicitor General (the government's lawyer before the Supreme Court), and the head of the Office of Legal Counsel.[1]

This is where I found myself on Monday, October 6, 2003, in a hastily organized ceremony in Attorney General John Ashcroft's fifth-floor conference room. With my wife, two young sons, and a handful of Justice Department friends looking on, Ashcroft asked me to swear on the large black Bible in his hand to "support and defend the Constitution of the United States against all enemies, foreign and domestic." After I did so, I became the twenty-fifth "Assistant Attorney General, Office of Legal Counsel."

The office suites of the Attorney General and the head of OLC are traditionally adjacent to one another and mutually accessible through a narrow back corridor, symbolizing their close working relationship. When my brief swearing-in ceremony ended, however, I did not go to the office suite adjacent to the Attorney General's. In 1993, Associate Attorney General Webster Hubbell, the Clintons' close friend and the number-three person in the department, occupied the prestigious suite next to the Attorney General's, and moved OLC down the hall, fifty yards away.[2]

This arrangement persisted throughout the Clinton years, and when John Ashcroft became Attorney General, he gave the traditional OLC offices to David Ayres, his Chief of Staff. Ayres was not a lawyer. He was a political consultant who had spent thirteen years on Capitol Hill, the last six as Senator Ashcroft's campaign manager, Chief of Staff, and loyal aide. In the two years before I arrived at the department, Ayres developed a public reputation as Ashcroft's "political bodyguard" who inserted himself in Justice Department legal policy decisions to ensure that they reflected a pro-Ashcroft political spin.[3] Ayres was also believed to limit lawyers' access to the Attorney General. The head of OLC traditionally had legal briefings with the Attorney General many times each week, and usually every day. But my predecessor, Jay Bybee, advised Ashcroft in person only a handful of times during his eighteen months in office.

In Washington, geography is one of the currencies of power. The traditional proximity of OLC and the Attorney General's office reflected OLC's influence and prestige within the department, and confirmed its reputation as "the Attorney General's lawyer."[4] As I was preparing for my confirmation hearings in the early summer of 2003, I spoke to former OLC officials about the job. Those who had heard about Ayres occupying the traditional OLC suite expressed astonishment and even bitterness about it. It was bad enough for the Clinton administration to give the space to a close personal friend of the President, even if he was an attorney and technically higher in rank in the department. It seemed much worse for a Republican Attorney General to give the space to a political consultant with no law degree, something the former OLC officials interpreted as evidence that OLC's "glory days" were over and, more ominously, as a sign that law in the Department of Justice had taken a backseat to politics.[5]

These forebodings did little to dampen my enthusiasm for the new job on that first Monday in October. I didn't much care that my office was fifty rather than ten yards away from the Attorney General's office. I was serving my country in time of war in one of the most important legal jobs in the government. I was working with many of the brightest lawyers in the executive branch. And a good deal of my time would involve crafting answers to the hard legal questions sparked by the war on terrorism—a topic at the core of my academic interest and expertise.

IN MANY RESPECTS, I was an improbable choice to lead the Bush administration's OLC. I was born in 1962 in Memphis, Tennessee. My mother was a former Miss Teenage Arkansas whose parents ran a famous nightclub across the Mississippi River in West Memphis, Arkansas. My father, who came from a prominent family in Memphis, blew through his trust fund at an early age, married and divorced my mom twice, and spent the rest of his life selling cars and fishing. I had two stepfathers—one a neurosurgeon in Lafayette, Louisiana, and the other a mob-connected Teamsters executive named Chuck O'Brien who was Jimmy Hoffa's right-hand man and for decades a leading suspect in Hoffa's disappearance. I attended college at Washington and Lee University and did a grandfather-sponsored two-year stint at Oxford. I then went to Yale Law School, where I entered without views on the law but emerged a conservative of sorts after an allergic reaction to Yale's political correctness and left-wing jurisprudence. After clerking for J. Harvie Wilkinson, a conservative federal appellate judge, and Supreme Court Justice Anthony Kennedy, I practiced law in a large Washington, D.C., firm before becoming a law professor.

Academic credentials are not enough to get the top spot in OLC. My Republican predecessors include two Supreme Court Justices (William Rehnquist and Antonin Scalia), President George H. W. Bush's Attorney General (William Barr), and other conservative icons like Theodore Olson and Michael Luttig. This lineage makes the head of OLC one of the most sought-after legal jobs in lawyer-laden Washington, D.C. And yet I lacked the usual political credentials for the job. I was conservative. But I didn't know any Republican Party politicians. I had never given money to a Republican candidate or to the party. I hadn't joined the legions of Republican lawyers who went to Florida to help out with *Bush v. Gore*. I hadn't even sought the OLC job.

A year earlier, in the spring of 2002, the Pentagon's top lawyer, Jim Haynes, convinced me to take a leave of absence from the University of Chicago Law School, where I was a professor, to work for him in the Department of Defense. Haynes heard about me from (among others) John Yoo, a friend and fellow legal academic at the University of California's law school at Berkeley who worked closely with Haynes on war-related issues from his perch as a deputy (the number two) in OLC. Yoo and I were part of a group of conservative intellectuals—dubbed "new sovereigntists" in *Foreign Affairs* magazine—who were skeptical about the creeping influence of international law on American law.[6] My academic objections to this trend were based on the need for democratic control over the norms that governed American conduct. My scholarship argued against the judicial activism that gave birth to international human rights lawsuits in U.S. courts. It decried developments in "customary international law" that purported to bind the United States to international rules to which the nation's political leaders had not consented. And it defended, on grounds of democratic legitimacy and national self-interest, the United States' refusal to enter into treaties like the Rome Statute establishing the International Criminal Court and the Kyoto Protocol regulating greenhouse gas emissions.

Haynes shared these attitudes. He also liked the op-eds and articles I had written supportive of military commissions. And he thought I could help him work through the array of novel issues that the Department of Defense faced after 9/11. So he offered me a position as his "Special Counsel," and in September of 2002 my wife, young son, and I moved to a small apartment in Alexandria, Virginia.

During my time at the Defense Department, Haynes gave me an endless stream of fascinating legal problems related to missile defense, Guantanamo detentions, military commissions, the Iraq invasion and occupation, the United Nations, and much more. I liked the work, and I learned a lot. But I had no ambitions beyond my relatively anonymous Defense Department job. In March of 2003, after seven months at the Pentagon, I told Haynes that I would leave the department that summer and return to academia. My wife was expecting our second child, and we had decided to move from the University of Chicago to the University of Virginia, closer to her family in North Carolina.

Around this time, Jay Bybee resigned as head of OLC to become a federal judge in Nevada. The White House's first choice to replace Bybee was John Yoo, who had come to OLC in June of 2001. Yoo was an expert in presidential war powers, but during his first few months on the job this topic was in little demand. Beginning on September 11, 2001, however, he suddenly became one of the most important lawyers in the government, a member of a secretive five-person group with enormous influence over the administration's antiterrorism policies.

The "War Council," as the group called itself, included the White House Counsel, Alberto Gonzales; the Vice President's Counsel, David Addington; Haynes; Gonzales's first deputy (and former OLC head under George H. W. Bush), Tim Flanigan; and Yoo. The War Council met every few weeks, either in Gonzales's White House office or behind closed doors in Haynes's Defense Department office. It would plot legal strategy in the war on terrorism, sometimes as a prelude to dealing with lawyers from the State Department, the National Security Council, and the Joint Chiefs of Staff who would ordinarily be involved in war-related interagency legal decisions, and sometimes to the exclusion of the interagency process altogether. The War Council also excluded Yoo's OLC boss, Jay Bybee. Bybee did not come to

OLC until several months after the 9/11 attacks. He had little expertise in war-related issues. The White House nominated Bybee to the federal bench soon after he arrived at OLC, and Bybee largely delegated OLC's war-on-terrorism responsibilities to Yoo and another of his deputies, Patrick Philbin.

Yoo played a vital role in the War Council. One of the Bush administration's biggest obstacles in responding to the 9/11 attacks was the vast array of post-Vietnam domestic and international criminal laws that governed many presidential war powers. These laws—concerning electronic surveillance, interrogations, and all manner of detainee treatment and trials—chilled counterintelligence officials from acting as aggressively as the White House believed necessary after 9/11. Yoo was crucial to addressing this problem. Unlike any of the others in the War Council, he was an OLC deputy with authority to issue legal opinions that were binding throughout the executive branch. And so after 9/11, Yoo, in coordination with the War Council and often in conjunction with Philbin (an important OLC lawyer but not a participant in the War Council itself), wrote opinion after opinion approving every aspect of the administration's aggressive antiterrorism efforts. These opinions gave counterterrorism officials the comfort of knowing that they could not easily be prosecuted later for the approved actions.

The opinions made Yoo enormously valuable to the White House after 9/11 and gave him extraordinary influence within the administration. Unfortunately for Yoo, his close working relationship with Gonzales and Addington alienated his Department of Justice boss, John Ashcroft. Ashcroft had uneven relations with the White House, and especially with Gonzales, his rival for influence over legal policy within the administration. Gonzales had been George Bush's lawyer for over a decade and was very close and intensely loyal to the President. He and others in the White House thought Ashcroft sometimes pushed his socially conservative political agenda at the expense of the President's. Ashcroft and Ayres, in turn, distrusted Gonzales, who because of his relationship with the President exercised unusual control over legal policy decisions usually reserved for the Attorney General. Gonzales and Ashcroft often clashed, and Gonzales usually won. He defeated Ashcroft's effort to take a hard-line stand against affirmative action before the Supreme Court; he led the creation of military commissions, which Ashcroft never liked; and he put the brakes on Ashcroft's attempt to implement an aggressive interpretation of gun rights under the Second Amendment.

The fight over Bybee's successor was another battle in this ongoing war. Yoo technically worked under Ashcroft, and his OLC opinions were issued under the authority of the Attorney General. But in practice Yoo worked for Gonzales. Yoo saw Ashcroft much more than Jay Bybee did, but he took his instructions mainly from Gonzales, and he sometimes gave Gonzales opinions and verbal advice without fully running matters by the Attorney General. This arrangement was an understandable affront to Ashcroft, who worried about the advice Yoo was providing in the Attorney General's name. So when the White House wanted to elevate Yoo to lead the office, Ashcroft put his foot down and vetoed Yoo for the job.

Gonzales and Addington realized Yoo's importance to the War Council and the administration's antiterrorism strategy more generally. They wanted to appeal Ashcroft's decision to the one person who could overrule him, the President. But Ashcroft told then-

Chief of Staff Andrew Card that Yoo was not competent to run OLC. It is unclear whether Ashcroft really believed this or whether he said it to kill Yoo's chances for other reasons. But in any event the gambit worked. Card declined to bring the fight to the President, and Ashcroft's veto stood. And suddenly, the War Council needed someone to fill John Yoo's shoes.

Soon after Yoo learned of Card's decision, he phoned me in my office in the Pentagon's D Ring. As he was telling me that Ashcroft had blackballed him and that he had recommended me to the White House for the OLC job, Jim Haynes burst in and asked me to hang up. "I know you're anxious to get back to teaching," he said excitedly, "but I think you're about to be offered an extraordinary opportunity to serve the country." Haynes then said that he had strongly recommended me to the White House for the OLC job, and that I had to take it if offered. As we were talking about what this meant, my phone rang again. It was Gonzales's assistant, asking me to come to the White House immediately.

I hung up the phone, put on my coat, and walked downstairs to the Pentagon Metro stop, where I took the train across the Potomac River and walked three blocks to the White House. I didn't bring anything with me, not even a résumé.

I had been to the White House before, but never to the cramped White House Counsel's suite in the West Wing, next door to Karl Rove's even tinier quarters. One of Gonzales's aides escorted me to the office of David Leitch, Gonzales's deputy, who was sitting at his desk. Leitch was a friendly face; I had known him for years, since we had both clerked for Jay Wilkinson on the court of appeals, and he had always been very kind to me. Sitting in chairs around

Leitch's desk as I entered the room were Gonzales and David Addington. I had met both men briefly before, but I had never had an extended conversation with either. I shook everyone's hand and was settling in on the couch at the opposite end of the room when Leitch kicked off the interview.

"Who's Henry Perritt?" he asked in a slightly accusatory tone.

I had no idea why he was asking me this. "He's the dean of Chicago-Kent law school," I replied. "And a well-known Internet scholar."

"Why did you give eight hundred dollars to his campaign?" Leitch followed up.

My heart sank. One of Leitch's jobs as Deputy White House Counsel was to vet candidates for political appointments. A few years earlier I had given my first, and at that point my only, campaign contribution to Perritt, who at the time was running for a seat in the House of Representatives from the Tenth District of Illinois. Perritt was not a Republican. He was a Democrat. A very liberal Democrat. I explained that Perritt was a friend, and that he had personally asked me to contribute to his campaign.

"Why have you never given money to a Republican?" Leitch continued. "*Are* you a Republican?"

The question seemed aggressive, but I knew that Leitch knew my party affiliation and legal views, and I sensed that he asked the question this way to help me. I responded that I considered myself conservative and a Republican, but that I had never had much interest in politics, and that it had never occurred to me to give money to any campaign until Perritt had asked.

"I'm not going to get this job," I thought to myself as this exchange played out. But then the topic abruptly shifted. Gonzales spoke for the first time, from the corner of the room.

"Jack, my job is to keep the President out of legal trouble," he said. "I rely on the head of OLC to make sure I do that." I nodded my head affirmatively but said nothing. Gonzales then began to ask questions. He wanted to know whether I was an expert on presidential war powers, the laws of war, terrorism, and international law. I assumed that he knew—from Haynes, Yoo, and Leitch—the answers to these questions, or else I wouldn't be in the room. But I assured him nonetheless that I was. I said I had worked on all of these issues for Haynes, and that I had taught them at the University of Chicago and written about them a great deal. I pointed to a book on the shelf that I had given Leitch a few months earlier. It was my coauthored casebook on foreign relations law, the area of law that he was asking me about. Things seemed to be going better now.

After a few more minutes of easy questions from Gonzales, David Addington finally spoke. He was the biggest presence in the room—a large man with large glasses and an imposing salt-and-pepper beard who had been listening to my answers intently. Addington was known throughout the bureaucracy as the best-informed, savviest, and most conservative lawyer in the administration, someone who spoke for and acted with the full backing of the powerful Vice President, and someone who crushed bureaucratic opponents. Haynes had known Addington since the two worked together under Secretary of Defense Richard Cheney in the Bush I administration, and was his close friend. Yoo spoke of Addington in reverential tones as a learned man with deeply conservative views about international law and presidential war powers. Yoo frequently told me stories about Addington slaying the legal wimps in the administration who stood as an obstacle to the President's aggressive antiterrorism policies. When Addington spoke, therefore,

I expected a sharp interrogation by an expert in my field who likely had more conservative views than I did.

"I saw that the Second Circuit cited your *Harvard Law Review* article," he said. He was referring to a recent New York federal court decision that had referenced my academic work in the course of clamping down on international human rights suits in the American legal system. I was surprised that Addington knew about the case, and even more surprised to learn that he knew the details of the arguments in my article. It was amazing that a man of his political status was intimately familiar with this relatively obscure academic debate. But as I would later learn, this was typical Addington. He cared a lot about the growing influence of international law in the U.S. legal system, and he closely followed the cases and scholarship on the issue. All the more impressively, he did this through his own research and without the assistance of staff summaries. For Addington had no staff. He had a single assistant who worked for him one morning each week. Otherwise Addington worked entirely alone.

Addington and I went on to have a congenial discussion about the Bush administration's antiterrorism legal policies. I agreed with and supported most of the policies I was aware of: the administration's critical stance toward the International Criminal Court and, more broadly, its suspicion about the influence of international institutions; the characterization of the conflict with al Qaeda and its affiliates as a "war," and the President's general wartime authority to detain enemy combatants and try them by military commission; the decision to deny al Qaeda and Taliban fighters prisoner-of-war status under the Geneva Conventions; and the legality of the invasion of Iraq the month before.

We did not, however, talk about things I didn't know about at the time, such as the National Security Agency's Terrorist Surveillance Program, or what President Bush would later describe as the CIA's "tough" interrogation regime. Nor did we talk about my disagreements with administration policy—disagreements that Haynes knew about but apparently did not convey to the White House. While I believed the government could detain enemy combatants, I thought it needed more elaborate procedures for identifying and detaining them, and had been working on this issue since I arrived at the Pentagon. I had long argued to Haynes that the administration should embrace rather than resist judicial review of its wartime legal policy decisions. I could not understand why the administration failed to work with a Congress controlled by its own party to put all of its antiterrorism policies on a sounder legal footing. And I had been critical, again only to Haynes, of what I viewed as unnecessarily broad assertions of presidential power in an obscure draft OLC opinion by John Yoo that Haynes had asked me to look at a few months earlier. None of these disagreements came out in my White House interview.

As the increasingly friendly discussion continued, it became clear that my interviewers had made up their minds. Finally Gonzales asked me whether I was interested in the OLC job. I said that I was but that I would have to talk to my wife and think about it for an evening. He then asked whether anything in my past would embarrass the President or stand as an obstacle to my confirmation. The only thing I could think of, I said, was that my stepfather was Jimmy Hoffa's right-hand man and a longtime suspect in Hoffa's disappearance. Everyone's eyes bulged with astonishment, but they quickly concluded—to my surprise—that this should not be a hurdle. These men were desperate for someone competent and loyal to fill Yoo's role, and neither my financial contributions to a liberal Democrat nor my accidental association with the mob would stand in the way.

"Jack, to get this job you have to convince the Attorney General to support you," said Gonzales. "I don't understand why, but Ashcroft doesn't like me, and he will be suspicious of you because your name came from my office." We talked for a bit about friends of mine in the Justice Department who might vouch for me to Ashcroft, and about how I might approach my interview with him. And then Gonzales and Addington rose, shook my hand, and left the room, leaving me to talk to Leitch about the remarkable series of events that had brought me to his office.

After convincing my wife that the OLC job was important enough for us to stay in Washington for a few more years, I found myself two days later standing alone on the fifth floor of the Justice Department building in a small wood-paneled room between the Attorney General's conference room and his office suite.

My subsequent interview with John Ashcroft, David Ayres, and another close aide was tense. Ashcroft was self-deprecating and charming. Ayres seemed grumpy and suspicious. After Ashcroft and I reminisced about the University of Chicago (where he attended law school and where I was still a professor, though on leave), the Attorney General came to the single issue that he and Ayres cared about: keeping the Attorney General in the loop. The two men repeatedly explained how important it was for the head of OLC to clear legal advice with the Attorney General, even—and especially—advice to the White House. I understood that the head of OLC speaks at the behest of the Attorney General, I said, and I assured them that I would not do anything significant without the Attorney General's prior knowledge and approval. I asked for much more access to the Attorney General than Jay Bybee had been given, and they enthusiastically agreed. Ashcroft and Ayres asked me no questions about international law or terrorism or any other questions about my competence for the job, which by that point was reasonably clear. They simply wanted to make sure that I would keep them informed about what I was advising the White House.

After the interview, I had lunch with an old friend, Hew Pate, an Assistant Attorney General in charge of the Antitrust Division who had lobbied Ashcroft's office on my behalf. At a restaurant near the Justice Department, I laughed when Pate gave me a present to congratulate me for what he hoped would be a thumbs-up from the Attorney General on my nomination. It was a DVD of *Being There*, a movie about Chance (played by Peter Sellers), a simple gardener from a cloistered estate who, through a series of improbable accidents and aided by vapid pronouncements mistaken for profound insights, is transformed into a powerful advisor to the President of the United States.

The next day I heard favorably from the Attorney General's office. I received the President's nomination to head OLC a few weeks later, and after an uneventful confirmation hearing and a summer of waiting, I was confirmed by the Senate on October 3, 2003.

THREE DAYS LATER, and a few hours after the Attorney General had sworn me in to office, I received a telephone call from White House Counsel Alberto Gonzales. Gonzales was the overseer of administration legal policies, and would become my most important and demanding client.

"Jack," Gonzales said after cursory congratulations on my new post, "we need you to decide whether the Fourth Geneva Convention protects terrorists in Iraq. We need the answer as soon as possible, no later than the end of the week," he added in his deadpan, nasally Texas drawl.

Gonzales's query about the legal status of terrorists in Iraq was typical OLC fare. Six months after the fall of Baghdad, Baathist remnants and al Qaeda fighters were engaged in increasingly deadly attacks on U.S. soldiers in Iraq, and the White House was worried. My job was to determine how far the U.S. military and the CIA could go in fighting the insurgency, consistent with the law.

It may seem odd that an obscure office of two dozen Justice Department lawyers rather than a court was deciding so momentous a question. But in fact most legal issues of executive branch conduct related to war and intelligence never reach a court, or do so only years after the executive has acted. In these situations, the executive branch determines for itself what the law requires, and whether its actions are legal. In theory, the President himself must construe the law as part of his constitutional duty to "faithfully execute" the law, for he must know what the law requires before he can enforce it. But the President and Congress have always delegated this power to the Attorney General, who has a duty to "give his advice and opinion on questions of law when required by the President of the United States."[7] And since the middle of the twentieth century, an increasingly busy Attorney General has delegated his legal advisory function to OLC.

It is crucial to the proper running of our government that OLC exercise this power wisely, and well. When John Adams used the famous phrase "a government of laws, and not of men" in the Massachusetts Constitution of 1780, he was speaking of the need to separate the legislative, executive, and judicial power, and in particular about the idea that "the executive shall never exercise the legislative and judicial powers, or either of them."[8] When the executive branch acts outside the reach of courts, however, it is both law interpreter and law enforcer, and runs the danger that Adams saw of interpreting the law opportunistically to serve its own ends. There are many other institutions besides courts that can check this tendency, including Congress, the press, and the electorate. But OLC is, and views itself as, the frontline institution responsible for ensuring that the executive branch charged with executing the law is itself bound by law.

The danger, of course, is that OLC lives inside the very political executive branch, is subject to few real rules to guide its actions, and has little or no oversight or public accountability. To ensure that OLC itself does not descend into Adams's nightmare, the office has developed powerful cultural norms about the importance of providing the President with detached, apolitical legal advice, as if OLC were an independent court inside the executive branch. OLC should provide "an accurate and honest appraisal of applicable law, even if that advice will constrain the administration's pursuit of desired policies," according to a group of Clinton administration OLC lawyers.[9] "Being a good legal advisor [to the President] requires that I reach sound legal conclusions, even if sometimes they are not the conclusions that some may deem to be politically preferable," echoes William Barr, who was the head of OLC and later the Attorney General under Bush I.[10] I embraced a similar view of OLC's responsibilities during my confirmation hearings before the Senate Judiciary Committee in July of 2003. "My main goal, if confirmed as head of Office of Legal Counsel, would be to continue the extraordinary traditions of the office in providing objective legal advice, independent of any political considerations," I testified.[11]

Once in office I would discover countervailing pressures that made it hard to implement this vision of the OLC job. For one thing, it wasn't an accident that the White House picked me to run OLC. "Any President, and any Attorney General, wants his immediate underlings to be not only competent attorneys, but to be politically and philosophically attuned to the policies of the administration," noted then-OLC head and later Chief Justice William Rehnquist.[12] As my interview in David Leitch's office made clear, the White House hired me in large part because I shared the basic assumptions, outlook, and goals of top administration officials. These "philosophical attunements" would shape my legal decisions as the head of OLC, as it would for any lawyer in any administration.

Philosophical attunement with the administration is legitimate because OLC "serves both the institution of the presidency and a particular incumbent, democratically elected President in whom the Constitution vests the Executive power," in the words of the Clinton OLC veterans, with whom I agree.[13] "Advice to a President needs to have the political dimension clearly in view, without a regard for any pejorative attached to the word political," explained Elliot Richardson, reflecting upon his short time as Richard Nixon's Attorney General and making a similar point.[14]

Having the political dimension in view means that OLC is not entirely neutral to the President's agenda. Especially on national security matters, I would work hard to find a way for the President to achieve his ends. Whenever I advised the White House that a proposed action was legally problematic, I would try to suggest ways to achieve its goals through alternative and legally available means.

I also came to believe that the President should receive what Robert Jackson, one of Franklin Roosevelt's Attorneys General, described as "the benefit of a reasonable doubt as to the law." The Attorney General should not "act as a judge and foreclose the Administration from making reasonable contentions," Jackson said, expressing a view that applies equally to OLC today.[15] Jackson also noted that he was not "quite as free to advocate an untenable position because it happens to be his client's position as he would if he were in private practice," because he "is the legal officer of the United States" and has "a responsibility to others than the President."[16] Legal advice to the President from the Department of Justice is neither like advice from a private attorney nor like a politically neutral ruling from a court. It is something inevitably, and uncomfortably, in between.

OLC also needn't look at legal problems the way courts do. Most Americans (including most lawyers) think the law is what courts say it is, and they implicitly equate legal interpretation with judicial interpretation. But the executive branch does not have the same institutional constraints as courts, especially on national security issues where the President's superior information and quite different responsibilities foster a unique perspective.[17] In addition, for many issues of presidential power there are no controlling judicial precedents. The Supreme Court has never resolved whether the President can use force abroad unilaterally without congressional authorization; or whether the President can terminate treaties; or the scope of executive privilege; or many other fundamental questions of presidential authority. What Robert Jackson said fifty-five years ago was still true during my time in office: "a judge, like an executive adviser, may be surprised at the poverty of really useful and unambiguous authority applicable to concrete problems of executive power as they actually present themselves."[18] When OLC writes its legal opinions supporting broad presidential authority in these contexts—as OLCs of both parties have consistently done— they cite executive branch precedents (including Attorney General and OLC opinions) as often as court opinions. These executive branch precedents are "law" for the executive branch even though they are never scrutinized or approved by courts.

Not surprisingly, OLCs of both parties have always held robust conceptions of presidential power. The Clinton-era OLC provides a telling example. The lawyers who worked at OLC from 1993 to 2000 tried to moderate what they perceived as their Republican OLC predecessors' overly aggressive conception of presidential power. On some matters they succeeded.[19] But on matters of war and national security, institutional imperatives and precedents almost always prevailed. We tend to forget that in its day the Clinton administration was excoriated for what political scientist David Gray Adler called its "absolutist pretensions" in military affairs.[20] Clinton's OLC wrote several opinions arguing that the President could disregard congressional statutes that impinged on the Commander in Chief or related presidential powers.[21] It signed off on the CIA's original rendition program of snatching people from one country and taking them to another for questioning, trial, and pun ishment.[22] And it approved unilateral uses of presidential military force in Bosnia, Haiti, and Kosovo. The Kosovo bombings were especially controversial because of their scale, because they began without congressional approval, and because they continued in the face of the House of Representatives' affirmative refusal, by a tie 213-213 vote, to authorize them. Kosovo was "the first time in our history that a president waged war in the face of a direct congressional refusal to authorize the war,"[23] as Adler noted. It also marked the first and only time that a president exceeded the limitations on the 1973 War Powers Act.[24]

The point here is not that the Clinton OLC was just like the Bush II OLC, for it was not. The Clinton OLC tended to invoke aggressive presidential military powers primarily for humanitarian rather than security ends, and its arguments for presidential power were more cautious than those in the Bush II OLC and relied more on congressional authorization. But these differences do not mask the fact that the Clinton lawyers—like all OLC lawyers and Attorneys General over many decades—were driven by the outlook and exigencies of the presidency to assert more robust presidential powers, especially during a war or crisis, than had been officially approved by the Supreme Court or than is generally accepted in the legal academy or by Congress.

The unusual pressures on OLC, the office's pro–President disposition, and the lack of real oversight may seem to belie the notion that OLC can bind the President to the rule of law. This is where the cultural norms in the office become crucial. Most important are the norms of detachment and professional integrity that permeate OLC and that transcend particular administrations.

The oath of office and a powerful professional concern to "do the right thing" help OLC lawyers to resist pressures for certain outcomes when they believe the law requires otherwise. I often felt responsible for upholding the reputation and integrity of OLC and the Department of Justice in ways that transcended Bush administration interests. I also thought I was serving the President even when the White House didn't like my legal advice, both because the President has a constitutional duty to faithfully execute the law and because skirting the law often leads to political trouble. Many of my predecessors emphasized to me the importance of occasionally saying "no" to the White House. "You won't be doing your job well, and you won't be serving your client's interests, if you rubber-stamp everything the client wants to do," Walter Dellinger, Clinton's OLC head, told me, echoing the views of OLC leaders from both parties.

For all of these reasons, I found myself at OLC managing what Jimmy Carter's Attorney General Griffin Bell described as the tension between the "duty to define the legal limits of executive action in a neutral manner *and* the President's desire to receive legal advice that helps him do what he wants."[25] This ever-present tension was unusually taut after 9/11, when what the President wanted to do was save thousands of American lives. There is no magic formula for how to combine legitimate political factors with the demands of the rule of law. The head of OLC must be a careful lawyer, must exercise good judgment, must make clear his independence, must maintain the confidence of his superiors, and must help the President find legal ways to achieve his ends, especially in connection with national security. OLC's success over the years has depended on its ability to balance these competing considerations—to preserve its fidelity to law while at the same time finding a way, if possible, to approve presidential actions.

WHEN I CONSIDERED the question that Gonzales posed to me during my first week on the job, my hunch was that the Geneva Conventions conferred legal protections—including protections against torture and physical coercion—on at least some terrorists in Iraq. In February 2002, President Bush had determined, correctly in my view, that in our conflict with al Qaeda and in Afghanistan the Third Geneva Convention, which governed prisoners of war, did not confer POW status on al Qaeda terrorists or on members of the Taliban who did not wear uniforms or comply with the laws of war. But Gonzales's question was whether a different Geneva Convention—the Fourth Convention, which governed the duties of an occupying power and the treatment of civilians—conferred legal rights on terrorists in Iraq. Everyone agreed that this convention applied to the traditional interstate war with Iraq. But the Fourth Convention's complex provisions cut in many different directions. The convention expressly denies protections to people who are citizens of neutral and allied nations. But it contemplates at least some legal protections for "spies and saboteurs," a class of belligerents that might be thought to include terrorists. But which terrorists? The Baathist Party remnants known as the Fedayeen Saddam? The al Qaeda soldiers, most of whom were not Iraqi citizens, who were fighting under the leadership of the Jordanian known as Abu Musab al-Zarqawi?

I had studied these questions a bit at the Pentagon, where seasoned military law experts disagreed about whether the Fourth Convention protected all terrorists in Iraq, some terrorists, or no terrorists. Patrick Philbin, who had been supervising OLC's terrorism-related work since Yoo left five months earlier, had been working on similar questions all summer with lawyers from the State Department, Defense Department, CIA, and the National Security Council. Near the end of my first week on the job, the lawyers around the government reached a consensus: the convention protected all Iraqis, including those who were members of al Qaeda or any other terrorist group, but not al Qaeda terrorists from foreign countries who entered Iraq after the occupation began.[26] I reviewed their work, and, after much discussion and my own independent analysis, I agreed.

I first ran my decision by Attorney General Ashcroft. Contrary to his reputation in some quarters, Ashcroft's Chief of Staff, David Ayres, was an outstanding manager of the department who made sure I saw Ashcroft as often and for as long as I needed. And in contrast to his reputation for being too political, Ashcroft was an intelligent interlocutor who took legal issues very seriously and was adept at legal argument. When we spoke, Ashcroft and Ayres were surprised that any terrorists in Iraq would receive Geneva Convention protections. Ashcroft asked me to explain the basis for this conclusion, and whether I was sure I was right. He emphasized that he had promised the President that the Department of Justice would do everything it could to give the President maximum discretion, within the law, to check Islamist terrorism. To underline the point, he related that CIA Director George Tenet (who had gotten wind of my impending decision, presumably from his lawyers) had called him to emphasize the importance of "flexibility" in tracking down and stopping the insurgents in Iraq.

I walked Ashcroft through my legal analysis. And I told him that many smart lawyers in several departments had vetted the Geneva Convention issue, that we had tried very hard to find ways to provide more flexibility, but that everyone agreed in the end that Iraqi terrorists had a legal right to protection. I also told Ashcroft that violation of the Geneva Conventions in Iraq could be punishable under the domestic war crimes statute. He assented to my conclusion and did not press me further.

"They're going to be really mad," Philbin told me as he and I were driving from the Justice Department to the White House to explain to Gonzales and Addington why the department had concluded that Iraqi terrorists were protected. "They're not going to understand our decision. They've never been told 'no.' "

Philbin was right.

"Jack, I don't see how terrorists who violate the laws of war can get the protections of the laws of war," said Gonzales, calmly, from his customary wing chair in his West Wing office. Gonzales was a quiet, placid, fatalistic man. He never became agitated or anxious, even in the face of bad news or pressure. He politely asked me to walk him through the provisions of the Geneva Conventions that supported my conclusion. And so I pulled out my black and red book collecting the laws of war and showed him the passages that we had interpreted to give legal protections to all Iraqi citizens in occupied Iraq. Gonzales's brow remained furrowed, but he didn't push further.

If Gonzales seemed puzzled and slightly worried, David Addington was just plain mad. "The President has already decided that terrorists do not receive Geneva Convention protections," he barked. "You cannot question his decision." Addington was referring to the President's February 2002 decision that al Qaeda and Taliban detainees did not receive POW or other protections under the Third Geneva Convention. I explained that I agreed with the President's 2002 decision, but that the situation of terrorists in Iraq was legally distinguishable because the very different Fourth Geneva Convention, not governed by the President's decision, applied there.

A few unpleasant minutes later, Philbin and I left the White House. As we were driving back to the Justice Department, I thought about the responsibilities of the OLC job in the terrorism era. I had just made a decision that conferred legal protections on the terrorists who were killing U.S. soldiers and threatening the Iraq project. In an administration bent on pushing antiterrorism efforts to the limits of the law, OLC's authority to determine those limits made it a frontline policymaker in the war on terrorism.

CHAPTER 2

The Commander in Chief Ensnared by Law

I n the days that followed my decision about Geneva Convention protections for terrorists in Iraq, I pondered why the
Attorney General and the White House accepted rather than
ignored my legal advice. My thoughts were drawn to Francis Biddle, Franklin Roosevelt's fourth Attorney General, whose portrait
(along with Elliot Richardson's) would hang for many months in
my OLC office.

Biddle was one of the preeminent lawyers of his era: a graduate
of Harvard Law School, a clerk for Oliver Wendell Holmes, and a
federal judge and the Solicitor General before becoming Attorney
General and later a judge at the Nuremberg trial of Nazi leaders.
He was also a member of the ACLU, and was generally "revered by
Amercian liberals," in the words of New Deal historian Geoffrey
Perrett.[1] One week after the December 7, 1941, attacks on Pearl
Harbor, Biddle spoke at the Library of Congress on the need to

protect civil liberties during the war. "[T]he war would test whether [our freedoms] could endure," he explained. And "although we had fought wars before, and our personal freedoms had survived, there had been periods of gross abuse, when hysteria and fear and hate ran high, and minorities were unlawfully and cruelly abused. Every man who cares about freedom must fight for it for the *other* man with whom he disagrees." The Director of the ACLU, Roger Baldwin, described Biddle's speech as "the most eloquent and practical words of any public man about civil rights in wartime."[2]

Two months after giving this speech, Biddle acquiesced in what the ACLU later called "the worst single wholesale violation of civil rights of American citizens in our history": the exclusion from the West Coast and detention of over a hundred thousand Japanese, including over seventy thousand Japanese-American citizens.[3] At first Biddle objected to the exclusion program. He advised Roosevelt that the Justice Department was opposed to and "would not under any circumstances evacuate American citizens," which Biddle described as not only illegal but also "ill-advised, unnecessary, and unnecessarily cruel."[4] Roosevelt ignored Biddle's counsel. On February 19, 1942, he accepted the advice of Secretary of War Henry Stimson and exercised "military judgment" to sign an executive order approving the exclusion program.[5]

"I do not think he was much concerned with the gravity or implications of this step," Biddle later said. Roosevelt acted in the belief "that rights should yield to the necessities of war." He thought that "[r]ights came after victory, not before," because he thought the Constitution did not prevent what military necessity demanded.[6] Once the President made his decision, Biddle recounted, "I did not think I should oppose it any further."[7] Biddle subsequently supported the President's decision and willingly transferred to the War Department the legal authorities needed to execute the President's order.[8]

Why was Biddle's experience so different from mine? Biddle, the civil libertarian, rolled over when Roosevelt, the "champion of freedom," ignored his advice about the legality of detaining tens of thousands of loyal Americans in the United States. Six decades later, a conservative Attorney General and a conservative White House acquiesced in legal advice from a conservative Assistant Attorney General about protecting terrorists who were killing American soldiers in Iraq—advice that they believed would hamper the war on terrorism. What had changed between 1942 and 2003?

LATE IN THE EVENING of June 2, 1919, Franklin and Eleanor Roosevelt were driving to their R Street home in Washington, D.C., following a dinner party when they heard a violent explosion. An anarchist had accidentally blown himself up while placing a bomb on the front steps of the residence of Attorney General A. Mitchell Palmer, who lived across the street from the Roosevelts. The bomb destroyed the front of Palmer's home, blew in every window on the block, and sprayed body parts all over the neighborhood. As the Roosevelts approached their home, they saw blood spattered on their front steps and heard screams from inside. The future President dashed upstairs (this was before he contracted polio), where he discovered James, the only of his children in the house at the time, standing in his pajamas among broken window glass. "I'll never forget how uncommonly unnerved Father was when he ... found me standing at the window," James later recalled. "He grabbed me in an embrace that almost cracked my ribs."[9]

After consoling James, Roosevelt rushed across the street. The Palmers were preparing for bed in the back of their house when the bomb went off, and were not injured. As firemen and federal agents arrived at the scene, Roosevelt gathered shreds of antigovernment pamphlets authored by "The Anarchist Fighters" that had been strewn about after the explosion, and began to realize that the bombing was part of a larger plot.[10] That evening anarchists detonated seven other bombs in cities across the United States. Attorney General Palmer declared the bombings an "attempt . . . to terrorize the country." With the eager assistance of twenty-four-year-old J. Edgar Hoover, whom he appointed to lead the Justice Department's new General Intelligence Division, Palmer began to prosecute, surveil, harass, and deport thousands of suspected communists, socialists, anarchists, and other antigovernment agitators in what came to be known as the "Red Scare."[11]

The Red Scare ended in the summer of 1920, but the R Street terrorist bombing that precipitated it cemented Roosevelt's long-held fears of fifth-column subversives inside the United States. These fears first took root during his service as Undersecretary of the Navy in the Wilson administration, when Roosevelt supervised the Office of Naval Intelligence's aggressive search for German secret agents suspected of attacks on U.S. weapons facilities before and during World War I.[12] When Roosevelt became President, his fear of terrorists grew. One week after Germany invaded Poland on September 1, 1939, he issued a directive beefing up domestic FBI authorities to detect and prevent the "sabotage" that had occurred before and during World War I.[13] When the FBI reported in the early months of 1940 that Nazi spies and saboteurs were operating throughout the United States, Roosevelt alerted the nation.[14]

"Today's threat to our national security is not a matter of military weapons alone," Roosevelt announced in a May 26, 1940, fireside chat, as Nazis were overrunning France, Belgium, and the Netherlands. "We know of new methods of attack. The Trojan Horse. The Fifth Column that betrays a nation unprepared for treachery. Spies, saboteurs and traitors are the actors in this new strategy."[15]

Then came the Japanese attack on Pearl Harbor. "I think the most effective fifth column work of the entire war was done in Hawaii," Navy Secretary Frank Knox told the nation one week after Pearl Harbor.[16] A commission led by Supreme Court Justice Owen Roberts deepened concerns about Japanese subversives when it concluded, in late January 1942, that many Japanese residents in Hawaii helped plan the Pearl Harbor attacks.[17] Within a month after Pearl Harbor, prominent journalists, West Coast politicians, and law enforcement officers, reflecting popular fears of Japanese air attacks or landings, assailed the President with shrill demands to rid the West Coast of Japanese conspirators.[18] At the same time, the Japanese military was stringing up impressive victories in the Pacific, and Japanese submarines were sinking American ships off the West Coast. These events lent credibility to intelligence reports Roosevelt was receiving about plans for Japanese attacks on California. And they lent urgency to advice from General John L. DeWitt, the commander of West Coast Command, that Japanese-Americans were "organized and ready for concerted action."[19]

Biddle and FBI Director J. Edgar Hoover argued, correctly in hindsight, that there was no hard evidence of disloyalty among Japanese-Americans. Roosevelt's decision to ignore their advice and to heed the alarmist warnings was informed, many historians have argued, by racist anti-Japanese sentiments. But the dominant motivations of Roosevelt and his military commanders were an intense feeling of responsibility to protect the nation, a persistent fear of domestic terrorists, and a painful regret that they had not acted aggressively enough in the face of pre–Pearl Harbor intelligence chatter that seemed, in retrospect, to point to something ominous. The military "had not forgotten that . . . they had been caught with their pants down at Pearl Harbor," noted Francis Biddle, and they "did not propose to be put in that awkward position again, or to take any chances."[20] Having failed once to prevent a surprise attack by people of Japanese ancestry, the Commander in Chief did not believe he could afford to ignore popular demands for security, especially when his military commanders insisted that the Japanese exclusion was necessary to protect the nation.

It would be wrong to infer from the Japanese exclusion episode that Roosevelt was indifferent to legal restrictions on his wartime authority. Roosevelt was a lawyer who read legal documents and court cases, engaged the brilliant lawyers around him in legal discussions, and sometimes refined or disagreed with their conclusions.[21] He also revered the U.S. Constitution and was sensitive to charges of aggrandizing executive power. But while Roosevelt was not hostile to law itself, he derided what he called "legalisms," and he was, according to Robert Jackson, "a strong skeptic of legal reasoning."[22] Roosevelt thought that laws and the Constitution should be interpreted flexibly and sensibly, in accordance with their broad purposes, to respond to the imperatives of the day. Technical lawyerly interpretations of legal abstractions did not suit his pragmatic mind or his experimental bent, especially in times of crisis.

Roosevelt could think this way because the law governing presidential authority during his era was largely a *political* rather than a *judicial* constraint on presidential power. When he considered bending the law, he did not worry about being sued or prosecuted, or about defending his actions before a grand jury or an international court. He worried instead about the reaction of the press, the Congress, and most of all, the American people. Roosevelt feared impeachment, not judicial trial; the democratic process, not courts, would be his judge. He sought the advice of his learned Attorney General because it was the right thing to do and because legal controversy was a potential measure of political controversy. But when the Commander in Chief disregarded Biddle's "legalistic" advice because he thought his responsibilities demanded that he do what was necessary to win the war, only politics stood as a potential sanction.

Roosevelt also acted in a permissive legal culture that is barely recognizable to us today. It was an era before Vietnam, before the revelations of Hoover's domestic espionage, and before Watergate. This was a time when the press, Congress, and intellectuals had a higher regard for the executive branch and the military. It was also a time, before the judicial civil liberties revolutions of the 1960s and 1970s, when America was much less solicitous of political and civil rights. In 1942, "neither the country, nor its political and intellectual leaders, nor such organizations as the American Civil Liberties Union, were truly libertarian in their outlook," noted historian Michal Belknap.[23]

No episode captures this lost legal culture better than the fate of eight Nazi saboteurs who were captured in the United States in late June 1942. The eight Nazis, one of whom was an American citizen, had traveled by submarine from France and landed on beaches in Long Island, New York, and the north coast of Florida. Their mission was the brainchild of Hitler himself, who wanted to cripple U.S. military production capacities and demoralize the American civilian population. The saboteurs' task was to blow up aluminum plants, railroad lines, canal locks, hydroelectric plants, and bridges. They also had plans for "nuisance bombings" of railroad terminals and Jewish-owned department stores.[24] Soon after their arrival in the United States, one of the saboteurs, fearing betrayal by the others or detection by U.S. officials, turned himself in. The FBI eventually rounded up the other seven, and on June 27 Hoover announced their capture publicly and suggested, falsely, that the arrests resulted from the FBI's infiltration of the Nazi system. The nation reacted with enormous joy, and with vengeance. "Demands immediately arose among members of Congress for swift justice to the saboteurs—for the death penalty if the law permits it," reported the *Washington Post*.[25] The public favored death for the saboteurs by a 10-1 margin.[26]

When Roosevelt learned of the saboteurs' capture, he insisted to Biddle that they be tried by a military court where ordinary procedural niceties would not stand in the way, justice would be swift, and the death sentence could be imposed. "Offenses such as . . . these are probably more serious than any offense in criminal law," Roosevelt argued. "The death penalty is called for by usage and by the extreme gravity of the war aim and the very existence of our American government."[27] Biddle worried about a Supreme Court decision from the Civil War, *Ex Parte Milligan*, that seemed to bar military trials in the United States when civilian courts were open for business. But Roosevelt had made up his mind, and on the basis of two brief presidential proclamations, Biddle arranged a military commission that had no written procedures or criminal laws. The President's public announcement that a military commission would try the saboteurs "met with general satisfaction in Washington, as it will throughout the country," and "calmed the fears of many who realized the delays and technicalities incident to civil trials," reported the *New York Times*.[28]

The saboteurs' military trial began on July 8 in an FBI assembly room on the fifth floor of the Justice Department—the same room that, after many renovations, would become my office sixty-one years later. The trial was conducted in total secrecy, and the windows were covered in heavy black curtains to block all daylight. An open trial would be "obviously rich in information that can be of value to the enemy, particularly to other saboteurs still on the loose," noted the *Nation*, expressing conventional wisdom.[29] Americans everywhere trusted the executive branch to conduct the secret trial. "The FBI vouches for the need of secrecy and the administration's lawyers support the legality of the procedure," wrote Arthur Krock of the *New York Times*. "Unless these lead to clear abuses, neither view is likely to be called into broad question," he added, expressing a faithful attitude toward government that would be unthinkable today.[30]

Three weeks into the secret trial, the Supreme Court announced that it would convene a special summer session to entertain the saboteurs' habeas corpus petitions challenging the legality of the military commission. "The decision to seek recourse in the Supreme Court did not meet popular approval in Washington," reported the *New York Times*. "On the contrary, there is great dissatisfaction here with the length to which the [three-week military trial] had already proceeded."[31] The *Detroit Free Press* was less restrained. "Realism calls for a stone wall and a firing squad, and

not a lot of holier-than-thou eyewash about extending the protection of civil rights to a group that came among us to blast, burn,
and kill," it opined.[32]

Roosevelt was also unhappy. "I want one thing clearly understood, Francis," he told the Attorney General. "I won't give them
up . . . I won't hand them over to any United States marshal armed
with a writ of habeas corpus. Understand?"[33] Biddle got the message. "I understood clearly," he revealed in his memoirs, but he
noted that Roosevelt's words "did not make things any easier for
his Attorney General, who was under a very special obligation to
obey the law, even if the words had the historical echo of some of
his obstinate predecessors, who, in times of crisis, had resisted what
they considered judicial interference with the President's duty to
act."[34] The Supreme Court got the message as well. "That would
be a dreadful thing," Chief Justice Harlan Fiske Stone said when he
learned that Roosevelt had threatened to execute the Nazis regardless of what the Supreme Court decided.[35] Within a few days, the
Court upheld the military commission's legality.

The country gasped a sigh of relief. "To handle [the saboteurs]
in the civil courts would be to help Hitler immensely, and that
would be intolerable," wrote the *Washington Post*. "We cannot afford
to give our enemy, in our present pass, the slightest assistance."[36]
The secret and juryless military court pronounced the saboteurs
guilty three days after the Supreme Court announced its judgment,
and less than a week later six of the eight Nazis were electro-
cuted. (Roosevelt commuted the sentences of the other two.) The
country congratulated itself on its commitment to the rule of law
throughout the six-week ordeal from capture to execution. "Even
in wartime and even toward the enemy we do not abandon our

basic protection of individual rights," gushed the *New Republic* in a typical editorial.[37]

SIX DECADES LATER, the President and the country were once again preoccupied with terrorist attacks on the homeland. But there were new concerns as well. In March 2005, the Department of Defense released the *National Defense Strategy of the United States*. Describing U.S. "vulnerabilities" in the "changing security environment," the *Strategy* noted that "our strength as a nation state will continue to be challenged by those who employ a strategy of the weak using international fora, judicial processes, and terrorism."[38]

Why would the mighty U.S. Defense Department include international organizations and judges as threats on par with terrorism? Who are "the weak," and why would the department worry so about its legal tactics? The answers to these questions stretch back three decades, and closely track the experiences of one man— former National Security Advisor and Secretary of State Henry Kissinger.

In August 1970, Philip Berrigan, a Catholic priest and famous anti–Vietnam War protester, was serving time in a Pennsylvania federal prison for burning draft files. Berrigan and a half-dozen friends on the outside jokingly conspired in a letter to kidnap Kissinger as punishment for war crimes he committed in Vietnam.[39] Berrigan was convicted of smuggling letters out of a federal prison. And the object of his ire won the Nobel Peace Prize in 1973 for his role in ending the Vietnam War. Peaceniks would continue to protest Kissinger's foreign policy decisions for decades, but the realist statesman barely noticed their words, which lacked the backing of a sovereign force. The modern international human rights movement was in its infancy. It wasn't obvious that Kissinger had violated any real laws. And there were no courts to enforce these laws in any event.

By 2002, things had changed. Memoirs and government disclosures over the years had highlighted Kissinger's involvement in the bombing of Cambodia, Pakistani massacres in Bangladesh, Indonesia's invasion of East Timor, and most of all, Operation Condor, the brutal effort by death squads of South American dictators to knock off their Marxist political opponents. And the words had grown louder and fiercer, as marginal protesters from the 1970s had grown into a cottage industry decrying Kissinger's impunity. In 2001 the *Village Voice* published *Manhattan's Milosevic: How You Can Do What the Government Won't: Arrest Henry Kissinger*, a how-to guide to citizens' arrests and judicial actions against Kissinger, and journalist Christopher Hitchens wrote *The Trial of Henry Kissinger*, a tendentious but vivid indictment of Kissinger's role in the controversies of the 1970s.[40] The next year a documentary movie of the same title toured around America and became a hit.

These mainstream attacks on Kissinger were a measure of how far the human rights culture had come since the 1970s. The 1975 Helsinki Accords, negotiated by Kissinger while Secretary of State, contained human rights principles that had given dissidents in the Soviet empire an organizational and motivational tool to challenge Soviet oppression. Jimmy Carter put human rights at the center of U.S. foreign policy, and the antiapartheid struggle, Tiananmen Square, South American death squads, and Pol Pot's genocide had galvanized a transnational network of human rights advocates.

Scores of well-funded nongovernmental organizations such as Amnesty International and Human Rights Watch, taking advantage of the CNN effect and later the Internet, had developed into powerful monitors and critics of human rights abuses, and leading advocates of an "end impunity" philosophy. The press lent credibility to these NGOs by writing stories around their reports and quoting their criticisms. Meanwhile, the end of the Cold War had sparked hopes of a world of liberal democracies under a human rights–dominated rule of law. Globalization and a more conservative Supreme Court motivated many in the academic American Left to replace the U.S. Constitution with international human rights law as the fount of progressivism.

What the movement lacked, however, was a way to enforce these norms. There was plenty of law available: treaties and international customs had for centuries governed the conduct of warfare—the treatment of prisoners and civilians, acceptable weapons and tactics, the rights of neutral parties, and the like. But the laws of war, as they are called, were often honored in the breach in the heat of battle, for they had no sanction behind them. Many hoped that the Nuremberg and Tokyo trials for war criminals following World War II would be models for enforcing prohibitions on war crimes and human rights abuses. But the decades that followed these trials saw national leaders continue to commit crimes in wartime and against their citizens, and the Nuremberg and Tokyo trials increasingly seemed like nonrecurrent examples of victor's justice rather than, as many had hoped, the beginnings of the rule of law on the international stage.

The enforcement gap finally began to close with the development of the idea of universal jurisdiction. Universal jurisdiction is the power of a national court to try citizens from another country, including government officials, for egregious human rights abuses, no matter where they are committed. The idea had been kicking around in human rights circles since World War II but got a big boost with two important events in the 1980s. The first was a 1980 case in New York called *Filartiga*, which allowed a Paraguayan citizen to sue a Paraguayan official who tortured his son in Paraguay. This decision has been described by Yale Law School Dean Harold Koh as the "*Brown v. Board of Education*" of the international human rights movement.[41] It sparked a wave of universal jurisdiction lawsuits in the United States for money damages against foreign government officials who allegedly committed torture, war crimes, and crimes against humanity outside the United States.

The second boost for universal jurisdiction came when Baltasar Garzón, a Spanish magistrate, began to investigate the South American dirty wars of the 1970s. In 1998, Garzón used universal jurisdiction to seek extradition of Augusto Pinochet, the former Chilean dictator and a leader of the Operation Condor movement, who was visiting London for a back operation. Garzón asked the London police to send Pinochet to Spain to stand trial for torturing and murdering Chileans in Chile during the 1970s. The House of Lords, in a landmark decision, ruled that universal jurisdiction was a valid concept, and that England must hand Pinochet over to Spain.[42] After a year of additional legal wrangling, England sent Pinochet back to Chile because he was unfit to stand trial.[43] But the Pinochet precedent remained on the books as a great victory for the "end impunity" movement. Sovereign immunity no longer stood as a roadblock to trials of government officials for gross human rights violations.

Garzón's near extradition of Pinochet rattled Kissinger in a way that Hitchens and the *Village Voice* never could. "The Pinochet precedent, if literally applied, would permit the two sides in the Arab-Israeli conflict, or those in any other passionate international controversy, to project their battles into the various national courts by pursuing adversaries with extradition requests," Kissinger warned in "The Pitfalls of Universal Jurisdiction," a defensive essay published in *Foreign Affairs* in July 2001.[44] The danger of universal jurisdiction, he added, "lies in pushing the effort to extremes that risk substituting the tyranny of judges for that of governments; historically, the dictatorship of the virtuous has often led to inquisitions and even witch-hunts."

Kissinger's article was a response to a summons he received in May 2001 while visiting France to give a speech. French Judge Roger Le Loire asked Kissinger to be a witness in an ongoing investigation into the Operation Condor deaths of French citizens. Kissinger quickly left the country.[45] Later that summer, courts in Chile and Argentina used diplomatic channels to ask Kissinger about Operation Condor. The following year the judicial noose tightened. In March of 2002, Kissinger canceled a speech in Brazil after leftist groups asked prosecutors to detain and question him—again about Condor.[46] In London the following month, the same Spanish magistrate who tried to prosecute Pinochet sought permission from the London police to question Kissinger for his knowledge of Operation Condor. No sooner was this permission denied on technical grounds than a human rights activist named Peter Tatchell sought an arrest warrant for Kissinger's "war crimes" in Vietnam, Laos, and Cambodia. Judge Nicholas Evans rejected the request because Tatchell was not "presently" able to submit a "suitably precise charge" against Kissinger. "Th[is] leaves open the possibility that at some point in the future he might give me a warrant if I come back with more detailed evidence," an optimistic Tatchell told the press.[47]

In public, Kissinger reacted discreetly to these growing judicial feints. "The decisions made in high office are usually 51-49 decisions so it is quite possible that mistakes were made," he said to a London audience during his April 2002 trip. "The issue is whether 30 years after the event courts are the appropriate means by which determination is made."[48] Kissinger made it seem as if he had no objection in principle to cooperating with these judges. "My position is that if the U.S. government thinks it is appropriate for me to answer the questions of foreign judges about the conduct of American policy, I will cooperate to the fullest extent."[49]

In private, however, Kissinger was livid, especially since he thought the U.S. government wasn't doing much to help. He decided to call an old friend from his government days, Gerald Ford's Chief of Staff and the current Secretary of Defense, Donald Rumsfeld.

Rumsfeld had already been worrying about this problem under the rubric of "lawfare," an idea that had been discussed in the Pentagon for years. Lawfare is "the strategy of using or misusing law as a substitute for traditional military means to achieve an operational objective," according to Air Force Brigadier General Charles Dunlap, who popularized the phrase.[50] Enemies like al Qaeda who cannot match the United States militarily instead criticize it for purported legal violations, especially violations of human rights or the laws of war. They hide in mosques so that they can decry U.S. destruction of religious objects when attacked. They describe civilian deaths as "war crimes" even when the deaths are legally permissible "collateral damage." Or they complain falsely that they were tortured, as we now know al Qaeda training manuals advise them to do. Lawfare works because it manipulates something Americans value: respect for law.

Rumsfeld viewed Kissinger's harassment in these terms. But there was a twist: the weak "enemy" using asymmetric legal weapons was not al Qaeda, but rather our very differently motivated European and South American allies and the human rights industry that supported their universal jurisdiction aspirations. Rumsfeld saw this form of lawfare as a potentially powerful check on American military power. He also saw it in more personal terms. He was leading the Department of Defense in a controversial war against al Qaeda and its affiliates, and was about to take it into a more controversial war in Iraq. Even before the revelations of abuse at Abu Ghraib and elsewhere, Europeans and human rights activists used the rhetoric of war crimes to criticize Guantanamo Bay detentions and military commissions. Rumsfeld believed that opponents incapable of checking American military power would increasingly rely on lawfare weapons instead. And as the widely detested critic of "Old Europe," he could expect to be at the top of the target list.

After hearing from Kissinger, the Secretary of Defense asked his Pentagon lawyer, Jim Haynes, to analyze and find a solution to what Rumsfeld termed "the judicialization of international politics." Soon after Rumsfeld's request, I arrived at the Department of Defense in September 2002 to be Haynes's Special Counsel. As a leading academic critic of many aspects of the international human rights movement, I was the perfect person for the assignment. Haynes quickly handed it off to me.

"In the past quarter century, various nations, NGOs, academics, international organizations, and others in the 'international community' have been busily weaving a web of international laws and judicial institutions that today threatens USG interests," began one of the memos I wrote on Rumsfeld's behalf. "The USG has seriously underestimated this threat, and has mistakenly assumed that confronting the threat will worsen it," the memo continued. "Unless we tackle the problem head-on, it will continue to grow. The issue is especially urgent because of the unusual challenges we face in the war on terrorism."

The United States, I explained, was a leading proponent of the international laws of war and of international human rights law. Recent controversies and abuses have obscured how seriously the U.S. military takes compliance with the laws of war. It has elaborate manuals on every aspect of warfare, it trains its soldiers thoroughly in the laws of war, and it sends lawyers known as Judge Advocates General into battle alongside military commanders. Every weapon used by the U.S. military, and most of the targets they are used against, are vetted and cleared by lawyers in advance.

Unfortunately, the Defense Department's efforts to comply with the laws of war do not prevent virulent criticism of U.S. military actions. The laws of war are often written in vague terms, and are subject to different interpretations. They prohibit, for example, "disproportionate" casualties and "outrages upon personal dignity"—terms that can mean very different things to different people, and that can easily be used as rhetorical weapons. The manipulability of international law became apparent in the spring of 2003 when a group of Iraqis brought universal jurisdiction criminal complaints in a Belgian court against George H. W. Bush, Colin Powell, and

Norman Schwarzkopf for their alleged war crimes during the 1991 Gulf War. A similar group filed a second criminal complaint the following month against Rumsfeld and Tommy Franks for alleged war crimes committed during the recent invasion of Iraq.

Rumsfeld immediately went on the offensive. "It's perfectly possible to meet elsewhere," he told reporters, implying that NATO headquarters could be moved to another country if Belgium tolerated lawsuits against NATO leaders. "Belgium needs to recognize that there are consequences for its actions."[51] Belgium quickly revised its universal jurisdiction law and eliminated the prosecutions against U.S. officials. But Rumsfeld and others worried more than ever about the judicialization of warfare. There were still many universal jurisdiction laws on the books in Europe, and the long war on terrorism would throw up innumerable opportunities for aggressive foreign prosecutors, especially after U.S. officials left office and their governmental immunities diminished.

It wasn't only foreign courts that Rumsfeld worried about—it was international courts too, such as the one the UN Security Council set up in 1993 to prosecute war crimes in the former Yugoslavia. Amnesty International alleged that during the 1999 Kosovo campaign, NATO countries committed "serious violations of the laws of war" by bombing a television station and electricity grids and by accidentally killing civilians.[52] The Yugoslav Tribunal in The Hague took the charges very seriously. After an elaborate investigation the tribunal determined that Amnesty International's accusations did not warrant prosecution, but only after the lead prosecutor overruled the advice of her assistants.

The near prosecution in an international court set up by the United States stoked worries about the International Criminal

Court, which came into being in July 2002. The ICC sets up a court and prosecutor not beholden to any government and a prosecutorial system without real political checks and balances. If the independent ICC prosecutor files charges against U.S. officials for war crimes or crimes against humanity, member states—there are currently 104—have an obligation to arrest and send them to the ICC for prosecution. The Clinton administration opposed the ICC, largely for its lack of political accountability. But President Clinton nonetheless signed the ICC treaty just before he left office because he wanted to send a signal of support for the project and keep open the possibility of the United States ratifying the treaty later. Determined to reverse this symbolically significant act, President Bush ordered the treaty "unsigned" soon after coming to power. The United States "does not intend to become a party" to the ICC treaty, Undersecretary of State John Bolton wrote to the United Nations, and "has no legal obligations" arising from Clinton's signature.[53] To underline how threatening the ICC seemed to U.S. interests, Congress in 2002 passed the American Servicemembers' Protection Act, colloquially known as the "Hague Invasion Act" because it authorizes the President to use "all means necessary and appropriate" to release any American imprisoned by the ICC.[54]

Few people outside the U.S. government think that an American will ever be hauled before the ICC, and most ICC watchers are puzzled at the United States' fierce resistance. The main reason for opposition, I explained in my memo for Rumsfeld, is that "the USG's unique global responsibilities expose it to a disproportionate risk of ICC prosecution." Unlike rogue dictators who hide behind walls of national sovereignty, hundreds of thousands of U.S. troops are deployed around the globe and thus are potentially easy to grab and bring to The Hague—especially in a world of rampant anti-Americanism. Even if no defendant is brought before the ICC, the ICC can still cause lawfare mischief by being a public forum for official criticism and judgment of U.S. military action. "The ICC is at bottom an attempt by militarily weak nations that dominated ICC negotiations to restrain militarily powerful nations," my memo for Rumsfeld explained. It is no accident that nations not joining the ICC include the United States, China, Russia, India, and Israel.

In 2003 Rumsfeld circulated my memo on the "judicialization of international politics" to the National Security Council, and demanded action. Several years of NSC meetings among lawyers and deputies followed. But a concrete plan never emerged. Lawfare has an important tactical advantage over warfare: the apparent moral high ground. The Department of State argued that any effort by the United States to oppose the increasingly powerful institutions of international justice would seem like a defensive admission of the very war crimes charges it wanted to avoid. The effort would also smack of hypocrisy, the State Department emphasized, since the United States aggressively used human rights institutions—including universal jurisdiction lawsuits—to check human rights abuses by other nations. The Department of Justice also opposed any anti–universal jurisdiction campaign on the ground that it would jeopardize its ability to bring its own universal jurisdiction prosecutions against foreign leaders and terrorists.

The NSC remained worried about the threat of foreign judges. But in the face of the bureaucratic squabbling, and preoccupied with weightier concerns, it couldn't figure out what to do about it. So by March of 2005, Rumsfeld acted alone, setting down a marker in the *National Defense Strategy* that he, at least, understood the threat posed to the United States by "the weak using international fora, judicial processes, and terrorism."

IT WAS NOT JUST international laws and foreign courts that the Bush administration had to worry about. Scores of domestic laws had made their way onto the battlefield as well. After the Supreme Court ruled in August 1942 that Franklin D. Roosevelt's secret military commission for the eight captured Nazi saboteurs was lawful, the liberal magazine the *Nation* joked that "had the Supreme Court granted [the saboteurs'] petitions, American soldiers would have to go into battle with John Doe summonses in place of rifles and a round of subpoenas in their cartridge belts."[55] Four months after 9/11, the World War II joke had become a reality. In February 2002, OLC gave the Department of Defense a thirty-page legal opinion titled "Potential Legal Constraints Applicable to Interrogations of Persons Captured by U.S. Armed Forces in Afghanistan."[56] The memorandum sounds like an ominous reference to aggressive interrogations. But in fact it was a detailed analysis of the complex ways that the famous *Miranda* rule ("you have the right to remain silent") applied on the battlefield in Afghanistan.

In addition to constitutional rules, domestic criminal laws had crept into war as well. A famous example can be found in the January 25, 2002, memorandum that White House Counsel Gonzales wrote President Bush to explain why he believed the President should conclude that the Geneva Convention on Prisoners of War (GPW) should not apply to the conflict with al Qaeda and the Taliban.[57] Gonzales's memo has become known for its statement that the war on terrorism "renders obsolete Geneva's strict limitations on questioning of enemy prisoners and renders quaint some of its provisions requiring that captured enemies be afforded such things as commissary privileges, scrip (i.e., advances of monthly pay), athletic uniforms, and scientific instruments." But its real significance lies in Gonzales's argument that the President should rule that Geneva does not apply in order to "[s]ubstantially reduce the threat of domestic criminal prosecution under the War Crimes Act." The War Crimes Act imposes criminal penalties (including the death penalty) for violations of provisions in the GPW or other laws of war. "A determination that the GPW is not applicable," Gonzales explained, would "guard effectively against misconstruction or misapplication" of the War Crimes law. It "would create a reasonable basis in law" that the law did not apply, and would "provide a solid defense to any future prosecution."[58]

It is unimaginable that Francis Biddle or Robert Jackson would have written Franklin Roosevelt a memorandum about how to avoid prosecution for his wartime decisions designed to maintain flexibility against a new and deadly foe. It is unimaginable because in 1942 neither the law nor the legal culture presented any real threat to aggressive presidential action. Between 1942 and the time Gonzales wrote his memorandum, however, law and legal culture had changed radically. The country had witnessed revolutions in freedom of speech, criminal law, civil rights, and military justice, and had become far more committed to the power and independence of courts, even in wartime. The rebellions and disclosures of the 1960s and 1970s had led the American people, the press, and criminal investigators to lose faith and trust in executive branch officers. In response to these events, Congress imposed more seri-

ous and palpable constraints on executive branch officials than anything done by international courts and international laws. Domestic
criminal laws and complex regulations had come to govern many
aspects of presidential war power. And they were enforceable by
an array of prosecutors, independent counsels, ethics monitors, and
inspectors general (investigators inside each executive agency who
are largely beholden to Congress).

The most famous 1970s-era legal restriction was the War Powers Act, which tried to limit presidential use of the U.S. military in
the absence of congressional approval. This law played little role in
the post-9/11 world, however, because President Bush sought congressional authorization before using force against al Qaeda and its
affiliates. But the 1978 domestic wiretapping law, the Foreign Intelligence Surveillance Act, had a big impact. It required the President
and his subordinates, on pain of jail, to get a special court's permission to listen to each electronic communication of suspected
foreign agents, including wartime enemies, in the United States.
Congress in the 1970s and 1980s also began to impose increasingly
complicated restrictions on the intelligence agencies, punishable by
criminal penalties. The criminalization of war continued in 1994,
when the Torture Statute made it a crime to inflict "severe physical or mental pain or suffering," and in 1996, when the war crimes
law at issue in Gonzales's memorandum brought criminal restrictions to bear on detainee treatment, conditions of confinement,
trial procedures, and military targeting of enemy property, among
other things.

There were many good reasons for these and scores of similar laws.
Nixon abused the prerogatives of office for personal ends. The FBI,

the CIA, and the National Security Agency had engaged in activities—such as spying on Americans for political gain, and assassinating foreign leaders—that sometimes exceeded their mandates and violated deeply held American values. On the international stage, nations in the twentieth century had a shameful record of committing or acquiescing in war crimes, torture, and crimes against humanity, especially against innocent civilians. Eradicating these evils through domestic criminal law is one of the goals of the human rights movement—a goal traditionally shared by the United States itself. It seems hard to sympathize with Gonzales's obsessions with avoiding prosecution for violating these laws. Why not just comply with them?

Gonzales's January 25 memorandum had answers to this question as it pertained to the Third Geneva Convention. "The nature of the new war places a high premium on other factors, such as the ability to quickly obtain information from captured terrorists and their sponsors in order to avoid further atrocities against American civilians."[59] More broadly, Gonzales noted, "it is difficult to predict the needs and circumstances that could arise in the course of the war on terrorism."[60] An administration under pressure to stop a second attack by an enemy it couldn't see and didn't fully understand was leery of tying its hands with vague criminal laws designed to govern traditional wars between nations and written before the advent of the Internet, cell phones, and miniaturized weapons of mass destruction.

The essential problem for Gonzales and company was that many of the laws criminalizing warfare—like the international laws on which some of them were based—were subject to multiple interpretations. "[S]ome of the language of the GPW is undefined (it prohibits, for example, 'outrages upon personal dignity' and 'inhuman treatment')," Gonzales wrote the President, "and it is difficult to predict with confidence what actions might be deemed to constitute violations of the relevant provisions of GPW."[61] He might have added that there were few precedents to give meaning to these laws, especially as they apply to non-state-actor terrorists.

These uncertainties made Gonzales worry that a prosecutor unfriendly to the administration would use criminal law to punish Bush administration officials who acted aggressively to prevent the next attack. It is "difficult to predict the motives of prosecutors and independent counsels who may in the future decide to pursue unwarranted charges,"[62] Gonzales told the President. This was a polite way of referring to the post-Watergate, post–Iran-Contra, post-Lewinsky legal culture in which independent counsels, inspectors general, and ethics monitors harass political officials for years after they leave office. And although Gonzales didn't worry about the Ashcroft Justice Department bringing a case, he did worry about a Justice Department in a subsequent administration of a different party prosecuting officials for wartime decisions with which it disagreed.

Gonzales's memo has been criticized as a conspiracy to commit a war crime. A more charitable and realistic view is that the President's counselor was trying to help his client avoid the pitfalls of the post-Watergate criminalization of warfare. President Bush faced national security imperatives akin to those that Roosevelt faced. But for the first time ever, the president's ultimate obligation to do what it takes to protect the nation from devastating attack was checked by a hornet's nest of complex criminal restrictions on his traditional wartime discretionary powers—restrictions that the White House feared would later be construed uncharitably in our shifting, polarized political culture. Many people think the Bush administration has been indifferent to wartime legal constraints. But the opposite is true: the administration has been strangled by law, and since September 11, 2001, this war has been lawyered to death. The administration has paid attention to law not necessarily because it wanted to, but rather because it had no choice.

It may be hard to believe that executive branch officials, many of whom risk their lives to protect the nation, really care much about criminal law, investigation, and possibly, jail. But they do care—a lot. In my two years in the government, I witnessed top officials and bureaucrats in the White House and throughout the administration openly worrying that investigators acting with the benefit of hindsight in a different political environment would impose criminal penalties on heat-of-battle judgment calls. These men and women did not believe they were breaking the law, and indeed they took extraordinary steps to ensure that they didn't. But they worried nonetheless because they would be judged in an atmosphere different from when they acted, because the criminal investigative process is mysterious and scary, because lawyers' fees can cause devastating financial losses, and because an investigation can produce reputation-ruining dishonor and possibly end one's career, even if you emerge "innocent."

Why, then, do they even come close to the legal line? Why risk reputation, fortune, and perhaps liberty? Why not play it safe? Many counterterrorism officials did play it safe before 9/11, when the criminalization of war and intelligence contributed to the paralyzing risk aversion that pervaded the White House and the intelligence community. The 9/11 attacks, however, made playing it safe no longer feasible.

CHAPTER 3

Fear and OLC

One morning in the spring of 2004, I went to the White House to deliver bad news. For months, Patrick Philbin and I had been trying to find a way to put an important counterterrorism initiative on a proper legal footing. We had come up empty, however, and we were now meeting with Alberto Gonzales and David Addington to explain that the Justice Department could not support the initiative's legality.

"If you rule that way, the blood of the hundred thousand people who die in the next attack will be on *your* hands," reacted David Addington, in disgust.

Addington's angry response reflected the profound anxieties that pervaded the Bush administration. Every morning the President sees a "threat matrix" that, as FBI Director Robert Mueller describes it, lists "every threat directed at the United States in the past 24 hours."[1] The matrix can be many dozen pages long. It includes warnings extracted from the tens of billions of foreign phone calls and email messages that fly around the world each day, from scores of human informants, from satellite photographs, and from other sources. It summarizes every known new threat, ranging from obviously false accusations to credible warnings about catastrophic weapons of mass destruction and conventional attacks in the United States and allied countries around the globe. For each threat the matrix lists possible targets, information on the group planning the attack, an analysis of the threat's credibility, and notes about actions taken in response.[2]

It is hard to overstate the impact that the incessant waves of threat reports have on the judgment of people inside the executive branch who are responsible for protecting American lives. "[Y]ou simply could not sit where I did and read what passed across my desk on a daily basis and be anything other than scared to death about what it portended," wrote George Tenet in his memoir *At the Center of the Storm*, capturing the attitude of every person I knew who regularly read the threat matrix. "You could drive yourself crazy believing all or even half of what was in" the threat matrix, he added.[3] Jim Baker, who until recently was the head of the Office of Intelligence Policy and Review, had a similar reaction. Reading the matrix every day is "like being stuck in a room listening to loud Led Zeppelin music," he told me. After a while, you begin to "suffer from sensory overload" and become "paranoid" about the threat.[4] Former Deputy Attorney General Jim Comey, the most levelheaded person I knew in government, says that reading about plans for chemical and biological and nuclear attacks over days and weeks and years causes you to "imagine a threat so severe that it becomes an obsession."[5]

One of the reasons the threats induce fear bordering on obsession is that—despite hundreds of billions of dollars in expenditures, round-the-clock efforts by thousands of people, and years of learning—the government has little "actionable intelligence" about who is going to hit us, or where, or when.[6] During World War II, Franklin Roosevelt would twice daily visit a "map room" filled with giant, frequently updated charts of the globe covered with differently colored and shaped pins and grease-penciled plastic covers that represented the size and location of Allied and enemy ships, airplanes, and troops, as well as the location of Churchill and Stalin. Roosevelt created the map room so that he "could visualize the progress of the war," according to historian Doris Kearns Goodwin.[7] The map room was a crude indicator of the geographic arc of the war. It contained representational errors, it revealed little about the enemy's intentions, and it didn't do much to forecast surprise attacks. But it did provide FDR with a macro picture of where the Germans and the Japanese were and the direction in which they were going.

We don't have the same luxury with our new enemy. General George C. Marshall, writing about World War I, decried war's "chronic obscurity"—the "scarcity or total absence of reliable information" about the enemy's strength and tactics.[8] But the open architecture enemy in the current war elevates chronic obscurity to new extremes. Jim Baker analogizes the task of stopping our enemy to a goalie in a soccer game who "must stop every shot, for the enemy wins if it scores a single goal." The problem, Baker says, "is that the goalie cannot see the ball—it is invisible. So are the players—he doesn't know how many there are, or where they are, or what they look like. He also doesn't know where the sidelines are—they are blurry and constantly shifting, as are the rules of the game itself." The invisible players might shoot the invisible weapon "from the front of the goal, or from the back, or from some other direction—the goalie just doesn't know."[9] Addington and the other goalies throughout the government lacked the information they needed to meet their responsibility to protect the nation. Their want of actionable intelligence combined with their knowledge of what might happen to produce an aggressive, panicked attitude that assumed the worst about threats and embraced a "better safe than sorry" posture toward them.

Two factors exacerbated this anxiety in the spring of 2004 when Philbin and I brought our bad news to the White House. The government was beginning to receive terrorist threat information that was more frightening than at any time since 9/11, according to then-CIA Director George Tenet.[10] And the 9/11 Commission was preparing to grill Condoleezza Rice, John Ashcroft, Robert Mueller, and George Tenet on national television about all the things that hindsight showed they might have done, but didn't, to prevent the September 11 attacks. "This was not something that had to happen," the Republican chair of the Commission, Thomas Kean, told the *New York Times,* summarizing his view of the evidence available before 9/11.[11] The Commission's finger-wagging made clear to every counterterrorism officer in the government that he or she, and ultimately the President, would be blamed harshly by the American people for failing to stop a second attack. The consistent refrain from the Commission, Congress, and pundits of all stripes was that the government must be more forward-leaning against the terrorist threat: more imaginative, more aggressive, less risk-averse. The Bush administration got the message.

It was not a new message. "Don't ever let this happen again," President Bush told my boss, John Ashcroft, during a National

Security Council meeting on September 12, 2001.[12] This simple sentence set the tone for everything Ashcroft's Justice Department would do in the aftermath of 9/11. Bush was not telling Ashcroft to do his best to prevent another attack. He was telling him to stop the next attack, period—whatever it takes. The Commander in Chief's order had an enormous impact on the Attorney General, who would invoke it to me years later when approving or urging me to approve aggressive counterterror actions. Through Ashcroft and other senior advisors, the President's personal mission to check Islamist terrorism at any cost trickled down and pervaded the administration. For counterterrorism officials inside the Bush administration, the 9/11 Commission hearings were simply a loud public affirmation, years after 9/11, of the President's directive.

Ron Suskind has labeled this attitude "the one percent doctrine."[13] He attributes its influence to Vice President Cheney's November 2001 decree to the CIA that low-probability threats must be treated like a certainty. But while Suskind accurately captures the attitude that pervades the government, he misunderstands its source and significance. It does not result from idiosyncratic Bush and Cheney marching orders. Its source lies deeper, and is not unique to this presidency. Rather, it flows from the same combination of factors that caused Roosevelt to take superaggressive actions in the Japanese internment to meet a threat of subversives that pales in comparison to the post-9/11 threat. The 9/11 directive to John Ashcroft and the one percent doctrine are natural responses by an executive branch entirely responsible for protecting the safety of Americans but largely in the dark about where or how the next terrorist attack will occur.

This is why Addington lost it when I told him and Gonzales that

I could not bless the initiative they thought crucial to preventing the next attack.

TO THOSE WHO KNOW how the White House Counsel's Office operates, it will seem very odd that the Counsel to the Vice President was even in the room when I conveyed the Department of Justice's legal advice to Alberto Gonzales. Franklin Roosevelt established the job of Counsel to the President in 1941, and during the next sixty years the "Counsel's Office" grew in importance as an all-purpose presidential advisor, ethics monitor, channel of communication between the White House and an increasingly professionalized and independent Department of Justice, and coordinator of administration legal policy.

Sometime during this period, the Vice President, too, began to hire a lawyer to advise him, but in no previous administration was the Vice President's Counsel so integrated into the operations of the powerful Counsel's Office. This changed in the Bush II presidency, when the Vice President's small office fused into the President's operating structures. The new arrangement reflected Vice President Cheney's enormous influence on President Bush. And it made Addington an altogether different type of Vice President's Counsel, one who received all of the important governmental documents that went to Alberto Gonzales, and one who was always in the room when Gonzales was discussing an important legal issue. Of probably a hundred meetings in Gonzales's office to discuss national security issues, I recall only one when Addington was not there.

Gonzales wanted Addington in the room because Addington knew things that he didn't. Gonzales came to Washington after a career as a corporate lawyer and a state court judge in Texas. He had thought little about presidential war powers, or national security law, or international law, and he had no experience with Washington bureaucratic politics, or with White House relations with Congress. But these subjects were at the heart of Addington's expertise. In the twenty years between 1981 and 9/11, he had been a lawyer in the CIA, the chief counsel for House of Representative committees on intelligence and international relations, a special assistant in the Reagan White House, the Republican counsel on the Iran-Contra committee, and special assistant and later general counsel to Dick Cheney when he was the Secretary of Defense. These experiences gave Addington a more comprehensive knowledge of national security law than anyone in the executive branch, and made him one of the savviest manipulators of the byzantine executive branch bureaucracy. It also gave him clout with Gonzales, who turned to Addington first for answers to the hard legal questions that arose after the 9/11 attacks.

Access wasn't the only source of Addington's power. Power also came from the full backing of his boss, the redoubtable Vice President. Addington had known Cheney and worked closely with him for nearly twenty years. I never once heard Addington invoke Cheney's authority. But it was clear to all that he was Cheney's "eyes, ears, and voice," as former Solicitor General Ted Olson put it.[14] When Addington spoke in Gonzales's office, everyone knew what the Vice President would be telling the President before a final decision was made.

Addington's power from above was supplemented by a deadly seriousness within: about the presidency, about separation of powers, about defeating the terrorists. Addington worked as hard as anyone in government and was always well prepared for meetings. His years of government service gave him much more knowledge than I possessed about many things, especially about how the bureaucracy worked. My years as an academic had given me an expertise about legal issues related to war and terrorism, which helped me to see that Addington's command of these issues, while impressive, was often idiosyncratic. Nonetheless, Addington's seemingly superior knowledge combined with a fierce temper, a sarcastic manner, and the Vice President's implicit backing make him an intimidating and effective advocate.

I was thus not surprised when Addington's broadside about blood on my hands was the first response to my bad news. I knew how he and other higher-ups viewed the stakes of my decision long before I gave it. This is why Philbin and I had been racking our brains for months. Michael Hayden, former NSA Director General and now the Director of the CIA, would often say that he was "troubled if [he was] not using the full authority allowed by law" after 9/11, and that he was "going to live on the edge," where his "spikes will have chalk on them."[15] Hayden's view permeated the executive branch after 9/11, and in light of the clear public demand to act aggressively to stop the terrorist threat, I agreed with it. My job was to make sure the President could act right up to the chalk line of legality. But even blurry chalk lines delineate areas that are clearly out of bounds. Congress had restricted what the President wanted to do here, and Philbin and I simply couldn't find any plausible argument that he could disregard these restrictions.

Addington had a different view. "Are you telling me that the Constitution doesn't empower the President to do what he thinks is necessary to prevent an attack?" he asked. Addington thought it did. He believed presidential power was coextensive with presidential responsibility. Since the President would be blamed for the next homeland attack, he must have the power under the Constitution to do what he deemed necessary to stop it, regardless of what Congress said.

In expressing this view, Addington was channeling the Vice President and ultimately the President. These men felt the same imperatives of responsibility that led Roosevelt and many other presidents to blow through "legalistic" restrictions on presidential authority during times of crisis. I too felt these pressures, and understood the personal consequences of a hand-tying legal decision that might lead to another successful attack. That's why I tried so hard to help the White House do what it wanted to do. But I also had other responsibilities. I was the person charged with interpreting legal restrictions that no President in time of national crisis had ever had to face before. Because many of the laws were criminal, and because we were acting in a super-legalistic culture, when I said "no" my superiors could not ignore me as easily as Roosevelt had ignored his Justice Department advisors.

"The President is free to overrule me if he wants," I told Gonzales and Addington after the latter had settled down.

This was not news. Gonzales and Addington were well aware that the President stood atop the executive branch and could in theory reverse any OLC decision and set legal policy for the executive branch. But overruling the head of OLC was not so easy in practice, especially since the White House had been relying heavily on "yes's" from OLC for the past two and a half years. "Your office is expert on the law and the President is not," FBI Director Bob Mueller once told me, explaining why he felt obliged to follow an

OLC legal opinion even if the President disagreed. The President is not a lawyer and his small legal staff is not well equipped to do the careful research and analysis needed for complicated legal problems. Even if the President, acting on the advice of his White House lawyers, determined that OLC's analysis was erroneous, the fact that OLC thought otherwise would give serious pause to the officials asked to act in the teeth of OLC's opinion. They might believe that OLC's legal analysis was more detached and thorough and thus a better interpretation of the law. And if a criminal restriction was in issue, they might worry that reliance on a President's legal imprimatur in the face of an OLC opinion to the contrary would not be respected by a future Justice Department of a different administration when deciding whether to prosecute.

"The President can also ignore the law, and act extralegally," I said.

Gonzales and Addington looked at me as if I were crazy. I was not urging the President to break the law, I emphasized. I was simply letting his legal advisors know that there were honorable precedents, going back to the founding of the nation, of defying legal restrictions in time of crisis. "A strict observance of the written laws is doubtless *one* of the high virtues of a good citizen, but it is not *the highest*," Thomas Jefferson wrote to a friend in 1810. "The laws of necessity, of self-preservation, of saving our country when in danger, are of higher obligation. To lose our country by a scrupulous adherence to written law, would be to lose the law itself, with life, liberty, property and all those who are enjoying them with us; thus absurdly sacrificing the end to the means."[16]

Jefferson was writing in a tradition of prerogative power that went back to the influential English philosopher John Locke, who believed that a leader's first duty was to protect the country, not

follow the law. But there was an important caveat to tl
tive, which I also conveyed to Gonzales and Addington.
prevent abuse, the leader who disregards the law should c
licly, throwing himself on the mercy of Congress and the
that they could decide whether the emergency was severe enough
to warrant extralegal action. "The line of discrimination between
cases may be difficult," Jefferson noted, "but the good officer is
bound to draw it at his own peril, and throw himself on the justice
of his country and the rectitude of his motives."[17] Public avowal of
extralegal actions, and after-the-fact political scrutiny, limited and
legitimized the dangerous presidential prerogative.

Gonzales, Addington, and their respective clients were not
remotely interested in this view. They believed their actions were
lawful, and even if they didn't, they could not confess error publicly, as the logic of the prerogative power required, because doing
so would tip off the enemy about our counterterrorist efforts. But
beyond these points, the idea of extralegal presidential actions simply wasn't feasible in 2004 in the way it was in 1810 or 1861 or
1942. It wasn't feasible for the same reasons that Roosevelt's political understanding of law and lawyers was no longer an option. The
post–Watergate hyper-legalization of warfare, and the attendant
proliferation of criminal investigators, had become so ingrained
and threatening that the very idea of acting extralegally was simply
off the table, even in times of crisis. The President had to do what
he had to do to protect the country. And the lawyers had to find
some way to make what he did legal.

The lawyers might have done this by reinterpreting laws to
make them more permissive, or by construing the President's
Commander-in-Chief power to forbid congressional intrusion.

But Addington often relied on a simpler idea that was implicit in his original hostile question to me: the Constitution empowers the President to exercise prerogative powers to do what is necessary in an emergency to save the country. And we are, after all, technically in an emergency. We have been since President Bush declared, on September 14, 2001, that "a national emergency exists by reason of the terrorist attacks at the World Trade Center, New York, New York, and the Pentagon, and the continuing and immediate threat of further attacks on the United States."[18]

The idea of an overriding emergency executive power is not the crazy notion that some have made it out to be. Addington probably got the idea from Abraham Lincoln, a president he admired and had studied carefully, and whom we often discussed. In response to the secession crisis that began when Confederate forces fired on Fort Sumter, Lincoln raised armies and borrowed money on the credit of the United States, both powers that the Constitution gave to Congress; he suspended the writ of habeas corpus in many places even though most constitutional scholars, then and now, believed that only Congress could do this; he imposed a blockade on the South without specific congressional approval; he imprisoned thousands of southern sympathizers and war agitators without any charge or due process; and he ignored a judicial order from the Chief Justice of the Supreme Court to release a prisoner detained illegally.[19]

No president before or since Lincoln has acted in such disregard of constitutional traditions, perhaps because no president has faced such an imminent threat to the nation's existence. Lincoln nonetheless informed Congress about all of these acts, publicly defended them as necessary to meet the crisis, and asked Congress to approve them. Many of these measures, "whether strictly legal or not, were ventured upon under what appeared to be a popular demand and a public necessity, trusting then as now that Congress would readily ratify them," Lincoln told Congress in a July 4, 1861, address that satisfied perfectly the Locke-Jefferson paradigm.[20]

But Lincoln ultimately went beyond Locke's and Jefferson's prerogative and laid the seeds for the very different and more dangerous idea that it was legal for the President to do whatever is necessary to protect the nation. The Constitution requires all federal officers to swear to "support this Constitution," but it requires the President alone to swear to the best of his ability, to *"preserve, protect* and *defend* the Constitution of the United States." Lincoln thought this special oath conferred upon him a special constitutional "duty of preserving, by every indispensable means, that government—that nation—of which that constitution was the organic law." He believed that "measures, otherwise unconstitutional, might become lawful, by becoming indispensable to the preservation of the constitution, through the preservation of the nation."[21]

This was a "striking innovation," in the words of historian Arthur M. Schlesinger, Jr., for "where Jefferson, like Locke, saw emergency power as a weapon outside and beyond the Constitution, Lincoln suggested that crisis made it in some sense a constitutional power."[22] It was an innovation that Franklin Roosevelt, who also studied Lincoln closely, would employ. In the late summer of 1942, Roosevelt was planning for the first great Allied offensive—Operation Torch, the invasion of North Africa designed to win control of the Mediterranean Sea. Roosevelt faced a much more sensitive and demanding problem at home, however: inflation. An emergency price control law enacted earlier that year denied the government the power to impose adequate farm price ceilings. The result was a sharp increase in the price of basic foodstuffs that hit poor families the hardest.

"[T]he war effort as a whole could survive a catastrophic failure of Torch," noted historian Kenneth Davis, "but could not survive the runaway inflation now immediately threatening."[23] Roosevelt faced a Congress, however, that did not want to revisit price control laws in the run-up to the 1942 midterm elections. After deliberating with his advisors, he threatened Congress into action, telling it on Labor Day that if it did not repeal the price control law soon, he would ignore it. "The President has the powers, under the Constitution and under Congressional acts, to take measures necessary to avert a disaster which would interfere with the winning of the war," Roosevelt warned, in words nearly identical to ones that Addington would often address to me. "In the event that Congress should fail to act, and act adequately, I shall accept the responsibility, and I will act."[24] Congress capitulated one month later.

Addington was thus not on entirely thin ice in thinking that President Bush, like Franklin Roosevelt and Abraham Lincoln, had the power under the Constitution to do what was necessary to save the country in an emergency. But Addington took this idea further than Roosevelt and Lincoln. Roosevelt's advisors urged him to invoke his emergency power to disregard the price control law without even consulting Congress. But although Roosevelt had an unusually broad view of his presidential authorities, he was "extremely reluctant," according to Davis, to take a step that was "normally constitutionally a legislative function," especially since price controls were not obviously something that fell within his military powers.[25] So Roosevelt compromised: he asserted the extraordinary emergency power, but in a way that forced Congress itself to act. Lincoln claimed and exercised similar emergency powers. But he too was sensitive to Congress's prerogatives and constitutional propriety. He invoked the emergency power to exercise powers reserved for Congress. But he did so only until Congress could meet in session and, at Lincoln's invitation, either ratify or reject his actions.

Addington had no such instincts. To the contrary, long before 9/11 he and his boss had set out to reverse what they saw as Congress's illegitimate decades-long intrusions on "unitary" executive power. The much-discussed phrase "unitary executive" first gained wide use in the 1980s, when the Reagan administration used the idea to fight off congressional attempts to check presidential power by creating executive officers and offices beyond the reach of the President's policy directives. Beginning in the fall of 2004, journalists began to use the term "unitary executive" to capture the very different Cheney-Addington view that Congress cannot unduly limit the Commander in Chief's prerogatives during wartime. "Even in a White House known for its dedication to conservative philosophy," said the *Washington Post*'s Dana Milbank in the first major newspaper article to use the term in the new way, "Addington is known as an ideologue, an adherent of an obscure philosophy called the unitary executive theory that favors an extraordinarily powerful president."[26]

After a while (but not at first), the White House too began to invoke the phrase "unitary executive" not only in its traditional 1980s version but also in its newer and more aggressive incarnation. In a famous signing statement that Addington doubtlessly had a hand in, for example, the President pronounced that he would

construe the 2005 Detainee Treatment Act's limitation on his interrogation powers "in a manner consistent with the constitutional
authority of the President to supervise the unitary executive branch
and as Commander in Chief and consistent with the constitutional
limitations on the judicial power, which will assist in achieving the
shared objective of the Congress and the President ... of protecting
the American people from further terrorist attacks."[27]

The views that ended up in this 2005 signing statement first took
root in the 1970s, when Richard Cheney was Chief of Staff during the last two years of Gerald Ford's presidency, a time when an
aggressive post-Watergate Congress was busy crafting many of the
laws that so infuriatingly tied the President's hands in the post-9/11
world. Cheney was at the President's side during what he would
later call "the nadir of the modern presidency in terms of authority
and legitimacy," and he would spend the rest of his distinguished
public career trying to restore the presidency to what he viewed
as its rightful place.[28] Addington began to embrace similar views
when he was a young CIA lawyer in the early 1980s. Colleagues
in the CIA remember Addington as relatively quiet and bookish,
a far cry from the brash bureaucratic browbeater he later became.
But it was his experience coming to grips with the unprecedented
restrictions that Congress, again in the 1970s, had placed on the
CIA and the presidency that led Addington to believe, in the words
of a former top CIA lawyer, that "the Presidency was too weakened," and that "in foreign policy the executive is meant to be quite
powerful."[29]

By 1987, both Cheney and Addington were, literally, on the same
page on executive power—the pages of the Minority Report of the
Congressional Committees Investigating the Iran-Contra Affair.

The Iran-Contra scandal grew out of the efforts by Oliver North in the White House to channel the proceeds from secret arms sales to Iran to support the Nicaraguan Contras, thereby circumventing Congress's ban on using appropriated funds for such a purpose. "A small group of senior officials believed that they alone knew what was right," the scathing investigating committee's Majority Report stated. These men "viewed knowledge of their actions by others in the Government as a threat to their objectives."[30] The Majority Report believed that the Iran-Contra policies resulted from "secrecy, deception, and disdain for the law," as well as "disrespect for Congress' efforts to perform its Constitutional oversight role in foreign policy."[31]

The Minority Report disagreed sharply. Issued in the name of then-Representative Richard Cheney and seven other congressmen, and researched by David Addington, a Counsel on the Committee, it claimed that the Majority Report rested "upon an aggrandizing theory of Congress' foreign policy powers that is itself part of the problem." The Minority Report explained that Congress was to blame for the Iran-Contra policies, which grew out of the White House's "legitimate frustration with abuses of power and irresolution by the legislative branch."[32] It then launched into an extraordinary twenty-two-page scholarly argument to demonstrate that Congress had overstepped its authority in tying down the presidency. The report noted that the "boundless view of Congressional power began to take hold in the 1970's, in the wake of the Vietnam War," and then recited two hundred years of constitutional history to argue that this view was wrong.[33] "Many, if not all, of the actions by representatives of the U.S. government that have been alleged to run counter to the Boland amendments," the Minority

Report concluded, "were constitutionally protected against limitation by Congress," and the "executive was not bound to follow an unconstitutional effort to limit the President's powers."[34] Almost twenty years later, at the height of the controversy over the Bush II administration's Terrorist Surveillance Program, Cheney would proudly point back to the obscure Minority Report as "very good in laying out a robust view of the president's prerogatives with respect to the conduct of especially foreign policy and national security matters."[35]

A few years after the Iran-Contra Affair, Secretary of Defense Cheney, acting in consultation with his general counsel, David Addington, expressed a similarly broad conception of presidential power in advising the first President Bush that he had the constitutional authority to invade Iraq without congressional authorization. Cheney testified before Congress that President Bush didn't require "any additional authorization from the Congress" before attacking Iraq.[36] "I was not enthusiastic about going to Congress to ask for an additional grant of authority," Cheney later said. "I was concerned that they might well vote NO and that would make life more difficult for us,"[37] he added, in perfect anticipation of arguments that a decade later would persuade the Bush II administration not to seek congressional input in the war on terrorism.

Colin Powell is reported to have said that David Addington "doesn't care about the Constitution."[38] If he said this, he was wrong. Addington always carried a tattered copy of the Constitution in his coat pocket, and would often pull it out and quote from it with reverence. Both he and his boss Cheney seemed to care passionately about the Constitution as they understood it. That is why they fought so hard to return the presidency to what they viewed as its rightful constitutional place. It is why Cheney and the President told top aides at the outset of the first term that past presidents had "eroded" presidential power, and that they wanted "to restore" it so that they could "hand off a much more powerful presidency" to their successors.[39] After 9/11, Gonzales and Addington would invoke these words like a mantra when we were deciding whether and how aggressive to be in the war on terrorism.

This underlying commitment to expanding presidential power distinguishes the Bush administration from the Lincoln and Roosevelt administrations. Lincoln and Roosevelt did not face anything like the congressional restrictions on presidential discretion that President Bush faced, and thus had a less pressing need to assert presidential prerogatives vis-à-vis Congress. But nor were Lincoln and Roosevelt executive power ideologues. Lincoln was ever anxious about his unprecedented assertions of presidential power. He made elaborate public efforts to explain them. And he almost always sought congressional support. Roosevelt was less timid about exercising broad presidential powers. But he consulted widely before exercising them, and he used the powers as a last resort to accomplish what he thought were vital ends, not as part of an aggressive program to expand presidential power for its own sake.

Vice President Cheney and David Addington—and through their influence, President Bush and Alberto Gonzales—had no qualms on this subject. They shared a commitment to expanding presidential power that they had long been anxious to implement. It is not right to say, as some have done, that these men took advantage of the 9/11 attacks to implement a radical pro-President agenda. But their unusual conception of presidential prerogative influenced everything they did to meet the post-9/11 threat.

MY CONFRONTATION WITH DAVID ADDINGTON that morning in the White House Counsel's office was a small episode in one of the underappreciated stories in the war on terrorism: the daily clash inside the Bush administration between fear of another attack, which drives officials into doing whatever they can to prevent it, and the countervailing fear of violating the law, which checks their urge toward prevention. After 9/11, the Bush administration feared for the nation's safety as much as Franklin Roosevelt had. But Roosevelt's political conception of legal constraints had largely vanished, and by 2001 had been replaced by a fiercely legalistic conception of unprecedented wartime constraints on the presidency. When President Bush and his senior advisors began to order the aggressive actions that they believed the post-9/11 situation demanded—covert military action, surveillance, detention, interrogation, military trials, and the like—they encountered these constraints for the first time in a major conflict.

The main problem was not that senior officials faced potential legal jeopardy. These officials worried intensely about violating the law and later being hauled before a grand jury or court. But they were usually willing to take risks to fulfill the enormous responsibilities that they had assumed to protect the country. And many of them, I think, implicitly believed they would likely be pardoned if they mistakenly crossed the line in executing the President's commands.

The main problem was the effect that the legalization of warfare and intelligence had on lower-level officials in the Defense

Department, the CIA, and the National Security Agency. The White House couldn't execute its plans to check al Qaeda without the cooperation of the military and intelligence bureaucracy. But these bureaucracies—especially in the intelligence community—had in the 1980s and 1990s become institutionally disinclined to take risks. The Church and Pike investigations of the 1970s and the Iran-Contra scandal in the 1980s taught the intelligence community to worry about what a 1996 Council on Foreign Relations study decried as "retroactive discipline"—the idea that no matter how much political and legal support an intelligence operative gets before engaging in aggressive actions, he will be punished after the fact by a different set of rules created in a different political environment.[40] "[I]t would simplify matters if at the time we were assigned to a covert action program, the letter of reprimand should accompany the orders, as receipt of one seemed inevitable," Melissa Boyle Mahle, a CIA Middle East field operative would tell her colleagues, half-jokingly.[41]

This mounting caution was reinforced by the swarm of lawyers that rose up in the military and intelligence establishment to interpret multiplying laws and provide cover for those asked to act close to the legal line. In the 1970s the CIA had only a handful of lawyers. But as legal restrictions on CIA activities grew, and despite huge personnel cuts in the 1990s, the number of CIA lawyers rose and rose, and today stands at well over one hundred. The number of lawyers in the Defense Department grew even more steeply during this period, and today stands at over ten thousand, not including reservists. As lawyers grew in number, they grew in influence. Commanding officers and intelligence operatives seeking to avoid "retroactive discipline" increasingly sought lawyers' permission before acting. If the lawyer said "no," the official had a perfect excuse for not acting. If the lawyer said "yes," the official was effectively immunized from legal liability, including jail. Seeking a lawyer's input thus became a way to avoid both blame and jail.

Lawyers are by nature and training a cautious bunch, and as their power grew, their caution spread. "I know from my work on this Committee for the past 10 years that lawyers at CIA sometimes have displayed a risk aversion in the advice they give their clients," Senator Bob Graham, the distinguished Democrat on the Senate Intelligence Committee, complained one year after 9/11, during the confirmation hearings of Scott Muller for the General Counsel of the CIA. Senator Graham and many others on the Senate and House intelligence committees in both parties were furious about what Graham called "cautious lawyering" at the CIA. "Unfortunately, we are not living in times in which lawyers can say no to an operation just to play it safe," he told Muller. "We need excellent, aggressive lawyers who give sound, accurate legal advice, not lawyers who say no to an otherwise legal operation just because it is easier to put on the brakes." Graham concluded by asking Muller to give "cutting-edge legal advice that lets the operators do their jobs quickly and aggressively within the confines of law and regulation."[42]

Senator Graham's disquisition reveals the national security lawyer's central dilemma. He is criticized for being too cautious, for putting on the brakes, for playing it safe in a dangerous world that cannot afford such risk aversion. But he is in the same breath cautioned to give "sound, accurate" legal advice within the "confines" of the law. It is often impossible to do both. The laws that govern the intelligence agencies are often not written in black and white, but rather in complex shades of gray. When intelligence clients ask lawyers whether aggressive counterterrorism actions are legal, clear answers don't always leap from the pages of the U.S. Code. Often the best a lawyer can do is to lay out degrees of legal risk, and to advise that the further the client pushes into the dark gray areas of legal prohibitions, the more legal risk he assumes. Even when the law is clear, lawyers sometimes offer muddy interpretations to serve a separate agenda. Some lawyers will use legal review as an opportunity to push their beliefs about the appropriateness of the proposed action, or to serve the institutional interests of their bureaucracy. Others will try to cover their behinds in case anything goes wrong by giving hedged answers when a clearer "yes" would have been more appropriate. Whatever its source, wishy-washy legal advice understandably infuriates the men and women who are asked to take aggressive action and want to know whether what they are about to do is legal or not, period. When they hear a government lawyer talking about shades of gray and degrees of risk, they understandably hesitate, especially when criminal laws are in play.

Lawyers weren't the only contributors to risk aversion. Inspectors general too sometimes engaged in "retroactive discipline" of lawyers themselves, making the lawyers even more cautious than usual. Each agency's "IG," as the office is called, reviews agency practices for waste, fraud, and abuse. IGs can also do criminal investigations and make criminal referrals to the Justice Department. Many IGs perform valuable audits that reveal bad practices and recommend improvements. The Department of Justice IG, for example, did outstanding work during my time there. I had a different experience, however, with the CIA Inspector General's office. In one investigation involving legal issues I knew a lot about, CIA IG investigators who weren't lawyers second-guessed complex legal interpretations that lawyers in the CIA General Counsel's Office had made under difficult circumstances. The investigators came across to me as aggressive prosecutors out to get their prey rather than neutral and helpful auditors trying to improve the agency's work. When I asked them whether they worried that this attitude would have a harmful, chilling effect on CIA lawyers, and thus on the agency itself, they said that wasn't their concern. I can only imagine the devastating impact this attitude had on the agency lawyers whom Senator Graham and others pressured daily not to engage in "cautious lawyering."

All of these factors combined to create a paralyzing culture of risk-averse legalism in the military and, especially, intelligence establishments before 9/11. In response to al Qaeda's August 1998 bombing of American embassies in Dar es Salaam, Tanzania, and Nairobi, Kenya, President Clinton issued several secret authorizations for the CIA to work with Afghan tribal elements to capture and if necessary kill Osama Bin Laden. The CIA had Bin Laden in its sights. But everyone in the CIA knew about Executive Order 12333, the 1970s-era ban on assassinations. Everyone also knew the fate of Robert Baer, a CIA case officer who, in the midst of organizing opposition to Saddam Hussein in 1995, was called home to Langley to face a career-ending FBI investigation for conspiring to murder Hussein.[43] This is one reason why George Tenet and other senior CIA managers insisted that the White House be unambiguously clear about what the CIA was authorized to do to Bin Laden. "CIA managers had been conditioned by history to read their written [authorizations] literally," notes Steve Coll in *Ghost Wars*, the most comprehensive history of CIA activity in Afghanistan before the 9/11 attacks. "Where the words were not clear, they recommended caution to their officers in the field."[44]

The clear authorization that the CIA sought never came. Clinton's OLC agreed that the assassination ban did not apply to a military target, like Osama Bin Laden, who posed an imminent threat to the United States.[45] So far so good. But then the ambiguities appeared. White House and Justice Department lawyers opposed an unrestricted lethal operation against Bin Laden, and would authorize his killing only if it were necessary for self-defense in the course of legitimately arresting him. This distinction was bad enough from the CIA's perspective, but the operation was further muddied by the lawyers' refusal to be clear about what constituted self-defense, or about how imminent a threat Bin Laden must pose before the CIA operation could commence. "Wiggle room" in the authorization led the CIA to worry, in Coll's account, "that if an operation in Afghanistan went bad, they would be accused of having acted outside the memo's scope."[46] Fear of retroactive discipline, induced by cautious legal authorizations, led the CIA to forego the covert operation.[47]

In this and many other episodes prior to 9/11, intelligence officers spooked by cautious lawyers failed to take actions that might have prevented the 9/11 attacks. The CIA was, in the words of the 9/11 Commission Report, "institutionally averse to risk," and law and lawyers were a big part of the problem.[48] It didn't help that CIA leaders encouraged their officers to buy professional liability insurance for legal expenses to be incurred in the expected criminal and related investigations.[49] "I think it's deeply disturbing that we have a system of government that asks young men and women to go overseas and take enormous risks for them and then say, 'Oh, by the way, you might want to get insurance to provide counsel because we might subsequently decide to prosecute you tomorrow for what we're asking you to do today,'" says Jeffrey Smith, a former CIA General Counsel.[50] Robert Baer, who was in a position to know, says the signal the insurance sends is clear. "Don't take risky assignments. Don't get involved in any contravention or possible contravention of American law. Just don't do it. It's not worth it. You can't afford the lawyers. The organization's not going to back you up. Take a nice safe assignment. Take no risks."[51]

After 9/11, of course, the threat from terrorism seemed much different, and pressure on the CIA to take risks increased. But all of the institutional factors contributing to risk aversion remained in place, and stood as an obstacle to the White House's aggressive go-it-alone strategy. This is where the OLC became crucial. More than any agency in the government, OLC could provide the legal cover needed to overcome law-induced bureaucratic risk-aversion. "It is practically impossible to prosecute someone who relied in good faith on an OLC opinion, even if the opinion turns out to be wrong," a senior Justice Department prosecutor once told me. OLC speaks for the Justice Department, and it is the Justice Department that prosecutes violations of criminal law. If OLC interprets a law to allow a proposed action, then the Justice Department won't prosecute those who rely on the OLC ruling. Even independent counsels would have trouble going after someone who reasonably relied on one. This is true even if OLC turns out to be wrong according to a court. One consequence of OLC's authority to interpret the law is the power to bestow on government officials what is effectively an advance pardon for actions taken at the edges of vague criminal laws. This is the flip side of OLC's power to say "no," and to put a brake on governmental operations. It is one of the most momentous and dangerous powers in the government: the power to dispense get-out-of-jail-free cards.

As the ambiguous 1998 advice about assassinating Bin Laden shows, however, OLC would have been of little help to the Bush II White House without someone in the office willing and able to write clear and forceful opinions supporting the President's aggressive counterterrorism program. By an accident of fate, the one person in the government who shared the Cheney-Addington view of presidential power—John Yoo—was sitting in OLC on September 11. (It was an accident of fate because Addington and Cheney did not know Yoo before he came to government, and had nothing to do with placing him in OLC.) Yoo was a prominent academic who possessed at the tip of his confident pen all of the crucial precedents from the founding era, the Civil War, and World War II that would be vital in helping the administration respond to al Qaeda. As a presidential war scholar, he was known for crafting historical arguments to support the President's power to use military force without congressional authorization. He believed that when the Constitution vested "the executive power" in the President, it gave him all of the military powers possessed by the King of England save those expressly given to Congress. He also thought that Congress could not limit the President's broad military powers, including his power to respond to terrorist attacks and threats.

A September 25, 2001, memorandum from Yoo to the White House, entitled "The President's Constitutional Authority to Conduct Military Operations Against Terrorists and Nations Supporting Them," set the tone for all that was to come.[52] In a mere two weeks after the attacks, while burdened with dozens of other emergency duties, Yoo cranked out a twenty-page document that collected over one hundred authorities—from the Constitution, statutes, presidential practice, and judicial opinions—to show that the President could legally "deploy military force preemptively against terrorist organizations or the States that harbor or support them, whether or not they can be linked to the specific terrorist incidents of September 11."[53] By itself this proposition is not terribly controversial, for presidents have long used the U.S. military to respond to various threats to U.S. interests abroad. But Yoo was not done. Completely in sync with Addington, he went a large and unsupported step further, and concluded that Congress could do nothing to check the President's power to respond to the terrorist threat. The first branch of government, Yoo argued without any citation of authority, cannot "place any limits on the President's determinations as to any terrorist threat, the amount of military force to be used in response, or the method, timing, and nature of the response. These decisions, under our Constitution, are for the President alone to make."[54]

For a White House deeply concerned by terrorism and facing an unprecedented array of legal barriers to action, Yoo was a godsend. In close coordination with the War Council, he pumped out opinions on all manner of terrorism-related topics with a clarity of approval that emboldened the hesitant bureaucracy.

CHAPTER 4

When Lawyers Make
Terrorism Policy

On September 26, 2002, three weeks after I began to work at the Department of Defense, I visited the forty-five-square-mile American naval base at Guantanamo Bay ("GTMO") in southeastern Cuba. The night before, as my wife and I were having dinner, Jim Haynes's assistant called to say that a spot had opened up on the plane Haynes was taking to Cuba the next morning. Nine hours later I drove to Andrews Air Force Base in Maryland, where just after dawn I and a dozen others took off in a Gulfstream jet for Cuba. It was my fortieth birthday.

The purpose of the trip was to review the facilities for Taliban and al Qaeda detainees in U.S. military custody. On the plane I was introduced to many important legal players in the administration, including David Addington, Patrick Philbin, John Rizzo (then the number-two lawyer in the CIA, and now its acting General Counsel), Alice Fisher (now head of the Criminal Division at the

Department of Justice), and several Pentagon lawyers. A little over three hours later, we landed in tropical Cuba, took a twenty-minute ferry across Guantanamo Bay, and boarded a bus for a brief ride to Camp Delta, the new detention facility. After a briefing on the operation of the camp from military officials, we walked through a detention building that held two-dozen orange jumpsuit–clad prisoners in mesh cells, each of which contained a bed, a sink, a toilet, and a copy of the Koran. Some of the detainees ignored us. Some stared at us with an empty gaze. Some looked at us with an anger that I had never before experienced. We next witnessed an ongoing interrogation, toured the camp's medical facilities, and saw the spot where construction was about to begin on a building to house military commissions. And then we took the bus and ferry trip back to the plane and, three hours after we arrived, left the island.

Our party did not head straight back to Washington. Instead, we flew to South Carolina to visit a military jail, the U.S. Naval Consolidated Brig in Charleston. We weren't there to see the dozens of sailors serving time for murder and assault. We stopped instead to see José Padilla, an American citizen arrested on May 8, 2002, in Chicago's O'Hare International airport on account of his connections to senior al Qaeda officials in Afghanistan and Pakistan, and, as Attorney General Ashcroft put it, his alleged intention to "build and explode a radiological dispersion device, or 'dirty bomb,' in the United States."[1] The government originally sent Padilla to New York, held him as a "material witness" in connection with the grand jury inquiries into the 9/11 attacks, and gave him a lawyer. A month later, however, President Bush designated him an "enemy combatant" whose detention without charge or trial was "necessary" to prevent him from "aiding al Qaeda in its efforts to attack the United States or its armed forces, other governmental personnel, or citizens."[2] The government then transferred Padilla to the naval brig in Charleston, where he occupied a cell in a wing to himself and was denied legal assistance.

After an hour-long tour and briefing at the supermodern Charleston brig, our party returned to the airport and reboarded the Gulfstream. We still weren't headed home. As evening approached, we flew to another naval brig, this time in Norfolk, to see another U.S. citizen enemy combatant, Yaser Hamdi. Hamdi had been captured in 2001 in Afghanistan fighting for the Taliban, designated an enemy combatant, and sent to Guantanamo Bay. When the U.S. military discovered that he was born in Baton Rouge, Louisiana, and thus was a U.S. citizen, it transferred him to the naval brig in Norfolk. By comparison to its sister prison in Charleston, the Norfolk brig was dilapidated. The briefing room had the look, feel, and smell of a 1950s classroom, and the entire facility seemed dark and old. After being briefed on the conditions of Hamdi's confinement and learning about the very limited contact he had had with any human being during the previous six months, we shuffled through gloomy corridors to a guard station command center to have a look at Hamdi himself. Top administration lawyers crowded around the small black-and-white closed-circuit television bolted in the back corner of the room, and witnessed the barely twenty-two-year-old Yaser Hamdi—it was his birthday as well[3]—in the corner of his small cell in an unused wing of the brig, crouched in a fetal position, apparently asleep.

Before I saw him on the closed-circuit television, I had no sympathy for Hamdi, whom I knew had volunteered to fight for the tyrannical Taliban. Witnessing the unmoving Hamdi on that fuzzy black-and-white screen, however, moved me. Something seemed wrong. It seemed unnecessarily extreme to hold a twenty-two-year-old foot soldier in a remote wing of a run-down prison in a tiny cell, isolated from almost all human contact and with no access to a lawyer. "This is what habeas corpus is for," I thought to myself, somewhat embarrassed at the squishy sentiment. (Habeas corpus is a process that allows judges to scrutinize the legality of executive detentions.) I immediately thought my reaction was misplaced. I didn't question the legality of holding Hamdi. I had no doubt that (as the Supreme Court would affirm twenty months later) the administration had legal authority to detain Hamdi, without charge or trial, just as Franklin Roosevelt had detained over four hundred thousand members of the German and Italian armies in the United States, including many American citizens, during World War II.[4] My real thought was whether it was prudent to do so in this way, in these circumstances.

That fleeting qualm on my fortieth birthday was my first insight into a characteristic mistake that the Bush administration made in the war on terrorism. On issue after issue, the administration had powerful legal arguments but ultimately made mistakes on important questions of policy. It got policies wrong, ironically, because it was excessively legalistic, because it often substituted legal analysis for political judgment, and because it was too committed to expanding the President's constitutional powers.

THE ADMINISTRATION'S FIRST and most fundamental post-9/11 decision occurred on September 11 itself. For decades the

U.S. government had officially viewed terrorism as a law enforcement problem. But when Andrew Card told President Bush in a Sarasota elementary school on the morning of 9/11 that America was under attack, the President decided that the conflict with Islamist terrorism must be viewed as a war. "They had declared war on us, and I made up my mind at that moment that we were going to war," Bush told Bob Woodward.[5] "Our war on terror begins with al Qaeda, but it does not end there," he told Congress and the American people, nine days later. "It will not end until every terrorist group of global reach has been found, stopped and defeated."[6]

The very notion of a "war on terror" has been much maligned, at home and especially abroad, and is increasingly out of fashion. The conflict with al Qaeda and other Islamist terrorist groups, critics say, does not qualify as a "real" war, but rather is war only in a metaphorical sense, akin to the war on drugs, or poverty, or crime. "War is traditionally defined as a state of belligerency between sovereigns," says Yale Law Professor Bruce Ackerman, in a typical formulation. "The wars with Afghanistan and Iraq were wars; the struggle against Osama bin Laden and al Qaeda is not."[7] Terrorism, by contrast, is a technique, and we can't be at war with a technique. "Once we allow ourselves to declare war on a technique, we open up a dangerous path, authorizing the president to lash out at amorphous threats without the need to define them," Ackerman adds.[8]

These criticisms capture important anxieties about using a war framework against uniformless non-state-actor terrorists in a seemingly endless conflict. But technically they are baseless. War is not, in fact, something only sovereign states do. International law recognizes that "armed conflicts," as modern wars are called, can take place between nations and non-state actors.[9] American history is replete with presidents exercising full military powers in wars with non-state actors such as pirates, the Chinese boxers, and Pancho Villa. More recently, the Office of Legal Counsel in the Clinton administration secretly concluded in the 1990s—as a prerequisite to its efforts to capture and if necessary kill Osama Bin Laden—that the United States was in an armed conflict with al Qaeda.[10]*

Nor, despite some soaring Bush administration rhetoric, is the "war on terror" a war against a technique. The basic contours of the war were established by Congress three days after 9/11, when it authorized the President to use "all necessary and appropriate force"—the traditional phrase that triggers the President's full military war powers—against the nations, organizations, and persons responsible for 9/11.[11] Congress also recognized that the President has authority under the Constitution, independent of congressional approval, "to take action to deter and prevent acts of international terrorism against the United States."[12] This is the authority Bill Clinton exercised when he launched Tomahawk missiles into Afghanistan and Sudan in 1998 in response to al Qaeda's attacks on the American embassies in Africa. These two sources of power—from Congress, and from the Constitution—allow war not against terrorism-the-technique, but rather against specific people, groups, and nations that commit terrorist attacks on the United States or that imminently threaten to do so. It is harder in this war than in past wars to identify the uniformless and ever-changing enemy with precision. But Congress has not authorized war against the Irish Republican Army, the Sri Lankan Tamil Tigers, the Basque ETA, or the many other terrorist groups that do not threaten the United States, and the President lacks the constitutional power to use military force against these groups.

In 2007 and beyond, it may be a good idea to stop using the rhetoric of a "war on terror," either because the phrase misleads the public to think we are fighting a tactic; or because, as Donald Rumsfeld noted in 2006, it "creates a level of expectation of victory and an ending within 30 or 60 minutes [like] a soap opera"; or because, as the British Foreign Office concluded at about the same time, the very use of "war" rhetoric strengthens terrorists and invites attacks; or for some other reason.[13] But whatever the right rhetorical approach may be, both Congress and the President decided in September 2001 that the conflict with al Qaeda and its affiliate Islamist terrorist organizations must be viewed through the legal prism of war. Congress reaffirmed this authorization in 2006, and the Supreme Court ruled in 2006 that the United States is in an "armed conflict" with al Qaeda.[14]

Our government chose to use the legal framework of war because after 9/11 it believed that military force would be necessary to defeat al Qaeda—not as a complete solution, or even the primary solution, but as a necessary part of the solution. The eight-year law enforcement approach to Islamist terrorism—which began with the 1993 World Trade Center bombings, which ignored Bin Laden's 1996 declaration of war, and which persisted even though the United States suffered many vicious blows from al Qaeda around the globe, and knew of plots to commit even more spectacular attacks inside the United States—failed.[15] The scale of the 9/11 attacks in lives, economic loss, and psychological trauma, and the suddenly credible knowledge of al Qaeda's efforts to obtain weapons of mass destruction and to commit ever-greater acts of terrorism with the aim of establishing a theocratic empire, transcended a mere violation of federal criminal law and demanded a more serious and sustained response than extradition, trial, and imprisonment for the perpetrators. It required, at least in part, a mix of military and paramilitary actions, preemptive strikes, deterrent threats, and surveillance in order to capture and incapacitate terrorist leaders, destroy training camps and structures of communication and control, and uncover valuable intelligence.

The government's decision to embrace a war framework was not only, or even primarily, about using the military in battle. The war lens also carries with it important legal powers that the government believed would be necessary to defeat al Qaeda and its friends. The most obvious such power is the power to kill enemy soldiers with impunity. The United States actually started asserting this war power long before 9/11. One of the reasons why Bill Clinton got an OLC determination that the United States was in an "armed conflict" with al Qaeda in 1998 was so that he and others involved in the capture-and-kill mission for Bin Laden didn't have to worry about violating murder laws or the ban on assassinations.[16] I believe (but do not know) that the Clinton Justice Department invoked a similar war powers rationale when it approved the rendition program in the 1990s.[17] That program, as originally conceived, snatched senior al Qaeda leaders in one country and took them to various Middle Eastern countries for trial and punishment.

After 9/11 the United States needed a more comprehensive program than rendition, because it needed to incapacitate not only senior al Qaeda leadership but also the Taliban and all al Qaeda and affiliate members who posed a threat to the United States. The government settled on another traditional wartime authority: the power to detain captured enemy soldiers, without charge or trial, until the conflict is over. The detention power, the Supreme

Court explained in a 2004 opinion upholding the detention of Yaser Hamdi, is a "fundamental and accepted . . . incident to war" that is designed "to prevent captured individuals from returning to the field of battle and taking up arms once again."[18] When the U.S. military and allies started capturing hundreds of Taliban and al Qaeda fighters in Afghanistan, Pakistan, and elsewhere, it detained them on precisely the same basis as it detained enemy fighters in past wars.

At first, thousands of captured enemy soldiers were kept in makeshift prisons in and around Afghanistan—in a mud-walled nineteenth-century fortress known as Qala Jangi near Mazar-i-Sharif; at a prison in Shibarghan; at the Kandahar airport; in temporary U.S. military bases around the country; and even on naval ships in the Arabian sea.[19] Within a month of the invasion of Afghanistan, however, it had become clear that these facilities would not suffice, especially for the more dangerous Taliban and al Qaeda detainees. Human rights groups had begun to complain about the prison conditions, and there was great pressure to release foot soldiers. But the administration's main fear was security. In late November 2001, a group of recently captured Arab Taliban fighters at Qala Jangi used concealed weapons to kill CIA agent Johnny Spann and others and took over the facility for a week until they were subdued in one of the most brutal battles in the Afghanistan campaign. Other facilities were subject to incessant sniper fire, rumors of attacks, and breakout attempts. It was becoming clear that the fanatical volunteer fighters in this war were not like World War II conscripts who were thrilled to be off the battlefield and in safe POW camps. The Islamist fighters would not stop fighting once captured, but would instead use any means at their disposal to kill their enemies.[20] "Get those guys out of here!" General Tommy Franks told top Pentagon officials, arguing that he couldn't maintain adequate security for the most determined al Qaeda and Taliban fighters.[21]

This was the background to the decision to use GTMO as a detention facility for dangerous detainees (although the most dangerous "high-value detainees" were kept at secret locations elsewhere).[22] The Pentagon considered other facilities besides GTMO, including military bases inside the United States and on the Island of Guam. But these bases were relatively easy targets for terrorists to attack. They would frighten and possibly endanger U.S. civilians. And detentions there were more likely to be subject to legal challenges since they were on U.S. soil. GTMO, by contrast, was isolated and well defended. And because it was technically not a part of U.S. sovereign soil, it seemed like a good bet to minimize judicial scrutiny. A similar calculus had motivated the Clinton administration to house over forty thousand Cuban and Haitian "boat people" on the naval base in the 1990s in order to preclude them from claiming political asylum, which they would be entitled to on U.S. soil.[23] But the legal case against judicial scrutiny on GTMO was not airtight. In a memorandum to Jim Haynes on December 28, 2001, Patrick Philbin and John Yoo concluded that a U.S. court probably "cannot properly entertain an application for a writ of habeas corpus by an enemy alien detained" at GTMO, but added that "[b]ecause the issue has not yet been definitively resolved by the courts . . . we caution that there is some possibility that a district court would entertain such an application."[24] This legal uncertainty is one reason why Donald Rumsfeld said, a day earlier, that GTMO was "the least worst place" available. "Its disadvantages, however, seem to be modest relative to the alternatives," he added.[25]

The United States planned not only to detain Taliban and al Qaeda fighters at GTMO but also, as President Bush announced on November 13, 2001, to try some of them in military commissions. Military commissions lack a jury and other procedural protections that accompany ordinary civilian trials. They are traditional wartime tools used to try war criminals quickly while at the same time preserving classified evidence and minimizing propaganda efforts by defendants, two concerns that are heightened when the enemy consists of terrorists. Military commissions were used extensively in World War II, the Spanish-American War, the Civil War, the War of 1812, and the Revolutionary War. Relying on legal advice provided by Patrick Philbin in OLC, Bush's military commission order was modeled on Roosevelt's order creating the commission that tried eight Nazi saboteurs.[26] The Supreme Court had unanimously approved the commission trial of the out-of-uniform Nazis, which included one American. This was a powerful precedent for trying out-of-uniform alien enemy fighters in a military commission on Guantanamo. "We relied on the same language in FDR's order, the same congressional statute that FDR did, and we had a unanimous Supreme Court decision on point," Brad Berenson, a White House lawyer who worked on the commissions in the fall of 2002, later told me. "As a lawyer advising a client, it doesn't get much better than that."[27]

The President's special wartime powers to detain Taliban and al Qaeda soldiers at GTMO and try some of them by military commission brought with them potential restrictions embodied in the laws of war, the congeries of international treaties and customs that govern conduct during warfare. The most immediately relevant treaty was the Third Geneva Convention, which conferred legal protections on a captured enemy fighter who complied with certain minimal requirements of the laws of war, such as distinguishing himself from civilians and carrying his arms openly. In February 2002, President Bush determined that al Qaeda fighters didn't qualify for POW status because the Geneva Conventions only apply to wars between nations and not wars with transnational non-state-actor groups like al Qaeda. He also ruled that Afghanistan (on whose behalf the Taliban technically fought) was a party to the Geneva Convention, but that because the Taliban did not wear uniforms, carry their arms openly, or follow other traditional wartime requirements, its fighters did not qualify for POW status either.

The bottom line was that none of the detainees in the war on terrorism would receive POW status or any other legal protection under the laws of war. This was a congenial conclusion to the administration, which wanted to maintain flexibility in the face of a new type of enemy with unknown capacities; to interrogate detainees in a way that POW status would have precluded; and to avoid future scrutiny under the War Crimes Act, which basically applies only if the Geneva Conventions do. But there was another, more fundamental reason for the administration's decision to deny al Qaeda and Taliban detainees POW protections under the Third Geneva Convention: it was the proper interpretation of the treaty, the traditional U.S. position that was designed to best protect both our troops and innocent civilians. This was not simply an argument of convenience. It was a principled view that many (including many in the Bush administration) had embraced since the 1980s, long before al Qaeda and the Taliban were even born.

During the Reagan administration a different battle about POW protections for terrorists arose in the context of deciding whether the United States should agree to amendments to the Geneva Conventions known as Protocol I. The POW protections in the Geneva Conventions were designed to give soldiers an incentive to fight in ways that minimized suffering among combatants and civilians alike. If a soldier wears a uniform and complies with the basic laws of war, he would be treated well if caught. But if (as terrorists do) he wears ordinary clothes and hides among civilians, he endangers the innocent and acts treacherously toward rival soldiers, and thus receives no rights under Geneva if caught. In the 1970s, so-called national liberation movements, led by supporters of the Palestine Liberation Organization, tried to alter this understanding of the laws of war in Protocol I by extending POW and other "combatant" protections to all fighters, including those (like members of the PLO) who hid among civilians. This effort dovetailed with the agenda of the nascent human rights movement and the traditional protector of the laws of war, the International Committee of the Red Cross. Both groups saw Protocol I as an opportunity to import more demanding human rights standards into the laws of war by rejecting Geneva's traditional reciprocity requirements and by ensuring that there were "no gaps" in the basic protections provided to even the most vicious and law-defying combatants.

Douglas Feith, a then-obscure mid-level official in Reagan's Defense Department who fifteen years later would become Donald Rumsfeld's controversial Undersecretary of Defense for Policy, led the opposition to Protocol I. The attempt to amend Geneva "sweeps away hundreds of years of law and morality by 'recognizing' that an armed combatant 'cannot' always distinguish himself from non-combatants and granting him the status of combatant anyway,"

Feith argued inside the Pentagon.[28] "As the essence of terroristic criminality is the obliteration of the distinction between combatants and non-combatants, it would be hard to square ratification of the protocols with our policy of combating terrorism." Feith convinced his Defense Department superiors—who included not only Secretary of Defense Caspar Weinberger and the Joint Chiefs of Staff, but also Colin Powell (Weinberger's two-star military assistant, and later Bush's Secretary of State) and William Howard Taft IV (the Deputy Secretary of Defense, and later Powell's top lawyer in the State Department)—that the United States should reject Protocol I. Secretary of State George Shultz was also convinced, and he reversed his department's support for the treaty. Protocol I "would afford legal protections to terrorists and 'national liberation movements' at the expense of non-combatants by granting combatant/ POW status to irregular fighters who do not wear uniforms and otherwise fail to distinguish themselves from non-combatants," he wrote to President Reagan.[29] Reagan accepted this determination and told the Senate that the United States could not ratify Protocol I because it was "fundamentally and irreconcilably flawed" and would "endanger civilians in war."[30]

The normally anti-Reagan establishment press embraced this view as well. In an editorial entitled "Denied: A Shield for Terrorists," the *New York Times* argued that the treaty might "give terrorists the legal status of P.O.W.'s," called this a "dangerous [loophole]," and agreed with Reagan that the provisions conferring Geneva rights on terrorists were "fundamentally and irreconcilably flawed" and should be rejected.[31] The *Washington Post* had a similar reaction. In an editorial entitled "Hijacking the Geneva Conventions," it argued against the idea of giving POW or any other combatant status to "terrorists," and agreed that Reagan was rejecting the amendments to the Geneva Conventions for "the right reason"—namely, "we must not, and need not, give recognition and protection to terrorist groups as a price for progress in humanitarian law."[32] The Senate never consented to the treaty, and the State Department informed the Swiss sponsors of the treaty that the United States had decided not to ratify it.

When the Bush administration decided in early 2002 to deny al Qaeda and Taliban forces legal protections under the Geneva Conventions, it was acting in step with this long-held U.S. position that terrorists and other enemy fighters who did not wear uniforms or carry their arms openly would be denied POW status. Contrary to conventional wisdom, this decision was not controversial inside the administration. It had the full support not only of the Justice Department but also of the Department of Defense and the State Department. "The lawyers all agree that al Qaeda or Taliban soldiers are presumptively not POWs," wrote Will Taft, the State Department's Legal Advisor, in February 2002.[33]

There *was* a very sharp internal dispute over the reasons for this conclusion. John Yoo floated the idea that the Taliban did not receive POW protections because Afghanistan was a failed state and thus did not deserve the protections of the Geneva Conventions at all.[34] The State Department vehemently opposed this argument. So did the Pentagon, where the normally mild-mannered Chairman of the Joint Chiefs of Staff, General Richard Myers, argued passionately against Yoo's position. He believed, according to Douglas Feith, that the Geneva Conventions were "ingrained in U.S. military culture," that "an American soldier's self-image is bound up with the Conventions,"and that "[a]s we want *our* troops, if captured, treated according to the Conventions, we have to encourage respect for the law by our own example."[35] Feith supported Myers and argued to Rumsfeld that the "failed state" approach harkened back to the subjective and politicized criteria in Protocol I that the United States had rightly rejected twenty years earlier.[36] These men did not believe or argue that Taliban soldiers should get POW protections. They simply thought it was important to affirm the treaty's applicability to the traditional interstate conflict with Afghanistan even if the United States denied Taliban soldiers rights under the treaty. Rumsfeld eventually agreed.[37]

Nothing whatsoever turned on this debate as far as the detainees were concerned. Colin Powell correctly argued to Alberto Gonzales in late January 2002 that both the Geneva-affirming approach of the Departments of Defense and State and the "failed state" approach of the Justice Department "provide the same practical flexibility in how we treat detainees, including with respect to interrogation," and that both approaches "allow us not to give the privileges and benefits of POW status to al Qaeda and Taliban." He also noted that neither approach "entails any significant risk of domestic prosecution against U.S. officials."[38] But the "failed state" idea, Powell insisted, would "reverse over a century of U.S. policy and practice in supporting the Geneva Conventions," would "undermine the protections of the law of war for our troops," and would produce a "negative international reaction."[39] President Bush ultimately adopted the Defense and State Departments' position.[40]

And so by February 2002, the administration had developed a coherent legal strategy for incapacitating terrorists. Congress had authorized the war and triggered the President's traditional war powers, and the President possessed independent war powers as

Commander in Chief. The President exercised these traditional powers to detain enemy soldiers and, possibly, to try them in military commissions. He chose Guantanamo Bay as the main detention site, a place that other presidents had used for similar purposes. And he had embraced the traditional American view that the Geneva Conventions did not give POW protections to combatants who fought out of uniform and failed to comply with the laws of war. Inside the administration the legal foundation for counterterrorism policies seemed strong.

BUT THIS IS NOT AT ALL the way things seemed outside the administration. The press, scholars, human rights groups, the International Committee of the Red Cross, and American allies balked loudly at decisions that in World War II would have been commonplace. The unusual nature of the war and extensive changes in the legal culture made previously uncontroversial wartime practices seem very controversial, illegal, and even radical.

At the most fundamental level, much of the country and most of our allies didn't think we were (or should be) at war with Islamist terrorists, and thus didn't think military detention and military commissions were appropriate tools for the President to use. They held these views for many reasons, but at bottom they simply did not trust the administration's claim that the threat of terrorism warranted a wholesale military response. Public judgments about the legality of presidential actions are colored by public perceptions of the stakes. When a nation is unambiguously at war and believes its future is at risk, practices that would have seemed wrong in peacetime are viewed as necessary and thus legitimate. Relatively few complained when Lincoln jailed thousands of antiwar agitators without charge or trial, or when Roosevelt used a military commission with few procedural niceties. But to the extent that a war appears phony or the threat appears exaggerated, wartime presidential powers like detention and military trial are viewed more skeptically by citizens, politicians, and courts, regardless of their technical legality.

The idea of military detention without charge or trial until the end of hostilities came in for special scrutiny. In traditional wars, soldiers wear uniforms and the war has a foreseeably finite duration (or at least one could imagine what the end of a war looked like). In this war, enemy soldiers do not wear uniforms and efforts to detain or kill them are much more likely than in traditional wars to mistakenly jeopardize or kill innocent civilians. (Provoking states into harming innocent civilians is one of the points of terrorism; it is one of the advantages that terrorists seek in hiding among civilians.) There were, of course, mistakes in past wars. But the legitimate worry—a worry once again caused by our enemy's purposeful failure to comply with traditional rules of warfare—is that mistakes are more likely and thus systematically more unjust in this one. And since this war has no apparent end, mistaken identifications of the enemy can result in indefinite and thus brutally unfair confinement, simply on the basis of mistakes about membership.

Yet another reason for suspicion about all-things-GTMO was that, for the first time ever, most of the enemy soldiers we were detaining were citizens of allied countries. This very awkward situation was made worse by the fact that the allies didn't accept the military framework we used to justify targeting, detention, and trial of combatants. Nor did they share our understanding of the Geneva

Conventions. The Reagan administration won a battle in rejecting the Protocol I amendments to the Geneva Conventions in 1987. But it lost the war, for by 2001 almost all of our allies had ratified Protocol I and come to view its extension of legal protections to all fighters, including terrorists, as absolutely necessary. These factors combined to give the Europeans a very different portrait of GTMO than the one administration lawyers had painted. The British and French weren't bothered by the American detention without trial of hundreds of thousands of German POWs in World War II. That was a "real" war in which all of the Allied forces agreed on the need for militarism, the detention of POWs without trial was a legitimate military function and complied with their conceptions of international law, and in any event no one cared about the Nazis. But when the British and French saw their own nationals blindfolded, wearing orange jumpsuits, and being detained at GTMO after 9/11 without charge or trial, they had a different attitude. The United States was exercising wartime powers against British and French citizens when it shouldn't be, and it was doing so in ways that violated what these countries saw as fundamental wartime legal requirements in any event.

Similar perception problems arose on the home front. The 9/11 attacks occurred in the United States. But many who might support enhanced wartime powers for the government on the battlefield were outraged when the Bush administration nabbed José Padilla, the U.S. citizen whom I visited in Charleston, in civilian clothes at O'Hare airport and designated him an enemy combatant. No one (including the Supreme Court) complained when Roosevelt used his military powers to capture, try, and execute the Nazi saboteurs caught in civilian clothes in the United States during World

War II, even though one of them, Herber Haupt, was an American citizen. But Haupt and his co-conspirators admitted they were Nazis, their uniforms were discovered, and everyone understood the stakes. Padilla had no uniform to discover, and his connection to al Qaeda and his dangerousness were questioned. Military action in the United States against someone in street clothes violates the deepest taboos of our constitutional system, and bears a heavy burden of suspicion—a burden exacerbated by doubts many have about whether this is really a war and whether the threat is exaggerated.

These novelties of the war on terrorism would have presented enormous challenges to any presidential administration exercising traditional war powers against non-state-actor Islamist terrorists. But the Bush administration exacerbated this problem. One mistake was to take a procedural shortcut with respect to the Geneva Conventions. While it was appropriate to deny al Qaeda and Taliban soldiers POW rights, there was a big question as to whether the people at Guantanamo were in fact members of the Taliban or al Qaeda. Geneva mandated that a "competent tribunal" assess whether individual combatants should receive POW protections in case of "any doubt" about their status.[41] The United States denied detainees these procedures on the ground that the President himself had made a "group status determination" that provided a "level and degree of attention [that] exceeds the type of attention envisaged by the drafters" of the Geneva Conventions, as Will Taft argued in March 2002.[42] Whatever its legal merits, this was an inadequate response to concerns that particular *individuals* were not enemy fighters but instead were innocent farmers scooped up in Afghanistan. To the skeptical slice of the American public and to most U.S. allies, it seemed as though a single and self-interested judge was consigning scores of people to indefinite detention without a modicum of due process.

The procedural shortcut was an early contributor to what European governments, human rights groups, and the media elite saw as a "legal black hole" on GTMO. To these groups, GTMO was a law-free zone where Americans were exercising arbitrary and abusive power over the increasingly sympathetic terrorists. The administration contributed to this perception when it refused, for many years after 9/11, to acknowledge any affirmatively binding legal restrictions on Guantanamo.. Will Taft in the State Department had argued in the 2002 Geneva debate that the United States should acknowledge that "Common Article 3" of Geneva—which contains minimal wartime protections originally designed for civil wars—governed GTMO as a matter of customary international law. Taft's argument was, I think, a stretch on the law. In light of President Reagan's 1987 rejection of Protocol I, the United States could not, in my view, be bound by any customary laws of war to confer legal protections on the terrorists detained at GTMO. Taft's belief to the contrary was not entirely baseless, but it was grounded less in the strict requirements of customary law than in larger imperatives, including concerns about honor and discipline of uniformed officials in the Defense Department (where he used to be a senior official); concerns in the State Department about allied reactions to an absence of law-of-war protections on GTMO; and a Protocol I–inspired "no gaps" philosophy that permeated thinking about the laws of war even if the philosophy had not been officially embraced by the U.S. government.

The administration chose to push its legal discretion to its limit, and rejected any binding legal constraints on detainee treatment under the laws of war. President Bush settled instead on treating the detainees "humanely and, to the extent appropriate and consistent with military necessity, in a manner consistent with the principles of Geneva."[43] This formulation sounded good. But it was very vague, it was not effectively operationalized into concrete standards of conduct, and it left all of the hard issues about "humane" and "appropriate" treatment to the discretion of unknown officials.

The "legal black hole" complaint was directed toward GTMO, but the source of complaint was more fundamental, especially in Europe. "A lot of the European reaction to Guantanamo is not because people care about the feelings of the prisoners there," Charles Grant, director of the Centre for European Reform, said in January 2002. "It's touched a neuralgic point, which is the European concern that America doesn't believe in international law, doesn't believe in submitting itself to rules, organizations or norms that limit its freedom of action."[44] Denying the detainees POW status and trying them in a military commission that lacked normal civilian safeguards seemed of a piece with America's refusal to join the Kyoto Protocol, its "de-signing" of the International Criminal Court treaty, its abrogation of the Anti-Ballistic Missile Treaty with the Russians, and what Europeans viewed as America's cowboyishly dismissive attitude toward international law prohibitions on the death penalty.

THIS WAS THE STATE OF PLAY when I arrived at the Department of Defense in the fall of 2002: the Bush administration had confidently exercised traditional wartime prerogatives, but these prerogatives were viewed with increasingly boisterous skepticism by allies, the press, Congress, and some in the administration, especially the State Department and military lawyers.

My boss, Jim Haynes, the Pentagon's top lawyer, was sensitive to these growing complaints. He was convinced (as was I) that the administration had strong legal arguments for the GTMO detention and military commission policies. But he also sensed that the twenty-first-century legal culture and the novelties of the war against terrorists demanded more elaborate safeguards for both military commissions and detentions than were provided in World War II.

Military commissions turned out to be much harder to implement than Haynes or anyone else had imagined, and six years after President Bush issued his military commission order there still hasn't been a trial in one. No one involved in issuing the President's November 2001 order had any idea how difficult it would be to, in effect, build a brand new court system from scratch. Roosevelt had issued a one-page order and his commission was up and running a few days later. But it took a half dozen or so Department of Defense lawyers years to craft, clear in the bureaucracy, and publish the many hundreds of pages of rules, procedures, and definitions that international and domestic law, and broader societal notions of justice, demanded for military commission trials in the twenty-first century. One big hurdle came from within the Defense Department itself, where some military lawyers committed to their own well-developed legal system—the Uniform Code of Military Justice—threw up roadblock after roadblock to the development of military commissions. Even after this monumental effort, the commissions were viewed by many military lawyers and many in the legal establishment as fundamentally unfair, and the commissions were subject to years of legal challenges and ultimately struck down by the Supreme Court in 2006.

Designing a system of long-term detention for the novel war against terrorists was also difficult. When I arrived at the Defense Department, Haynes asked me to craft a regime that would minimize mistakes about who is a true enemy combatant and ensure that the military detained only those who remained truly dangerous. There were lots of hard questions about how much legal representation to give the detainees, how to allow the detainee to bring in new evidence, how to ascertain future dangerousness, and the like. My efforts and the efforts of others under Haynes's supervision resulted in a plan similar to the one the administration would be forced to adopt years later under pressure from the Supreme Court. But we got nowhere with these plans in 2002–2003. One obstacle was that the White House and Department of Justice opposed even a discretionary expansion of detainee rights. A second obstacle was Paul Wolfowitz, the Deputy Secretary of Defense whom Rumsfeld had put in charge of questions regarding detainees at GTMO. Wolfowitz hated making decisions about detainee issues, and simply ignored Haynes's proposals on the topic.

My time in the Pentagon led me to doubt whether the Defense Department could, without the legitimizing impact of congressional ratification, craft long-term legal policies for incapacitating terrorists. The World War II precedents were very helpful. But there were too many nagging uncertainties about how to apply these precedents to a very different, twenty-first-century conflict—uncertainties that critics, including many in Congress, were exploiting with greater and greater success. The administration had two basic options at this point. It could stick to the go-it-alone approach in the face of the growing criticisms, placing a bet that the courts (which were not yet hostile) would defer to the President's updating of the World War II structures. Or it could ask for Congress's explicit help with its detention and military commission policies. "When the President acts pursuant to an express or implied authorization of Congress, his authority is at its maximum," and is "supported by the strongest of presumptions and the widest latitude of judicial interpretation," Justice Jackson wrote in his famous concurring opinion in the *Youngstown* case.[45] Getting Congress on board would thus place whatever emerged from the process—an admitted risk—on a solid legal foundation appropriate for this new type of war, and would diminish many complaints about legitimacy.

The administration of course chose the go-it-alone route. When I was working at the Defense Department in 2002–2003 I did not really understand why. After I came to OLC in October 2003 and started going to White House meetings, however, I discovered the reason: the White House was afraid of tying the President's hands in ways that would prevent him from doing what he thought was necessary to protect the American people—a fear grounded in an unquestioned commitment to a peculiar conception of executive power.

A hastily arranged meeting in late February 2004 was typical of a dozen or so meetings I attended (and, I suspect, of many meetings before I arrived at OLC). Gonzales asked a group of lawyers to convene in his office to assess the implications of the Supreme Court's announcement that it would review a lower court's approval of the government's detention, without charge or trial, of Yaser Hamdi. Paul Clement, the deputy to Solicitor General Ted Olson and the best Supreme Court litigator of his generation, said the Court's action was bad news. He explained that although we had solid legal arguments, the Supreme Court might not accept traditional wartime detention in the seemingly indefinite and ill-defined war on terrorism.

"Why don't we just go to Congress and get it to sign off on the whole detention program?" I asked, explaining that the Supreme Court would have a much harder time striking down a wartime detention program that had Congress's explicit support. Clement concurred, as did John Bellinger, Condoleezza Rice's legal advisor, and Department of Defense General Counsel Jim Haynes. Those men had made this argument before. They had always been shot down, just as I was about to be.

"Why are you trying to give away the President's power?" Addington responded. He believed that the very act of asking for Congress's help would imply, contrary to the White House line, that the President needed legislative approval and could not act on his own. The President's power would diminish, Addington thought, if Congress declined its support once asked, especially if it tried to restrict presidential power in some way. Congress had balked, during the month after 9/11, at giving the President everything he had asked for in the congressional authorization to use force and the Patriot Act. Things would only be worse in 2004 and beyond, Addington believed.

Addington would always ask two simple questions whenever someone proposed that the White House work with Congress to clear away a legal restriction or to get the legislature on board: "Do we have the legal power to do it ourselves?" (meaning on the President's sole authority), and "Might Congress limit our options in ways that jeopardize American lives?" In the Hamdi meeting and in many others, everyone agreed that the President had the lawful authority to detain enemy soldiers during wartime. We also could not deny that going to Congress might limit the President's power at the margins, or that the limitation might conceivably cause us to release a detainee or fail to get information that resulted in another attack.

Of course there was an obvious counterargument: the relentlessly unilateral approach in a novel war might lead us to lose in the Supreme Court in a way that tied the President's hands much tighter than Congress would, thus jeopardizing American lives (if one thought this way) even more. This argument had at least a little traction. Whenever the Supreme Court threatened to review one of the administration's terrorism policies, Paul Clement was able to eke out small concessions from the White House. On the day of the Hamdi meeting, for example, the White House agreed to push harder on the efforts already in progress to establish, as a matter of executive discretion, more formal procedural protections for detainees like the ones Haynes and his subordinates had crafted over a year earlier.

Relatively small steps of this sort would, over several years, eventually add up to nontrivial protections for the GTMO detainees. Addington never liked these developments. But at least they were decisions by the executive alone, and thus were consistent with his fundamental stance of nonaccommodation toward Congress. They were also consistent with his relentlessly short-term perspective. Addington awoke every morning primed to do battle with the terrorists and focused on preventing an attack that day or that week, and not on what might happen next year or beyond. "We'll deal with that when and if it is necessary to do so," he would say when someone raised the possibility of difficulties that might result later from being overly aggressive now.

Addington once expressed his general attitude toward accommodation when he said, "We're going to push and push and push until some larger force makes us stop." He and, I presumed, his boss viewed power as the absence of constraint. These men believed that the President would be best equipped to identify and defeat the uncertain, shifting, and lethal new enemy by eliminating all hurdles to the exercise of his power. They had no sense of trading constraint for power. It seemed never to occur to them that it might be possible to increase the President's strength and effectiveness by accepting small limits on his prerogatives in order to secure more significant support from Congress, the courts, or allies. They believed cooperation and compromise signaled weakness and emboldened the enemies of America and the executive branch. When it came to terrorism, they viewed every encounter outside the innermost core of most trusted advisors as a zero-sum game that if they didn't win they would necessarily lose.

Addington's hostility to working with Congress was mild compared to his hostility to accommodating the concerns of allies and international organizations. "They don't have a vote" was how he would invariably respond when someone—usually John Bellinger—would object to a policy (or lack of one) by invoking allied protestations.

Behind Addington's sarcastic chauvinism was an elaborate theory of international relations. Addington and, I inferred, the Vice President and President viewed conflicts with allies—especially European allies—as inevitable and unbridgeable. Their belief was reinforced by Robert Kagan's influential June 2002 essay "Power and Weakness," which was widely circulated inside the administration when I arrived in September 2002. "When it comes to setting national priorities, determining threats, defining challenges, and fashioning and implementing foreign and defense policies," Kagan argued, "the United States and Europe have parted ways."[46] The militarily powerful United States, he claimed, is strategically devoted to maintaining peace and security through unilateralism and coercion, and is naturally hostile to international law restrictions on its power. Militarily weak Europeans, by contrast, were strategically devoted to securing these ends using international laws and institutions, and through persuasion and negotiation.

Kagan's essay gave structure to intuitions that top administration officials already possessed. Influenced by Kagan, and armed with the knowledge that Europeans were themselves dismissive of international law when it clashed with demands of national security (such as in Kosovo in the summer of 1999), the White House viewed sharp public disagreements over international law as the inevitable outcome of different strategic capabilities and goals. The "international community" seemed dead set against the military approach to counterterrorism that the United States thought necessary, and the administration didn't think much of this community in any event. There seemed no room for compromise.

This attitude was reinforced by Addington and company's belief that there were few if any real strategic costs to not compromising. They thought the heated public reaction to GTMO and military commissions was rhetorical froth that had few real consequences for the war on terrorism. The same allies that complained bitterly in public were vigorously cooperating behind the scenes on issues like intelligence sharing and interdiction of terrorist financing, where they had much to gain. And the same allies that railed against GTMO were also privately resisting the United States' years-long behind-the-scenes efforts to return dangerous detainees in GTMO to their own countries for detention.[47] This hypocritical posture led the White House to interpret the allies' sharp rhetoric about the international laws of war as strategic lawfare driven by larger disagreements—about the invasion of Iraq, the Kyoto Protocol, the ICC, and the like—that wouldn't dissipate no matter what the United States did on Guantanamo Bay. England and Australia were always exceptions because of the President's close relationship with Tony Blair and John Howard, and because England and Australia were perceived as genuine allies who were making genuine sacrifices to help the United States. But the solicitude and seriousness with which everyone took the complaints of the English and Australians only underscored the relative disinterest in the public complaints of other nations.

Addington's hard-line nonaccommodation stance always prevailed when the lawyers met to discuss legal policy issues in Alberto Gonzales's office. During these meetings, Gonzales himself would sit quietly in his wing chair, occasionally asking questions but mostly listening as the querulous Addington did battle with whomever was seeking to "go soft." It was Gonzales's responsibility to determine what to advise the President after the lawyers had kicked the legal policy matters around. But I only knew him to disagree with Addington once, on an issue I cannot discuss, and on that issue the President overruled Gonzales and sided with the Addington position.

"When history looks back, I want to be in the class of people who did the right thing, the sensible thing, and not necessarily the fashionable thing, the thing that met the aesthetic of the moment," Douglas Feith told Jeffrey Goldberg in the *New Yorker* in 2005, referring to his controversial decisions in the Pentagon.[48] This was precisely David Addington's attitude to hard legal decisions about terrorism. The Vice President's influential lawyer had unshakable beliefs about executive power, about the correctness of his legal positions, about the nature and severity of the terrorist threat, and about what was necessary to defeat the threat. He thought that others had less information than the White House did about the threat, and were motivated by concerns other than what would best protect the American people. He believed that faced with tough decisions, true leadership required him to do what was right, even, and especially, if it was unpopular. As the complaints grew and grew, as the pressure to change course increased, Addington became more and more insistent that the administration was doing the right thing, and he stuck to his guns with an ever-firmer grip. Many times when Addington faced enormous resistance, I thought to myself, "He'll have to back down now." But he rarely did. And he never did on something he thought was important unless an immediate and unavoidable disaster would result. I grudgingly admired Addington's perverse integrity, even when I thought his judgments were crazy.

PERHAPS THE ODDEST THING about my fortieth-birthday trip to GTMO and the naval brigs was that the plane was full of lawyers. This was an apt metaphor for many of the Bush administration's terrorism policies: never in the history of the United States had lawyers had such extraordinary influence over war policy as they did after 9/11. The lawyers weren't necessarily expert on al Qaeda, or Islamic fundamentalism, or intelligence, or international diplomacy, or even the requirements of national security. But the lawyers—especially White House and Justice Department lawyers—seemed to "own" issues that had profound national security and political and diplomatic consequences. They (and, after October 2003, we) dominated discussions on detention, military commissions, interrogation, GTMO, and many other controversial terrorism policies. We also played an unusually large role debating and deciding whether and how the President should work with Congress or allies on basic issues related to counterterrorism.

The main reason why lawyers were so involved is that the war itself was encumbered with legal restrictions as never before. Everywhere decisionmakers turned they collided with confining laws that required a lawyer's interpretation and—in order to avoid legal liability—a lawyer's sign-off. "There is no operation at the CIA that is conducted without approval of lawyers," Michael Scheuer, the longtime chief of the Bin Laden Unit at the CIA, told Congress in 2007. "I can't go to the bathroom at CIA without a lawyer," he added.[49] The national security lawyers' omnipresent cover-your-ass role cannot fully explain why lawyers were so often involved in making national security *policy*. Policymakers needn't do everything the lawyers tell them they are allowed to do. Instead, they normally ask lawyers what is legally possible, and then do a separate calculus about which legally possible things are worth pursuing.

A different cover-your-ass logic provides a more plausible additional reason for lawyers' unusual influence on terrorism policy. After 9/11 the White House believed that the President could decline to pursue a particular policy or action that might save thousands of lives only if he had a very good reason. Haunted by 9/11 and the 9/11 Commission, the White House was obsessed with preventing a recurrence of the expected harsh blame after the next attack. When declining to take some action that might conceivably save American lives, the White House would ask itself whether it would have a good excuse to the American people if the failure to act resulted in deaths. A lawyer's advice that a policy or action would violate the law, especially a criminal law, was a pretty good excuse. But fear of offending allies or Congress often was not. This is why the question "What should we do?" so often collapsed into the question "What can we lawfully do?"[50] It is why Addington always asked the same two questions: "Is the policy legal?" and "Might seeking others' support tie down the President and thus jeopardize lives?" It is why there was so much pressure to act to the edges of the law. And it is why what the lawyers said about where those edges were ended up defining the contours of the policy.

A White House confident about what it wanted to do also used lawyers, and especially legal opinions by OLC lawyers, as a sword to silence or discipline a recalcitrant bureaucracy. Many people in the government were nervous or upset about implementing the President's post-9/11 counterterrorism policies: military lawyers objected to military commissions, which departed from well-settled ways of conducting modern military trials; so too did some Justice Department prosecutors, who preferred the civilian trial system where they were in charge; the State Department objected to parts of the GTMO detention program; and some in the CIA were reportedly anxious about the special interrogation program for high-value detainees. Some of the objections were grounded in genuine concern about violating the law, while others were policy differences or bureaucratic-turf protection expressed in the language of law. Because an OLC ruling that a proposed course of action is lawful made it practically impossible for anyone who relied on the advice to be prosecuted, it could effectively blunt most legal objections. This left bureaucrats who wanted to stop or not implement policies with few options other than political objections the White House could easily overrule, or leaking information to the press, the usual fallback position. In this way OLC gave the White House freer reign to do as it wished, and to insist that others do so as well.

There is a final reason why lawyers played such a dominant role. The President and the Vice President always made clear that a central administration priority was to maintain and expand the President's formal legal powers. In any policy debate, a lawyer could gain traction for a particular course of action—usually, going it alone—by arguing that alternative proposals would diminish the President's power. Addington in particular used this tactic effectively to thwart efforts to work with Congress. If Lincoln or Roosevelt had done something in their wars without seeking specific congressional approval, then any Bush administration effort to seek congressional approval for a similar wartime action would be interpreted as creating a bad precedent that would diminish the presidency. This gave lawyers with a pro-executive bent ammunition in any policy debate.

Whatever the reason, the lawyers had a huge impact on terrorism policy, and much of it wasn't salutary. "A lot of times lawyers dominate our deliberations and we get in trouble down the line," National Security Advisor Stephen Hadley, himself a Yale-trained lawyer, once complained in an NSC meeting. "When lawyers get together they consider things in their sphere of expertise, but they exclude a lot of issues that matter, like public relations, congressional politics, and diplomacy."[51] Hadley would often complain about the lawyers' role in the years after 9/11, both when he was Condoleezza Rice's deputy from 2001 to 2004 and after he assumed control over the NSC in 2005. He was not the only one to complain. I heard, or heard of, similar objections by Condoleezza Rice and Donald Rumsfeld.

Lawyers "naturally look to *legal sources* to find the answers [and then] they construct whatever answers they can from the available legal sources and pronounce it as a legal opinion," said Philip Zelikow, the Executive Director of the 9/11 Commission, later a top advisor in Condoleezza Rice's State Department, and later still a public critic of the role that Bush administration lawyers played in developing antiterrorism policy.[52] When advising the President about what he should do in wartime, some lawyers often confound the formal legal powers they discover in statutes or precedents with the actual determinants of presidential power, which include the context of action, political support, credibility, and reputation. Lawyers advising the President also tend to be backward-looking rationalizers rather than forward-looking problem solvers. Asked to craft detention and trial policies in the war on terrorism, they looked to laws and precedents from past wars. Since the White House had taken working with Congress off the table, a lot of sensible policy options—such as establishing criminal laws for military commissions that were specifically tailored to the problem of modern terrorism, or creating a long-term preventive detention regime under the supervision of a national terrorism court—simply were not available. The lawyers were forced to squeeze the twenty-first-

century war with al Qaeda into Civil War and World War II precedents, which did not account for the massive differences between
the 1860s and 1940s and today.

The irony of the lawyer-dominated approach to counterterrorism policy is that the lawyers who didn't do so well at statecraft
also ended up not doing so well in the arena of their expertise:
the Supreme Court. David Addington would often predict that
the Supreme Court would not countermand the Commander in
Chief in wartime. He was surprisingly naive about the factors that
influenced Supreme Court decisionmaking. In his characteristi-
cally legalistic fashion, he looked at the scores of Civil War and
World War II precedents that supported the President's actions, and
was oblivious to how changes in context and culture might influence the Court's decision to approve presidential action.

Starting in the summer of 2004, however, the Court handed the
administration a series of defeats on terrorism policy. In its least
bad ruling for the President, the Court held that he could exercise his traditional military powers to detain Yaser Hamdi until the
end of the Afghanistan conflict. But the Court questioned whether
the President could exercise these traditional powers indefinitely
in the war against al Qaeda, and for the first time it imposed constitutional due-process shackles on the President during wartime.[53]
Much worse for the Bush administration, on the same day in a different opinion, the Court announced, after turning somersaults to
distinguish an important World War II precedent that the government had relied on heavily, that it had the authority to scrutinize
the legality of the government's actions on Guantanamo.[54]

The June 2004 Supreme Court decisions responded much less
to the requirements of controlling legal precedents than to broader,

extralegal factors. Almost three years after 9/11, the threat from terrorism seemed to have waned. The legal culture had become very suspicious of the administration's grand assertions of executive power in the face of growing complaints. In the two months before the decisions the critics' worst fears seemed to have been confirmed with the revelations of the Abu Ghraib abuses and OLC's opinions on interrogations, which argued that the President could disregard legal prohibitions on torture. And yet while the government's losses in the Supreme Court made front-page news, the decisions were really little more than slaps on the wrist. Contrary to the Court's civil liberties rhetoric, it did not at that time require the President to alter many of his actions. What the Court really did was send a signal to the President that GTMO could not be a law-free zone, that the President did not have a "blank check" (as the Court put it) to conduct the war on terrorism, and that the Court was willing to step in to do more if the executive did not get its legal house in better order.

The June 2004 decisions gave the administration the perfect opportunity to go to a Congress controlled by Republicans to get the entire terrorism program on a stronger and more explicit legal footing not driven by backward-looking legalisms. But in some of my last meetings in government following those Supreme Court rulings, Addington again prevailed. Refusing to read the Court's tea leaves, and taking advantage of the fact that the Court had not in fact technically required the executive to do very much, Addington successfully argued once again that the administration should continue push-push-pushing until a stronger force required otherwise, something the Supreme Court had not done yet. The administration exercised its discretion to confer more procedural rights on detainees and to improve their conditions of confinement, and it redoubled its efforts to release nondangerous detainees from GTMO. But it still refused to go to Congress to put the detention program on a strong statutory foundation.

Two years later, in the summer of 2006, the Supreme Court spoke again, this time invalidating the administration's efforts to try Salim Ahmed Hamdan, Bin Laden's driver and bodyguard, in a military commission.[55] The Court once again stretched to distinguish its World War II precedents, and it once again wrote an opinion that was informed more by the atmospherics of executive extravagance and a seemingly waning terrorist threat than by strict analysis of legal materials. But this time the Court's decision seemed to have more bite. The Court ruled that the administration could not go forward with military commissions without Congress's explicit approval. And it held that the basic legal protections of "Common Article 3" of the Geneva Conventions applied in the war against al Qaeda and its affiliates, not, as Will Taft had urged in 2002, as a matter of customary international law, but rather as a treaty obligation. The Common Article 3 holding was legally erroneous, in my view, but it was hugely consequential. It meant that a small portion of the Geneva Conventions *did* apply in the war on terrorism, and it provided detainees with more elaborate legal rights of humane treatment and legal process than the administration had ever acknowledged. And more ominously, the Court's holding implied that the 1996 War Crimes Act, which the independent counsel–fearing executive branch had tried to neuter since 2002, was in play and applicable to many elements of the administration's treatment of detainees.

I was not in the government when the *Hamdan* decision was

announced, but both news reports and friends in government say that the decision created alarm inside the administration that summer. The press reported that the CIA had grown more and more anxious about its classified but increasingly public program for detaining and interrogating high-level detainees at secret locations abroad. The Court's decision that the Geneva Conventions and the War Crimes Act applied in the fight against al Qaeda brought CIA worries about retroactive discipline to new highs.[56] The same concerns preoccupied the National Security Council and Attorney General Gonzales. And beyond these personal concerns, the Supreme Court's decision had called into question the legal basis for many aspects of the administration's post-9/11 detainee policies, including the treatment of detainees on GTMO, military commissions, and interrogation policy. The decision was "a sweeping and categorical defeat for the administration," said the *New York Times'* Linda Greenhouse, the dean of Supreme Court reporters, adding that its announcement was an "historic event, a defining moment in the ever-shifting balance of power among branches of government."[57] Her colleague Adam Liptak reported a few days later that "the effect of the decision, constitutional lawyers across the political spectrum agreed, could devastate the administration's main legal justifications for its campaign against the terrorist threat."[58]

The "stronger force" that Addington had anticipated had finally arrived. Now only Congress could help the administration out of its predicament. On September 6, 2006, two months after the Supreme Court's decision and two months before the midterm elections of 2006, President Bush sent a bill to Congress about military commissions and related detainee issues. When he announced the draft bill, the President made the stakes of the legislation concrete and very high. He lifted the veil of secrecy on the CIA's secret detention and interrogation of "the key architects of the September the 11th attacks [who are] dangerous men with unparalleled knowledge about terrorist networks and their plans for new attacks." He also revealed that the "tough" set of "alternative" interrogation procedures applied to some of these men had revealed information "that has saved innocent lives by helping us stop new attacks—here in the United States and across the world."[59] And he announced that he was bringing the fourteen men in CIA detention to Guantanamo Bay for possible trial in the military commissions for which he was seeking congressional authorization.

A little over three weeks later, a Congress still (but not for long) controlled by the President's party enacted a law that gave the President a surprising victory. The Military Commissions Act of 2006 explicitly authorized many aspects of the military commission regime that the Supreme Court had invalidated three months earlier. And it gave the President much more, including a broadened definition of "unlawful enemy combatant"; implicit approval for aggressive interrogations short of torture; immunity from prosecution for those who participated in past interrogations that crossed the prohibited line; narrowing interpretations of the Geneva Conventions and amendments to the War Crimes Act that minimized the impact of the Supreme Court's decision; elimination of judicial habeas corpus review over Guantanamo; and a prohibition on the judicial use of the Geneva Conventions to measure the legality of the Guantanamo detentions. "Taken as a whole," Scott Shane and Adam Liptak noted in the *New York Times*, "the law will give the president more power over terrorism suspects than he had before the Supreme Court decision" in the *Hamdan* case three months earlier.[60]

One might imagine that David Addington and his superiors felt at least a little vindicated by this outcome. These men had fought hard, inside the administration and with Congress, to ensure the victory in Congress's approval of the Military Commission Act of 2006. For five years the administration had pushed unilateral executive power to its limits. When the Supreme Court finally forced it to seek Congress's help, it emerged with a congressional ratification of most of what the Supreme Court rejected, and in some respects more. And throughout this period the administration had achieved its main goal of preventing a second terrorist attack on the homeland.

And yet the administration had lost much as well. The Military Commission Act was a victory for it only against the baseline of expectations established by the Supreme Court a few months earlier. Measured against the baseline of what it could have gotten from a more cooperative Congress in 2002–2003, the administration had lost a lot. If it had earlier established a legislative regime of legal rights on Guantanamo Bay, it never would have had to live with the Court's Common Article 3 holding, or with the War Crimes Act. If the administration had simply followed the Geneva requirement to hold an informal "competent tribunal," or had gone to Congress for support on their detention program in the summer of 2004, it probably would have avoided the more burdensome procedural and judicial requirements that became practically necessary under the pressure of subsequent judicial review. It surely could have received an even more accommodating military commission system if they had made the push in Congress in 2002–2003 instead of the fall of 2006.

I am not suggesting that the Military Commission Act was a bad development. To the contrary, it was an important first step in the right direction of putting counterterrorism policy on a more secure and sensible legal foundation. For a White House trying to minimize restrictions on the presidency, though, the new law was, from the 2002–2003 baseline, unfortunate. But most unfortunate of all was the effect on the status and reputation of executive power generally. It was said hundreds of times in the White House that the President and Vice President wanted to leave the presidency stronger than they found it. In fact they seemed to have achieved the opposite. They borrowed against the power of future presidencies—presidencies that, at least until the next attack, and probably even following one, will be viewed by Congress and the courts, whose assistance they need, with a harmful suspicion and mistrust because of the unnecessary unilateralism of the Bush years.

CHAPTER 5

Torture and the Dilemmas of Presidential Lawyering

I learned about the Abu Ghraib abuses for the first time in late April of 2004 from a television news program playing, volume down, in the back corner of Alberto Gonzales's White House office. "This is going to kill us," Gonzales quietly muttered, as I and a few other lawyers were assembling to discuss an unrelated matter. While I stared in astonishment at the photos of sadistic violence on the television screen, my mind began to race. Was I indirectly responsible for the abuses? Could I have done something to stop them?

I had begun worrying about the possibility of excessive interrogations about eight weeks after I arrived in the Justice Department in October 2003. During October and November of that year I spent a lot of time in SCIFs—supersecret Sensitive Compartmented Information Facilities that are immune from bugging—being briefed by somber officials from the White House, CIA, and National Security

Agency about some of the government's highly classified counterterrorism programs. Each of the programs, I learned, had been approved by OLC and backed by an OLC opinion.

At first, I was too busy answering a stream of questions from the White House, and getting to know the OLC staff and other lawyers in the Justice Department and around the government, to read these opinions. But then about six weeks into the job, Patrick Philbin, the deputy in OLC who had been responsible for legal advice on the classified programs after John Yoo's departure and until my arrival, told me about an OLC opinion that was "out there," that may contain serious errors, and that he had been working to correct. Coming from Philbin this news was alarming. Philbin is a careful lawyer, but he was not squeamish about pushing the President's power to its limits. He was a longtime friend of Yoo and had worked closely with Yoo on counterterrorism issues since 9/11. Any worries he had about flaws in OLC's post-9/11 national security opinions were informed and credible.

I began to read the opinion Philbin worried about, and I asked him to bring me any other opinions that he believed might have similar problems. After reading a short stack of opinions, two stood out. The first—entitled "Standards of Conduct for Interrogation under 18 U.S.C. §§ 2340–2340A"—was the infamous "torture memo" of August 1, 2002.[1] This opinion was addressed to Alberto Gonzales from my predecessor, Jay Bybee, but according to press reports and John Yoo's public comments, it was drafted by Yoo himself. The opinion formed part of the legal basis for what President Bush later confirmed were "alternative" interrogation procedures used at secret locations on Abu Zubaydah, a top al Qaeda operative; Khalid Sheikh Mohammed, the al Qaeda mastermind behind the 9/11 attacks; and other "key architects of the September 11ᵗʰ" and other terrorist attacks.[2] The second opinion, from Yoo to Jim Haynes (my former boss in the Pentagon) and dated March 14, 2003, was entitled "Military Interrogation of Alien Unlawful Combatants Held outside the United States." This opinion remains classified, but it has been publicly confirmed that it was the "controlling authority" for a subsequent April 2003 Department of Defense interrogation "Working Group" report that contained much of the same analysis as the August 1, 2002, OLC opinion.[3]

The primary legal issue in both opinions was the effect of a 1994 law that implemented a global treaty banning torture and that made it a crime, potentially punishable by death, to commit torture.[4] Congress defined the prohibition on torture very narrowly to ban only the most extreme of acts and to preserve many loopholes. It did not criminalize "cruel, inhuman, and degrading treatment" (something prohibited by international law) and did not even criminalize all acts of physical or mental pain or suffering, but rather only those acts "specifically intended" to cause "severe" physical pain or suffering or "prolonged mental harm."[5] Even with these narrow definitions, uncertainties about the legal limits of torture remained. How should pain be measured? How does one draw the line between severe (and therefore prohibited) pain and nonsevere (and thus not prohibited) pain? What does "mental pain" mean? And how much mental pain can one impose before producing "prolonged" mental harm? The answers to these questions are not obvious.

"Our intent in the Justice Department's original research was to give clear legal guidance on what constituted 'torture' under the law, so that our agents would know exactly what was prohibited, and what was not," John Yoo later said of the August 1, 2002, interrogation opinion.[6] The opinion identified torture with acts that cause the amount of pain "associated with a sufficiently serious physical condition or injury such as death, organ failure, or serious impairment of body functions."[7] Any action that fell short of these extreme conditions could not, in OLC's view, be torture. Even if the interrogators crossed this hard-to-reach line and committed torture, OLC opined, they could still avoid criminal liability by invoking a necessity defense (on the theory that torture may be necessary to prevent a catastrophic harm) or self-defense (on the theory that the interrogators were acting to save the country and themselves). Finally, OLC concluded, the torture law violated the President's constitutional commander-in-chief powers, and thus did not bind executive branch officials, because it prevented the President "from gaining the intelligence he believes necessary to prevent attacks upon the United States."[8]

The message of the August 1, 2002, OLC opinion was indeed clear: violent acts aren't necessarily torture; if you do torture, you probably have a defense; and even if you don't have a defense, the torture law doesn't apply if you act under color of presidential authority. CIA interrogators and their supervisors, under pressure to get information about the next attack, viewed the opinion as a "golden shield," as one CIA official later called it, that provided enormous comfort.[9]

ON THE SURFACE the interrogation opinions seemed like typically thorough and scholarly OLC work. But not far below the surface there were problems. One was that the opinions interpreted the term "torture" too narrowly. Most notorious was OLC's conclusion that in order for inflicted pain to amount to torture, it "must be equivalent in intensity to the pain accompanying serious physical injury, such as organ failure, impairment of bodily function, or even death."[10] OLC culled this definition, ironically, from a statute authorizing health benefits. That statute defined an "emergency medical condition" that warranted certain health benefits as a condition "manifesting itself by acute symptoms of sufficient severity (including severe pain)" such that the absence of immediate medical care might reasonably be thought to result in death, organ failure, or impairment of bodily function.[11] It is appropriate, when trying to figure out the meaning of words in a statute, to see how the same words are defined or used in similar contexts. But the health benefit statute's use of "severe pain" had no relationship whatsoever to the torture statute. And even if it did, the health benefit statute did not define "severe pain." Rather, it used the term "severe pain" as a sign of an emergency medical condition that, if not treated, might cause organ failure and the like. It is very hard to say in the abstract what the phrase "severe pain" means, but OLC's clumsy definitional arbitrage didn't seem even in the ballpark.

These and other questionable statutory interpretations, taken alone, were not enough to cause me to withdraw and replace the interrogation opinions. OLC has a powerful tradition of adhering to its past opinions, even when a head of the office concludes that they are wrong. The tradition is akin to the doctrine of stare decisis, which counsels a court to stand by erroneous prior decisions except in very special circumstances. Stare decisis reflects the judgment that "in most matters it is more important that the applicable rule of law be settled than that it be settled right," as Justice Louis

Brandeis once said.[12] If OLC overruled every prior decision that its new leader disagreed with, its decisions would be more the whim of individuals than the command of impersonal laws. Constant reevaluation of prior OLC decisions would make it hard for OLC's many clients to rely on its decisions. A few reversals of OLC opinions had occurred when an administration of one party with one legal philosophy replaced an administration of another party with another legal philosophy. I knew of no precedent for overturning OLC opinions within a single administration. It appeared never to have been done, and certainly not on an important national security matter.

Despite the superstrong stare decisis presumption, I decided in December 2003 that opinions written nine and sixteen months earlier by my Bush administration predecessors must be withdrawn, corrected, and replaced. I reached this decision, and had begun to act on it, before I knew anything about any interrogation abuses. I did so because the opinions' errors of statutory interpretation combined with many other elements to make them unusually worrisome.

First was the subject matter, torture, a universally condemned and morally repugnant practice. The administration's aim was to go right to the edge of what the torture law prohibited, to exploit every conceivable loophole in order to do everything legally possible to uncover information that might stop an attack. At first I was anxious to learn about this. Was it right for the administration to have gone right up to the line? Was it right for OLC to have gone there? And was it right for me personally to go there, even in the process of trying to fix prior legal errors?

I quickly set aside these considerations. I was no expert on what our enemies were up to or on what it would take to stop them. The methods of interrogating high-value al Qaeda detainees known to have information of al Qaeda plans had been fully vetted at the highest levels of the executive branch by officials who had much more information about the terrorist threat than I had, and who would be personally and politically responsible if another attack occurred as a consequence of the government declining to take these aggressive steps. I had very little basis for second-guessing my superiors' judgment that certain detainees should be questioned as aggressively as legally possible. When appropriate, I put on my counselor's hat and added my two cents about the wisdom of counterterrorism policies. But ultimately my role as the head of OLC was not to decide whether these policies were wise. It was to make sure that the policies were implemented lawfully.

Nor did I think there was anything inherently wrong with exploring the contours of the torture law. Some have argued that OLC should decline to provide legal advice about the torture law because any advice might result in humans being subject to hurtful techniques short of torture, even if they are legal. Hardly anyone would be completely immune to such concerns, but in the end a government lawyer, and especially a lawyer at OLC, must put them aside. A lot of legal advice related to war and covert action touches on morally problematic subjects, and might be relied on to harm other humans. Should the United States bomb an enemy leader hiding in a mosque, knowing it will destroy the mosque and kill a thousand innocent civilians? Should the President approve a covert operation to assassinate a foreign leader or rig a foreign election? Presidents cannot avoid making these and hundreds of other ugly calls. And in so doing, they must know whether their actions are consistent with our laws and Constitution. OLC's ultimate responsibility is to provide information about legality, regardless of what morality may indicate, and even if harm may result.

Although the proper role of OLC in this context was limited to interpreting the torture law, the nature of the question informed how OLC should answer. Interpreting the torture law is not like resolving an interagency dispute about regulatory control over a merger, or commenting on the constitutionality of an appropriations bill in Congress. The stakes in the interrogation program were unusually high. On the national security side of the balance potentially stood tens of thousands of lives, economic prosperity, and perhaps our way of life. On the other side of the balance lay the United States' decades-long global campaign to end torture, relations with the Muslim world, and the nation's moral reputation and honor. In this context, it was unusually important for OLC to provide careful and sober legal advice about the meaning of torture.

Which leads to the second problem with the interrogation opinions: the unusual lack of care and sobriety in their legal analysis. Nowhere was this more evident than in the opinions' discussion of the President's commander-in-chief powers. Many prior OLC opinions had advised that the President could ignore statutes that in concrete instances conflicted with his commander-in-chief powers.[13] But none had done so quite the same way as the interrogation opinions. OLC might have limited its set-aside of the torture statute to the rare situations in which the President believed that exceeding the law was necessary in an emergency, leaving the torture law intact in the vast majority of instances. But the opinion went much further. "*Any* effort by Congress to regulate the interrogation of battlefield detainees would violate the Constitution's sole vesting of the Commander-in-Chief authority in the President," the August 2002 memo concluded.[14] This extreme conclusion has no foundation in prior OLC opinions, or in judicial decisions, or in any other source of law. And the conclusion's significance sweeps far beyond the interrogation opinion or the torture statute. It implies that many other federal laws that limit interrogation—anti-assault laws, the 1996 War Crimes Act, and the Uniform Code of Military Justice—are also unconstitutional, a conclusion that would have surprised the many prior presidents who signed or ratified those laws, or complied with them during wartime.

OLC's conclusion about presidential power was all the more inappropriate because it rested on cursory and one-sided legal arguments that failed to consider Congress's competing wartime constitutional authorities, or the many Supreme Court decisions potentially in tension with the conclusion. When I led OLC, I was not shy about pushing wartime presidential power very far. But when one concludes that Congress is disabled from controlling the President, and especially when one concludes this in secret, respect for separation of powers demands a full consideration of competing congressional and judicial prerogatives, which was lacking in the interrogation opinions.

Another problem with the opinions was their tendentious tone. "It reads like a bad defense counsel's brief, not an OLC opinion," a senior government lawyer said of the August 2002 opinion when he learned that I was withdrawing it in the summer of 2004. The opinions lacked the tenor of detachment and caution that usually characterizes OLC work, and that is so central to the legitimacy of OLC. In their redundant and one-sided effort to eliminate any hurdles posed by the torture law, and in their analysis of defenses and other ways to avoid prosecution for executive branch violation of federal laws, the opinions could be interpreted as if they were designed to confer immunity for bad acts. Its everyday job of interpreting criminal laws gives OLC the incidental power to determine what those laws mean and thus effectively to immunize officials from prosecutions for wrongdoing. This is a hazardous power for an anonymous office to possess, and it is crucial that it be exercised judiciously. But the interrogation opinions seemed to do the opposite: they seemed more an exercise of sheer power than reasoned analysis.

The final nail in the interrogation opinions' coffin was that their legal arguments were wildly broader than was necessary to support what was actually being done. When OLC is asked whether proposed government actions comply with criminal laws, it usually has precise actions in mind, and it usually conforms its analysis to these precise actions. "Even Bill Barr," a former OLC head and later Attorney General who was not shy about approving aggressive exercises of executive branch power, "would write narrow and precise opinions about particular practices and say, 'Come back to me if you go one millimeter beyond this opinion,'" a CIA lawyer told me after I left the government.[15] This is a prudent practice, especially in the context of secret government operations that bump up against criminal laws. It ensures that the government acts in the darkness of secrecy no more aggressively than necessary. And it improves the quality of OLC's legal analysis, for legal interpretation is easier, and contains fewer inadvertent mistakes, when the law is applied to particular concrete facts.

The interrogation opinions did not take this approach. The August 1, 2002, opinion analyzed the torture statute in the abstract, untied to any concrete practices. Then, in a second August 1, 2002, opinion that still remains classified, OLC applied this abstract analysis to approve particular and still-classified interrogation techniques.[16] These separately and specifically approved techniques contained elaborate safeguards and were less worrisome than the abstract analysis in the public torture opinions themselves, which went far, far beyond what was necessary to support the precise techniques, and in effect gave interrogators a blank check. The same bifurcation occurred with the Defense Department: The March 2003 OLC opinion to the Defense Department contained abstract and overbroad legal advice, but the actual techniques approved by the department were specific and contained elaborate safeguards.

In sum, on an issue that demanded the greatest of care, OLC's analysis of the law of torture in the August 1, 2002, opinion and the March 2003 opinion was legally flawed, tendentious in substance and tone, and overbroad and thus largely unnecessary. My main concern upon absorbing the opinions was that someone might rely on their green light to justify interrogations much more aggressive than ones specifically approved and then maintain, not without justification, that they were acting on the basis of OLC's view of the law. And so in December 2003 I concluded that I must withdraw and replace OLC's analysis.

But how? There were no precedents to guide me. I knew that withdrawing the opinions would have serious reverberations. My bosses considered interrogation of detainees with knowledge of al Qaeda's plans to be the most effective way to prevent the next attack. The program "is worth more than [what] the FBI, the Central Intelligence Agency and the National Security Agency put together have been able to tell us," George Tenet would later claim, expressing the view that permeated the executive branch during my time in office.[17] The program had been approved by the National Security Council, legally blessed by the Attorney General, and briefed to congressional leadership.[18] But the entire interrogation edifice was built on the OLC opinions, and might collapse if I withdrew them. I then would be responsible for the increased vulnerability of the country that resulted from these pullbacks. More broadly, withdrawing the opinions would be unfair to the men and women who had engaged in dangerous and controversial actions in reliance on OLC's blessing, and who might view withdrawal of the opinions as a treacherous first step in a Justice Department effort to hold them legally responsible for past acts. Withdrawal would also dissuade operatives from viewing OLC opinions as reliable authorization when they were asked to perform controversial acts in the future. On top of this, I worried that withdrawing the opinions drafted by my friend John Yoo would be a painful stab in his back, even if it was the right thing to do.

After many conversations with Philbin, I decided that I should not withdraw the opinions until I could affirmatively inform the Defense Department and CIA precisely what interrogation practices were legally available under a proper analysis. Although I was worried by what the sloppy interrogation opinions might be used to justify, I had not concluded that the actual interrogation techniques approved by the Justice Department were illegal. I hoped that providing replacement guidance when I withdrew the opinions would minimize the expected panic throughout the government about the consequences of the withdrawal.

The plan worked well with respect to the OLC opinion issued to the Department of Defense in March 2003. In April 2003, the

Secretary of Defense had relied on the March OLC opinion to approve twenty-four interrogation techniques.[19] Most of these techniques had long been in the military manual and viewed by military lawyers to be consistent with the Geneva Conventions.[20] None involved anything rough. Philbin, I, and others in OLC had a relatively easy time concluding that these twenty-four precisely defined and procedurally restricted techniques did not violate the torture statute or any other applicable law.[21]

During a meeting in December 2003, I told Ashcroft that I intended to withdraw the March 2003 OLC opinion but allow the Defense Department to continue to employ the twenty-four techniques. Ashcroft was not terribly surprised and did not resist. He knew that OLC had discovered some significant problems in its prior analyses, and he supported my and Philbin's efforts to straighten things out, especially since in this instance we wouldn't (at least to the best of our knowledge) be telling the Pentagon to stop doing anything. I didn't inform the White House about my decision. The March 2003 opinion was addressed to the Department of Defense, and although its withdrawal would have enormous implications later for matters the White House cared a lot about, I knew that running the matter by Gonzales and especially Addington would make it much harder to fix the opinions. I technically didn't need White House approval, so I didn't seek it.

I called Jim Haynes—my friend, and former boss—during the quiet week between Christmas 2003 and the New Year. I knew that my withdrawal of the March 2003 OLC opinion would be painful for him. Ever since 9/11, Haynes had been in the middle of a struggle between a White House and Department of Justice bent on pushing the President's war powers to their limits, and the armed forces bent on upholding what Haynes once admiringly described as a "tradition of restraint" on interrogation and detainee treatment.[22] This clash came to a head in the spring of 2003 when Haynes convened a Defense Department civilian-military Working Group to determine the military's interrogation policy in the war against al Qaeda and the Taliban. In this connection, Haynes properly sought OLC's legal views on the law of interrogation— views that resulted in the 2003 opinion I was about to withdraw. When military lawyers strenuously objected to the OLC legal analysis, Haynes correctly insisted that the Defense Department, like the rest of the executive branch, was bound by OLC's legal rulings. Despite OLC's legal ruling, Haynes acted within his discretion and, invoking the traditions of the military and other policy considerations, recommended that Rumsfeld approve only the twenty-four uncontroversial techniques.[23] Nonetheless, Haynes's acceptance of Yoo's March 2003 analysis resulted in a bruising battle with military lawyers, and would later be the basis for misleading and unfair attacks by the press and others on his motives and judgment. My withdrawal of the Yoo opinion less than a year after this battle would, I feared, weaken him within the department and harm his reputation.

"Jim, I've got bad news," I began. "We've discovered some errors in the March 2003 opinion that John wrote you on interrogation. The opinion is under review and should not be relied upon for any reason. The twenty-four techniques you approved are legal, but please come back for additional legal guidance before approving any other technique, and do not rely on the March 2003 opinion for any reason."

There was a long silence. "OK, Jack," Haynes eventually replied.

After another silence, he asked, quite fairly, what was wrong with the opinion.

"There are many potential problems with it," I told him, and briefly explained my concerns with the interpretation of the torture statute and other statutes, the overbroad commander-in-chief analysis, and the criminal defense analysis.

The conversation lasted less than five minutes. Haynes never pushed back, he and I never spoke at length about the issue again, and he never told me how he implemented the withdrawal within the Defense Department. I later learned, however, that he acted promptly on my request. "We were asked not to rely upon [the March 2003 memo] going back to December of 2003. I have not relied upon it since," Haynes's deputy Dan Dell'Orto testified in the summer of 2005.[24] And the department later informed OLC that "to the extent that the March 2003 Memorandum was relied on from March 2003 to December 2003, policies based on the substance of that Memorandum have been reviewed and, as appropriate, modified to exclude such reliance."[25]

Fixing the March 2003 opinion was easy compared to the challenges of fixing the August 2002 opinion to the White House that underlay the CIA interrogation program. I couldn't simply withdraw the opinion but reapprove the interrogation techniques, as I had done with the Defense Department. The 2002 opinion and the attendant CIA techniques, unlike the ones approved by the Pentagon, had been vetted in the highest circles of government. And in contrast to my sense of the Defense Department techniques, I wasn't as confident that the CIA techniques could be approved under a proper legal analysis. I didn't affirmatively believe they were illegal either, or else I would have stopped them. I just didn't yet know. And I wouldn't know until we had figured out the proper interpretation of the torture statute, and whether the CIA techniques were consistent with that proper legal analysis.

Reaching this conclusion took much longer than I expected. In the early months of 2004, I didn't have the time or the resources to devote to the problem, which despite its obvious importance wasn't the highest priority for me or my office. The August 2002 opinion wasn't the most difficult or consequential of the flawed legal opinions that needed fixing at the time. Other matters that remain classified, but that everyone in the government agreed were a higher priority, preoccupied my time, day and night and weekends, during the first four and a half months of 2004. And these responsibilities came on top of OLC's normal business, including the daily deluge of very hard terrorism-related questions to which the White House, CIA, Defense Department, and other agencies needed quick answers.

Just as these other matters were reaching partial resolution in the spring of 2004, the Abu Ghraib scandal broke. When those horrible pictures began to be published, everyone in the government scrambled for cover. My first reaction was to wonder whether any of my decisions in OLC were connected to the abuses. My October 2003 decision (described in chapter 1) that all Iraqis, including Iraqi citizens who were members of al Qaeda, were "protected persons" under the Fourth Geneva Convention included an exception for members of al Qaeda in Iraq who were not Iraqi citizens. I was confident that this conclusion, which was supported by experienced law-of-war attorneys in the State and Defense Departments and in OLC, was legally correct. But I still wondered whether anyone had exploited this loophole as a justification for abusing non-Iraqi al Qaeda members found in Iraq. I also worried about OLC's flawed March 2003 opinion and the legal analyisis by the Department of Defense Working Group that was based on it, both of which blew through a number of legal restrictions on interrogation. These legal analyses were designed, I knew, for GTMO detainees. But had they somehow had influence beyond the Cuban naval base? And had my direction to Haynes five months earlier not to rely on the March 2003 OLC opinion been too late?

The White House and Justice Department were pretty successful in distancing themselves from the Abu Ghraib abuses during May of 2003. But then in early June, the interrogation opinions began to leak to the press. On June 7, the *Wall Street Journal* reported on a draft of the April 2003 Department of Defense Working Group Report that had relied on the March 2003 OLC opinion. "Bush administration lawyers contended last year that the president wasn't bound by laws prohibiting torture and that government agents who might torture prisoners at his direction couldn't be prosecuted by the Justice Department," it said.[26] The next day, the *Washington Post* reported on the August 2002 opinion: "In August 2002, the Justice Department advised the White House that torturing al Qaeda terrorists in captivity abroad 'may be justified,' and that international laws against torture 'may be unconstitutional if applied to interrogations' conducted in President Bush's war on terrorism, according to a newly obtained memo."[27]

Both the August 2002 OLC opinion and the Defense Department Working Group Report that relied on the March 2003 OLC opinion were now on the Internet and flying around the world. The August 2002 opinion, OLC's original effort at defining torture, received the most scrutiny, and the reviews were, to put it mildly, not favorable. There were no defenders of the interrogation opinions inside the administration either, save Addington. Many people vehemently argued, however, that it would be unfair to those who had relied on OLC to withdraw the opinion now. I was keenly aware of this. That was why I had hesitated to withdraw the August 2002 opinion until I could provide a replacement opinion that specified exactly what was legal. But now I was in a bind. I was under pressure from all quarters in the administration to stand by and reaffirm the August 2002 opinion. But five months earlier I had withdrawn the March 2003 OLC opinion after concluding that the identical legal analysis of torture contained in the August 2002 opinion was flawed beyond repair. I couldn't unwind my fundamental decision about the flaws in OLC's interrogation analysis, and had no desire to. But I also hadn't done the independent analysis of the torture law that would allow me to say with certainty whether and which of the CIA's special interrogation techniques were legal, and thus my reasons for delaying withdrawal of the August 2002 opinion still held.

For a week I struggled with what to do. In the end I withdrew the August 2002 opinion even though I had not yet been able to prepare a replacement. I simply could not defend the opinion. I had rejected its reasoning in the March 2003 opinion, and I knew that the August 2002 opinion would eventually suffer the same fate. Delaying the inevitable was only making matters worse, especially since it had become apparent that every day the OLC failed to rectify its egregious and now-public error was a day that its institutional reputation, and the reputation of the entire Justice Department, would sink lower yet.

The White House, the CIA, and many others believed I "buck-led" under the pressure of public outcry, someone in the CIA later told me. John Yoo has charged that I and others in the Justice Department "panicked when the Abu Ghraib scandal erupted," that my decision to withdraw was "really just about politics," and that the department was "too worried about the public perceptions of its work."[28] Obviously, the public release of the opinions and the resulting outcry precipitated my decision. But the fact was that I had made my decision six months earlier under a veil of ignorance about government abuses or public perception.

The decision to withdraw the August 2002 opinion was mine alone, but during that crucial week I received indispensable advice from Philbin and from the Deputy Attorney General, Jim Comey. Ever since Comey had come on board in December of 2003, he had been my most powerful ally, not only in correcting the flawed interrogation opinions but also in many other significant and diffi-cult matters as well. Comey is a seasoned prosecutor and one of the quickest and shrewdest lawyers I have ever met. He thinks clearly in times of crisis and possesses a keen sense of proportion that is the mark of good judgment. And he always acted with a sensitivity to upholding the integrity of the Justice Department.

Comey was out of town during the week I deliberated about what to do with the August 1, 2002, opinion. But I telephoned him twice that week in the late evening, and in both conversa-tions he helped me think through the implications of withdraw-ing the opinion. When I finally informed John Ashcroft and David Ayres about my decision on Tuesday morning, June 15, 2004, they were understandably shaken. The opinion had been issued under Ashcroft's delegated authority. And just the week before, the Attorney General had taken dozens of spears in the chest for the administration on the interrogation issue in testimony before Congress. I had helped prepare Ashcroft for that testimony. Although he knew (and approved) of my withdrawal of the problematic legal advice about the torture law contained in the March 2003 opinion to the Department of Defense, and although he knew the August 2002 opinion had the identical problems, I had not previously told him that I would also withdraw the August 2002 opinion. And yet here I was less than a week after his testimony telling him that I believed that he, and the Justice Department, would have to confess error. My timing was unfair to the Attorney General, and I wished then and wish now that I had made my decision a week earlier in order to spare him this additional embarrassment. Ashcroft was, in context, extraordinarily magnanimous and, as always, supportive. But I sensed for the first time that he might be questioning my judgment, and I wondered when I left his office whether he would agree with my decision or exercise his prerogative to overrule me.

That evening Ashcroft spoke with Comey. I later learned that Comey backed me fully. He told Ashcroft that the August 2002 interrogation opinion was "deeply flawed" and argued to Ashcroft that my decision was "the right thing" for OLC, for the Department of Justice, and for the government.[29] The next morning, Wednesday, June 16, I met again with the Attorney General and Ayres. It was immediately clear that the Attorney General had accepted my decision to withdraw the August 2002 opinion and had made the decision the department's official position.

In that same meeting I handed the Attorney General my letter of resignation. I had been thinking for a while about resigning, but my timing was driven by a desire to ensure that my withdrawal of the interrogation opinion would stick. Comey and I agreed that this timing would make it hard for the White House to reverse my decision without making it seem like I had resigned in protest.

As for the reasons for my resignation, there were many. I had an offer for a tenured position at Harvard Law School, and I had had enough of government. The interrogation opinions were not the only or even the most difficult problem I had faced at OLC. I had fought other much more contested battles, and I was physically and mentally drained. I missed my wife and two young sons, whom I rarely saw, and whom I never saw when I wasn't exhausted and distracted.

But the main reason I resigned was that important people inside the administration had come to question my fortitude for the job, and my reliability. The White House put up no resistance, at least in my presence, to my withdrawal of the August 2002 interrogation opinion. And after I submitted my resignation letter, Gonzales and his deputy, David Leitch, several times asked me to stay. But a week or so earlier, David Addington had pulled a 3-by-5-inch card out of his jacket pocket in Alberto Gonzales's office, in the presence of many top administration lawyers. The card contained his handwritten list of OLC opinions that I had rescinded or modified. "Since you've withdrawn so many legal opinions that the President and others have been relying on," Addington said sarcastically, "we need you to go through all of OLC's opinions and let us know which ones you still stand by." It was a biting point, and not entirely unfair. No one except Addington disputed that the opinions I had withdrawn and redone (or started to redo) were deeply flawed. But the fact was that in a mere nine months in office I had reversed or rescinded more OLC opinions than any of my predecessors. Many of the men and women who were asked to act on the edges of the law had lost faith in me. What else might I withdraw, and when? In light of all I had been through and done, I did not see how I could get that faith back. And so I quit.

MY MAIN GOAL after tendering my resignation, I told Ashcroft and Comey, was to write replacements for the August 2002 and March 2003 interrogation opinions before my departure, which was scheduled for six weeks later. This proved to be a naive ambition. I and many others in my office worked hard on the opinions during that time, but for many reasons it was impossible to finish them.

During those last few weeks in government, my relations with the CIA, and especially with CIA lawyers, were, to put it mildly, strained. I had done something I had tried very hard to avoid: I had changed the rules in the middle of the game in a way that potentially jeopardized national security and that certainly harmed an institution I had come to admire, the CIA. The lawyers I worked with in the CIA were among the best in government: smart, careful, resourceful, and cool under pressure. Every day, they and their clients were exposed to a buzzsaw of contradictory commands: stay within the confines of the law, even when the law is maddeningly vague, or you will be investigated and severely punished; but be proactive and aggressive and imaginative, push the law to its limit, don't be cautious, and prevent another attack at all costs, or you will also be investigated and punished. The agency had been asked to go out on a limb in 2002, and it had demanded and received absolute legal assurances from the Department of Justice and the White House. I had done the unthinkable in withdrawing its golden shield.

And I had done so at a time that George Tenet would later describe as one of the most threatening since 9/11.[30] The agency was understandably angry and anxious, and quite predictably disinclined to continue with aggressive interrogations despite the increasing threats. "Confusion about the legal limits of interrogation has begun to slow government efforts to obtain information from suspected terrorists," even though it was the "start of a critical summer period when counterterrorism officials fear that Al Qaeda might attack the United States," reported the *New York Times* in late June.[31]

My actions in June 2004 contributed to a problem that has bedeviled the intelligence community since the 1960s. The executive branch and Congress pressure the community to engage in controversial action at the edges of the law, and then fail to protect it from recriminations when things go awry. This leads the community to retrench and become risk averse, which invites complaints by politicians that the community is fecklessly timid. Intelligence excesses of the 1960s led to the Church committee reproaches and reforms of the 1970s, which led to complaints that the community had become too risk averse, which led to the aggressive behavior under William Casey in the 1980s that resulted in the Iran-Contra and related scandals, which led to another round of intelligence purges and restrictions in the 1990s that deepened the culture of risk aversion and once again led (both before and after 9/11) to complaints about excessive timidity, which after 9/11 led to renewed aggressive action, which once again (following the interrogation and rendition and terrorist surveillance controversies) is leading to retrenchment by the intelligence community in the face of complaints that it has gone too far.

These cycles of timidity and aggression are the bane of the

intelligence community, and are a terrible problem for our national security. They flow from the confluence of three related Washington pathologies: the criminalization of warfare, the blame game, and the cover-your-ass syndrome. Everyone agrees that risks must be taken to confront the terrorist threats. But no one wants to be blamed when the inevitable errors occur. Everyone wants cover. The President wants plausible deniability, or blames bad intelligence. Congressional intelligence committees demand to be informed, but not in a way that will prevent them from being critical when things go badly. Intelligence agencies want explicit instructions from the White House and Congress, which are rarely forthcoming. The agencies thus increasingly demand cover from their lawyers. Their lawyers, in turn, increasingly seek cover from OLC. And, as my actions demonstrate, OLC opinions are not always reliable.

Some of these pathologies could have been avoided with respect to interrogation. It took my temporary successor, Dan Levin, a former prosecutor and very experienced executive branch lawyer, almost six months of hard work to complete, vet, and publish the replacement for the flawed August 2002 opinion.[32] The Levin opinion gave the torture law a much more rigorous and balanced interpretation, correcting the errors and exaggerations of the original opinion. The new opinion declined to address the presidential override issue analyzed in the earlier memo, reasoning that consideration of these matters "would be inconsistent with the President's unequivocal directive that United States personnel not engage in torture." And then, in an important footnote, the Levin opinion stated that "[w]hile we have identified various disagreements with the August 2002 Memorandum, we have reviewed this

Office's prior opinions addressing issues involving treatment of detainees and do not believe that any of their conclusions would be different under the standards set forth in this memorandum."[33] In other words, no approved interrogation technique would be affected by this more careful and nuanced analysis. The opinion that had done such enormous harm was completely unnecessary to the tasks at hand.

HOW COULD THIS have happened? How could OLC have written opinions that, when revealed to the world weeks after the Abu Ghraib scandal broke, made it seem as though the administration was giving official sanction to torture, and brought such dishonor on the United States, the Bush administration, the Department of Justice, and the CIA? How could its opinions reflect such bad judgment, be so poorly reasoned, and have such a terrible tone? And why would OLC write an opinion that was so unnecessary and overbroad? I was not in government when the original August 1, 2002, opinion was written, but I can hazard some informed guesses.

The main explanation is fear. When the original opinion was written in the weeks before the first anniversary of 9/11, threat reports were pulsing as they hadn't since 9/11. Newspapers reported increases in intelligence chatter in August 2002. But inside the administration the "end-of-summer threat," as it was called, seemed much worse. "We were sure there would be bodies in the streets" on September 11, 2002, a high-level Justice Department official later told me. Counterterrorism officials were terrified by a possible follow-up attack on the 9/11 anniversary, and desperate to stop it. The administration had in its custody Abu Zubaydah, "a senior terrorist leader and a trusted associate of Osama bin Laden" who, as President Bush later explained, possessed "unparalleled knowledge about terrorist networks and their plans for new attacks."[34] The President believed that "the security of our nation and the lives of our citizens" depended on our ability to get this information from Zubaydah.[35] So did George Tenet. "I've got reports of nuclear weapons in New York City, apartment buildings that are gonna be blown up, planes that are gonna fly into airports all over again . . . Plot lines that I don't know—I don't know what's going on inside the United States," Tenet later said of the context in which the initial aggressive interrogations took place. "And I'm struggling to find out where the next disaster is going to occur. Everybody forgets one central context of what we lived through. The palpable fear that we felt on the basis of the fact that there was so much we did not know."[36] I'm sure that when the CIA's interrogation techniques came for approval to OLC in 2002, the lawyers felt the same pressure as everyone else to do everything possible to get information related to the expected attack.

Fear explains why OLC pushed the envelope. And in pushing the envelope, OLC took shortcuts in its opinion-writing procedures. On the theory that expert criticism improves the quality of opinions, OLC normally circulates its draft opinions to government agencies with relevant expertise. The State Department, for example, would normally be consulted on the questions of international law implicated by the interrogation opinions. But the August 2002 opinion, though it contained no classified information, was treated as an unusually "close hold" within the administration. Before I arrived at OLC, Gonzales made it a practice to limit readership of controversial legal opinions to a very small group of lawyers. And so, under directions from the White House, OLC did not show the opinion to the State Department, which would have strenuously objected. This was ostensibly done to prevent leaks. But in this and other contexts, I eventually came to believe that it was done to control outcomes in the opinions and minimize resistance to them.

There is something to be said for this approach in times of genuine emergency. But I did not follow the practice when I was head of OLC in 2003–2004. I always insisted that the State Department chime in on issues of international law, even if the issues were highly classified. And though the process was often painful, it always improved my work. I also insisted, sometimes in the face of White House resistance, that more lawyers in the Justice Department be given access to classified programs so that we had the manpower to do a proper legal analysis. In August 2002, however, only a small handful of lawyers in the White House, Justice Department, and CIA were involved in drafting and reviewing the interrogation opinion, and few of them had a critical stance toward the opinion's interpretation of torture or the President's power.

All of these men wanted to push the law as far as it would allow. But none, I believe, thought he was violating the law. John Yoo certainly didn't. He has defended every element of the opinion to this day, and I believe he has done so in good faith. Yoo was indispensable after 9/11; few people had the knowledge, intelligence, and energy to craft the dozens of terrorism-related opinions he wrote. The poor quality of a handful of very important opinions is probably attributable to some combination of the fear that pervaded the executive branch, pressure from the White House, and Yoo's unusually expansive and self-confident conception of presidential power.

Yoo is not the first Justice Department lawyer to write a legal opinion in a time of crisis that was later widely repudiated. The same was true of the unconvincing opinion that Attorney General Edward Bates wrote for Abraham Lincoln justifying Lincoln's suspension of the writ of habeas corpus. Historian Nancy Baker said the Bates opinion was a product of "military utility" and "political exigencies,"[37] and historian Arthur M. Schlesinger, Jr., described it as "exculpatory."[38] Similar judgments were leveled against the opinion that the revered Attorney General Robert Jackson wrote to authorize, in the face of several congressional statutes to the contrary, Franklin Roosevelt's destroyers-for-bases deal in the tense summer of 1940. The Jackson opinion was "an endorsement of unrestrained autocracy in the field of our foreign relations" that was the most "dangerous opinion . . . ever before penned by an Attorney General of the United States," according to the esteemed Princeton constitutional scholar Edward Corwin.[39] Fifty years later Senator Daniel Patrick Moynihan claimed that Jackson "subverted the law" and rendered Roosevelt "clearly subject to impeachment."[40] Bates and Jackson, like Yoo, acted under enormous pressure to help the President avoid what he saw as a disaster in time of crisis.

Whatever explains how Yoo came to write the interrogation opinions, it is wrong to lay the blame for the interrogation opinion fiasco entirely at his feet. Yoo was, after all, only a Deputy Assistant Attorney General, a position that requires neither nomination by the President nor confirmation by the Senate. The ultimate responsibility for giving Yoo such power and influence, and for failing to better supervise his activities, must lie with the Assistant Attorney General in charge of OLC, the Attorney General in whose name OLC exercises authority, and the White House.

Yoo's superiors probably failed to supervise him adequately for two reasons: under pressure to push the envelope, they liked the answers he gave; and lacking relevant expertise, they deferred to his judgment. Yoo was a war powers scholar at a prestigious law school. He also had enormous personal charm, and he was extremely persuasive in explaining his views. On the surface the interrogation opinions appeared thorough and scholarly. It was thus not easy for the men under pressure in the summer of 2002 to critically analyze Yoo's opinion. Jay Bybee, who actually signed the August 2002 opinion, is a fine lawyer and judge. But he had no training in issues of war or interrogation, and he tended to approve Yoo's draft opinions on these topics with minimal critical input. Nor were Yoo's boss, Attorney General John Ashcroft, or the nominal recipient of the opinion, White House Counsel Alberto Gonzales, in positions to raise informed questions. Ashcroft had come to the Justice Department from thirty years in politics, and Gonzales had been a corporate lawyer and state judge before coming to the White House. Addington, of course, was a very informed observer. But he possessed nearly the same characteristics that led Yoo to be so incautious and aggressive in the interrogation context.

I used to think that another reason why Gonzales and Addington never perceived problems in the interrogation opinions (and other problematic opinions) was that they didn't think it their role to question the merits of OLC's legal analysis. Robert Jackson once famously said of the Supreme Court's authority, "We are not final because we are infallible, but we are infallible only because we are final."[41] Early in my tenure at OLC, Gonzales and Addington expressed the similar view that OLC's legal reasoning was irrelevant to the authority of an OLC opinion. All that mattered, they believed, was OLC's bottom line approval. My earliest disagreement with both men was about whether this was the right way to view OLC. I maintained that the correctness and quality of the OLC opinions mattered. OLC's getting it right was important to making sure the government acted legally. Revelation of a flawed opinion could be politically damaging. And one might not necessarily receive "immunity" from future Justice Department prosecution—an issue they were obsessed with—if one relied on an obviously flawed legal opinion.

I eventually came to believe that Gonzales's and Addington's charitable hands-off attitude toward OLC's authority extended only to opinions that gave them answers they liked. They acquiesced in my withdrawal of the OLC interrogation opinions, but they did not always acquiesce in OLC opinions that reached uncongenial conclusions. Addington in particular had a reputation for ensuring that those who crossed swords with him never received White House approval for advancement, even when it was widely believed that approval was deserved. I was immune to this pressure because the Senate had confirmed me, because I loved my "real" job as an academic, and because I had no higher government ambition. But others were not. At the beginning of President Bush's second term, Solicitor General Paul Clement wanted to hire Patrick Philbin, the brilliant conservative lawyer who helped me correct some of OLC's prior errors, as his principal deputy to argue cases before the Supreme Court. Addington, presumably acting with the implicit blessing of the Vice President, expressed opposition to the promotion, and newly minted Attorney General Gonzales demurred. Others suffered a similar fate for similar reasons.

Alberto Gonzales went along with Addington's strict enforcement of the party line on promotions in the Justice Department. But in the end he was much less rigid than Addington about the flawed OLC opinions I had struggled to correct. In Gonzales's mind, he had taken all the proper steps in coordinating the government's legal policy decisions related to interrogation. He had surrounded himself in the White House with two very experienced national security lawyers, David Addington and Tim Flanigan, and had heeded their advice; he had taken great care to secure the Department of Justice's blessing for the interrogation policy; and he could take comfort from the fact that the department's lawyer doing the analysis, John Yoo, was an academic expert on war and national security. Gonzales was, I think, genuinely stunned when the legal foundation for the interrogation policy imploded in the spring and summer of 2004. After the devastating revelations and bruising reverberations in that period, and after I had announced my resignation and was about to leave government, Gonzales and I had a friendly chat—he was always very friendly toward me, no matter how difficult I made his life—about our time working together. "I guess those opinions really were as bad as you said," he told me near the end of our talk.

IN DECEMBER 2004, four months after I left OLC and a few weeks after I started work at Harvard Law School, the front page of the *Boston Globe* reported on an "angry debate" among my new colleagues in connection with my alleged role in working on the "torture memos" while in government.[42] A few weeks earlier the *Washington Post* wrote about a draft opinion I had circulated in March 2004 advising Alberto Gonzales that the Fourth Geneva Convention permitted the United States to temporarily remove Iraqis from Iraq for purposes of interrogation.[43] The *Post* reported that the CIA and White House pressured me into writing the draft, that Iraqis were taken out of Iraq in reliance on the draft, and that the draft was a part of the CIA's rendition policy of taking suspected terrorists from one country to another where they would have "no access to any recognized legal process or rights."[44]

Most of this was inaccurate. I was often pressured by many people to do many things in government. But for this draft opinion, which was not a high priority in my office, I was not. The question about taking Iraqis temporarily out of Iraq for questioning arose in the fall of 2003 after I ruled that even Iraqi terrorists were "protected persons" under the Fourth Geneva Convention. I believe the draft opinion reached the right conclusions, but for the reasons I stated in the draft, the issue was not clear.[45] In any event, I never finalized the draft, it never became operational, and it was never relied on to take anyone outside of Iraq.[46] I do not know whether the request for legal advice about relocating Iraqi prisoners outside Iraq for questioning was associated with a broader rendition program. But I do know that the draft opinion could not have been relied upon to abuse anyone, not only because it was never finalized, but more importantly because it stated that the suspect's Geneva Convention protections must travel with him outside Iraq.[47]

The *Post* story missed most of these points, and instead emphasized that my opinion was written by the same office (OLC) that wrote the torture opinions. This gave a handful of my new Harvard colleagues—who disliked my scholarship and the Bush administration, and who opposed my appointment to the faculty—an opportunity to speculate publicly about my role in facilitating torture. "I believe that the faculty was seriously at fault for not inquiring more deeply, prior to making this appointment, into any role Jack Goldsmith may have played in providing legal advice facilitating and justifying torture," one new colleague told the *Boston Globe*.[48] Another suggested that even if I weren't directly involved in the "torture memos," those memos nonetheless "reflected ideas developed by a group of academic lawyers in and out of government in which Jack has played an active role."[49] Although many of my new colleagues publicly stood by me, the *Globe* story still stung, for it gave public credence to the suggestion, contrary to the painful reality of what I had been through during the year before, that I was an architect of what many saw as the administration's torture policy. The *Globe* story was not the greatest of introductions to the new neighbors my family and I were just beginning to meet. But I was too timid to defend myself at the time, and while I publicly denied drafting the interrogation opinions, I said nothing about my role in withdrawing them and trying to fix them.

A little over a year later, *Newsweek* ran a story that painted me as "the opposite of what [my] detractors imagined," namely, "the central figure in a secret but intense rebellion of a small coterie of Bush administration lawyers." *Newsweek* recounted my withdrawal of the two interrogation opinions and also reported that I had raised "serious questions" about the NSA Terrorist Surveillance Program, which resulted in a dramatic confrontation with the White House and "tougher legal standards" for the program. *Newsweek* said that in my "frequent face-to-face confrontations" with David Addington over these matters, the Vice President's Counsel was "beside himself" with anger and accused me of "putting brave men at risk." And it quoted Jim Comey praising me and others at his 2005 Department of Justice farewell speech for being "committed to getting it right—and to doing the right thing—whatever the price."[50]

I must confess that I liked the *Newsweek* story better than the *Boston Globe* story. And yet I laughed in agreement when my conservative Harvard colleague Charles Fried said of the reaction to the *Newsweek* story that "the only thing worse than being demonized by the left is being lionized by the left." I didn't see myself as a Bush administration opponent, and I still had many friends working in government. It was unsettling and somewhat embarrassing that so many people who detested the administration, and until the *Newsweek* article didn't much like me, were calling me a "hero" and suggesting that my actions in government confirmed their views of the administration. I worried that praise from administration opponents would make it appear, incorrectly, that I had been currying favor in my new environment at the expense of my old colleagues.

But more than anything else I felt uncomfortable with the Mani-chean tone of the *Newsweek* story, a tone one sees so often when the press and intellectuals criticize the Bush administration's attempts to balance security and liberty. My fights with David Addington and others were not struggles between the forces of good and evil. Our sharp disagreement over the requirements of national security law and the meaning of the imponderable phrases of the U.S. Constitution was not a fight between one who loves the Constitution and one who wants to shred it. Whether and how aggressively to check the terrorist threat, and whether and how far to push the law in so doing, are rarely obvious, especially during blizzards of frightening threat reports, when one is blinded by ignorance and desperately worried about not doing enough. Addington and I had different experiences, different perspectives, different roles, and different responsibilities. Despite our many fights, and despite what I view as his many errors of judgment, large and small, I believe he acted in good faith to protect the country.

I have been critical of my predecessors' actions in writing the interrogation opinions. But I was not there when they made the hard calls during the frightening summer of 2002. Instead, I surveyed the scene from the politically changed and always-more-lucid after-the-fact perspective. When I made tough calls in crisis situations under pressure and uncertainty, I realized that my decisions too would not be judged from the perspective of threat and danger in which they were taken. They would instead be judged, as Jim Comey once said, "in a quiet, dignified, well-lit room, where they can be viewed with the perfect, and brutally unfair, vision of hindsight," and "where it is impossible to capture even a piece of the urgency and exigency felt during a crisis."[51] Recognizing this, I often found myself praying that I would predict the future correctly. Some people have praised my part in withdrawing and starting to fix the interrogation opinions. But it is very easy to imagine a different world in which my withdrawal of the opinions led to a cessation of interrogations that future investigations made clear could have stopped an attack that killed thousands. In this possible world my actions would have looked pusillanimous and stupid, not brave.

CHAPTER 6

The Terror Presidency

On Friday, April 27, 2007, after a morning spent working on this book, I left my office and walked in the rain to meet FBI Special Agents Ronald Doe and Tim Smith (aliases) in the Au Bon Pain café in Harvard Square in Cambridge, Massachusetts. Doe and Smith looked like archetypal FBI G-men: they had short hair and wore white shirts, dark suits, and black lace-up shoes. As we sat down among the swirl of scruffy Harvard students playing chess and studying for exams, the out-of-place FBI agents cracked uneasy smiles when I joked that if their identities were revealed the FBI-hating lefties around us would tear them limb from limb.

I had met Doe and Smith twice before in a small windowless room in the FBI building in Washington, D.C. They were leading the criminal investigation into the leaks to James Risen and Eric Lichtblau that resulted in stories in the *New York Times* and a subsequent book about the National Security Agency's secret program of warrantless monitoring of international communications involving people associated with al Qaeda.[1] I had worked on the legal aspects of this program in 2003–2004 while I was at OLC. In prior meetings at the FBI, I had told Doe and Smith about a meeting I had in October 2004, three months after I resigned from OLC, with Lichtblau, the *Times* reporter who covered the Justice Department. I had never spoken to Lichtblau until he called me out of the blue in my temporary office at the American Enterprise Institute and asked to meet for coffee. I agreed, and at the end of a friendly hour-long chat about his career in journalism and the colorful figures in the Bush administration, he asked me a few questions about what he called a secret NSA program. Panicked inside, I told Lichtblau, untruthfully, that I didn't know what he was talking about. As soon as our meeting ended, I went straight to the Justice Department to tell Jim Comey, the Deputy Attorney General with whom I had worked intimately on NSA matters, about the conversation.

I had last spoken with the FBI about six months earlier, and was surprised when Doe called to say that he and Smith wanted to come to Cambridge for a brief meeting. A few moments after I sat down at the table in Au Bon Pain, Doe looked apologetic as he handed me a manila envelope that contained a subpoena. "You are commanded to appear and testify before the Grand Jury of the United States District Court in Alexandria, Virginia"—the same court where al Qaeda operative Zacarias Moussaoui was tried and convicted—in connection with the leak investigation, it read. I was stunned, and Doe seemed embarrassed. "We wanted to serve you in person as a favor because we expected you'd be mad," Doe said. "We believe you told us the truth," he added, assuring me that he did not suspect me as the source of the leak. He said he was not sure why the lawyers at the Justice Department had decided to subpoena me, but he suspected it was because of my contact with Lichtblau.

The subpoena required me to turn over to the Justice Department evidence of any communication with any reporter from the *New York Times*. In the course of complying with this request, I found a September 2006 email from Scott Shane, a *New York Times* reporter who had been working on a story about CIA agents' fear of prosecution for the activities they had been asked to perform in the war on terrorism. Shane's email sought my permission to use a quotation from a prior conversation where I had said that even "a failed prosecution or a lawsuit that goes nowhere can produce 'devastating' headlines and legal fees." I agreed to let Shane use the quote, and urged him to say that it was not only lawsuits that counterterrorism officials worried about but also "threatened prosecution, grand jury proceedings, etc.—any of this stuff sucks big time." How right I was. In the midst of writing a book about how fear of legal process after government service influenced people during their government service, my ideas and concerns had suddenly become concrete.

Doe correctly predicted I would be angry about the subpoena. I understood the government's need to question me under oath in light of my contact with Lichtblau. But, I told the FBI agents, I worried very much about the expense of the attorneys I would need to help me prepare for the grand jury.[2] I also told them that I worried about a perjury trap. The verdict against Scooter Libby for false statements and perjury was just six weeks old, and I knew that Washington investigations for governmental abuse often lead to ruinous grand jury investigations for lying. I of course had no intention of lying. But I could not remember many of the details of the hours of conversations I had with the FBI, and I feared that I might make statements under oath inconsistent with ones made in those conversations. When investigators and prosecutors ask a witness repeatedly about the same events, inconsistencies are inevitable. The inconsistencies put the witness in the position of having to show that they are unintentional, and thus not a crime. The prosecutor who sought my grand jury testimony would later disclaim any purpose to rehash my lengthy agent interviews, and he kept his word. But I wouldn't know that until months after I was served with the subpoena, when I was actually in the grand jury room.

What angered me most about the subpoena I received on that wet day in Cambridge was not the expense of lawyers or a possible perjury trap, but rather the fact that it was Alberto Gonzales's Justice Department that had issued it. As Doe and Smith knew, I had spent hundreds of very difficult hours at OLC, in the face of extraordinary White House resistance, trying to clean up the legal mess that then–White House Counsel Gonzales, David Addington, John Yoo, and others had created in designing the foundations of the Terrorist Surveillance Program. It seemed rich beyond my comprehension for a *Gonzales*-led Department of Justice to be pursuing *me* for possibly illegal actions in connection with the Terrorist Surveillance Program, I told the two wide-eyed FBI agents in Harvard Square. They understood what I was talking about. But Doe nervously said that the legality of the foundations of the program was "outside [their] jurisdiction," and the agents quickly changed the subject to tell me about the recent progress they had made on the source of the leak.

I was not opposed to the leak investigation itself or to vigorous surveillance of terrorists. I agreed with President Bush that the revelations by Risen and Lichtblau had alerted our enemies, put our citizens at risk, and done "great harm" to the nation.[3] I hoped the FBI would find and punish the leakers, and I had spent many hours trying to help them do so. I also shared many of the White House's concerns with the Foreign Intelligence Surveillance Act (FISA), the 1978 domestic wiretapping law that required executive officers, on pain of jail, to get a court warrant before wiretapping suspected enemies in the United States. We were at war with terrorists who were armed with disposable cell phones and encrypted emails buried in a global multibillion-communications-per-day system. It seemed crazy to require the Commander in Chief and his subordinates to get a judge's permission to listen to each communication under a legal regime that was designed before technological revolutions brought us high-speed fiber-optic networks, the public Internet, email, and ten-dollar cell phones.[4]

But I deplored the way the White House went about fixing the problem. "We're one bomb away from getting rid of that obnoxious [FISA] court," Addington had told me in his typically sarcastic style during a tense White House meeting in February of 2004. The Vice President's Counsel, who was the chief legal architect of the Terrorist Surveillance Program, was singing the White House tune on FISA. He and the Vice President had abhorred FISA's intrusion on presidential power ever since its enactment in 1978. After 9/11 they and other top officials in the administration dealt with FISA the way they dealt with other laws they didn't like: they blew through them in secret based on flimsy legal opinions that they guarded closely so no one could question the legal basis for the operations. My first experience of this strict control, in fact, had come in a 2003 meeting when Addington angrily denied the NSA

Inspector General's request to see a copy of OLC's legal analysis in support of the Terrorist Surveillance Program. Before I arrived in OLC, not even NSA lawyers were allowed to see the Justice Department's legal analysis of what NSA was doing.

I am not permitted to say much about how Jim Comey, Patrick Philbin, and I, with the crucial support of former Attorney General John Ashcroft and others, struggled to put the Terrorist Surveillance Program on a proper legal footing. I first encountered the program in 2003–2004, long after it had been integrated into the post-9/11 counterterrorism architecture. Putting it legally aright at that point, without destroying some of the government's most important counterterrorism tools, was by far the hardest challenge I faced in government. And the whole ordeal could have been avoided. On January 17, 2007, Gonzales informed the Congress that the executive branch, under pressure from Congress and the courts following the leak, had worked out an "innovative" arrangement with the Foreign Intelligence Surveillance Court—the secret court that runs the FISA system, and that the administration had originally bypassed—to achieve the government's goals of "speed and agility" in surveillance within the four corners of the FISA law.[5] In 2004 I and others in the Department of Justice had begun the process of working with the FISA court to give the Commander in Chief much more flexibility in tracking terrorists. From the beginning the administration could have taken these and other steps to ramp up terrorist surveillance in indisputably lawful ways that would have minimized the likelihood of a devastating national security leak. But only if it had been willing to work with the FISA court or Congress. The White House had found it much easier to go it alone, in secret.

The American people expect the President to take imaginative and aggressive actions like the Terrorist Surveillance Program to keep the terrorists at bay. And they blame the President and no one else when the terrorists strike. "The whole government is so identified in the minds of the people with his personality," said the twenty-seventh President, William Howard Taft, "that they make him responsible for all the sins of omission and of commission of society at large."[6] Nowhere is Taft's dictum truer than with national security. But at the same time that we expect the President to keep us safe, we also question his motives and fear his power when he acts to do so. When James Madison told Thomas Jefferson that "it is a universal truth that the loss of liberty at home is to be charged to the provisions against danger, real or pretended, from abroad," he had the presidency in mind.[7] The President's control over the military and intelligence agencies, his ability to act in secret, and his power to self-interpret legal limits on his authority create extraordinary opportunities for abuse.. Presidents throughout American history have used the threat of war or emergency to expand presidential powers in ways that later seemed unrelated or unnecessary to the crisis.

"The problem is to devise means of reconciling a strong and purposeful Presidency with equally strong and purposeful forms of democratic control," said Arthur M. Schlesinger, Jr., in his famous 1973 book, *The Imperial Presidency*.[8] Schlesinger's argument, written in the shadow of Watergate, was that presidents had arrogated national security power in ways that threatened to upset the mechanisms of democratic accountability. The presidency in the age of terrorism—the Terror Presidency—suffers from many of the vices of Schlesinger's Imperial Presidency. But these vices appear in new forms, and the Terror Presidency also faces new challenges to its twin and sometimes incompatible obligations to keep us safe and maintain our trust. The best-intentioned and best-prepared presidents, exercising uncommon leadership and good judgment, will make mistakes in managing the difficult trade-offs between security and liberty that the seemingly endless terror threat presents. But future presidents can learn from the experiences of the last six years, and from other crisis presidencies, about how to minimize these mistakes.

FIFTEEN MONTHS BEFORE I was subpoenaed, I attended a dinner at a Cambodian restaurant in Cambridge in honor of Elaine Scarry, a Harvard English professor who was the inaugural speaker for the "Age of Terror" lecture series sponsored by Harvard's Humanities Center. During dinner, the center's director, Homi Bhabha, asked the two-dozen intellectuals around the table whether the Bush administration's "discourse of threat" (color-coded threat-level symbols, the rhetoric of fear, and the like) was an overreaction to a real threat or a cynical effort to cover up poor intelligence and justify military action abroad and restrictions at home. I answered that the administration was describing its perception of the threat in good faith. A young professor at the table strongly disagreed. "The threat is entirely made up by the Bush administration, and is designed to scare us," he said. Al Qaeda and its affiliates are not as menacing or competent as their lucky 9/11 strike made them seem, he said. Nuclear weapons are hard to get or make, and chemical and biological weapons, while easier to make, are hard to use effectively. The administration's mendacious reaction to 9/11, he concluded, is akin to past presidential overreactions to perceived threats, like the Red Scare, the Japanese internment, and McCarthyism. A murmur of agreement spread around the room, as many others concurred that the government's reactions to 9/11 were pretextual attempts to expand presidential power.

Almost a year later, in a Boston suburb about four miles away, a subway passenger noticed a small device attached to the ramp support for Interstate 93, Boston's main north-south highway. Wires and tubes emerging from the device appeared to be connected with electrical tape to a circuit board and batteries. Local authorities feared the package was a bomb planted by terrorists. Sirens soon filled the air as the Boston bomb squad, police cars, fire trucks, ambulances, and television helicopter crews descended on the scene, closing northbound traffic on I-93 and the subway station below it. An officer from the explosive detection unit, wearing thick green bomb squad armor, attached cables to the device and destroyed it with a water cannon. Authorities later closed train stations, highways, and bridges when similar devices were discovered around the city.[9]

It turned out that the package was not a terrorist bomb, but rather a 12-by-18-inch electronic placard covered with magnetic lights, akin to a children's Lite-Brite toy. The lights represented a character called a "Mooninite" from *Aqua Teen Hunger Force*— a cartoon about a talking box of french fries and his fast-food friends—flipping the world his middle finger. Hippy video artists had placed thirty-eight of these devices around Boston as part of a "viral marketing" publicity stunt to generate buzz for the cartoon. They succeeded beyond their wildest dreams. Everyone in Boston now knew about the cartoon characters that ground portions of the city to a halt and cost it nearly a million dollars in response fees and more in lost business caused by transportation delays.[10]

"For those who responded to it, professionals, it had a very sinister appearance," said Massachusetts Attorney General Martha Coakley, explaining why Boston officials reacted so forcefully to what turned out to be harmless blinking lights. "It had a battery behind it and wires."[11] The Boston police later issued a "message" listing "all the facts and circumstances" behind the city's reaction to the cartoon lights. During the morning it was responding to the light devices, Boston police had also learned that British authorities had arrested several terror suspects, that a Washington, D.C., Metro station had been closed because of a suspicious package, and that four people had been overcome by fumes from a package in a New York City post office. And as Boston police officials were responding to reports about multiple packages with protruding wires and tubes, the New England Medical Center reported finding a possible pipe bomb after a man ran out of its building screaming, "God is warning you that today is going to be a sad Day."[12] With these reports pouring in, and under conditions of great uncertainty, the Boston police decided that they had to assume the worst about the packages being reported around the city.

The actions of the Boston police in response to the Mooninite incident put the President's staggering responsibilities in perspective. Every morning the President sees threats that are hundreds of times more harrowing than the ones that led the police to lock down Boston's transportation routes. Inside the federal government counterterrorism officials are genuinely fearful, every day, of a devastating homeland attack. These fears are fueled by their knowledge of terrorists' aims and the infinite number of targets, and by their relative ignorance about when, where, or how the next attack will occur.

The American public largely shared the government's anxieties on 9/11. But since that time public concern about the terror threat has waned. One month after 9/11, 85 percent of the American public believed that another attack was likely to happen in the near future; by the summer of 2007, this figure had dropped to 40 percent.[13] During this same period, the percentage of the country that saw terrorism as the nation's most important problem dropped from 46 to 4 percent.[14] "A democracy cannot fight a Seven Years' War," General Marshall once said.[15] A democracy has an especially hard time fighting a long war with few obvious public signs of the threat. The absence of an attack at home since 9/11 naturally makes Islamist terrorism seem less scary than many once believed. "Five years is a short time for jihadists who think in terms of epochal struggles, the rise and fall of civilizations, and rewards in an afterlife," Paul Pillar, the former Deputy Chief of the CIA's counterterrorism center, wrote on September 11, 2006.[16] But in a democracy at war it is a long time, and it is natural for public vigilance to fade over time, even if to the President's eye the threat has not faded one bit.

Public support is especially likely to be short-lived in this war, which lacks the usual indicia of wartime crisis. Unlike in World War II and the Civil War, when the stakes to the nation were obvious, this war has brought no draft, little mobilization, relatively few casualties, and no shortages, rationing, or economic controls. Nor have we seen alarming army divisions, or decisive public victories such as the battles at Midway and Gettysburg. We have suffered defeats in this war, but victories are largely invisible, and consist mostly of capturing or killing individual terrorists. The best evidence of our success—the absence of a second homeland attack—has had the self-defeating effect of enhancing public skepticism about the reality of the threat. This skepticism is reinforced by years of government threat alerts that, in the absence of an attack, seem like exaggerations or manipulations. It is also reinforced by the government's practice of arresting domestic groups with evil plans but seemingly minimal capacities, such as the Lackawanna Six, the Virginia paintball jihadists, the Miami-based "Seas of David" group, and the JFK airport plotters. The executive branch believes it must stop terror plots very early, before they are fully hatched, but over the years these early arrests have caused many people to grow cynical.

As the public perception of the terror threat has dimmed, the downsides of our counterterrorism efforts have become more salient.[17] The public naturally focuses less on the threat it cannot see, and more on things it can see: false alarms, the alienation of allies, terrorist recruitment, misallocated resources, and diminished American honor. Iraq is exhibit number one on the cost side of the ledger. Guantanamo Bay is exhibit number two. The island detention facility is nothing like its shabby portrayal in the press: most of it is a supermodern prison facility where the terrorist detainees are treated better than convicted inmates in high-security prisons in the United States. But years of public misinformation about GTMO, made credible by government secrecy and mistakes, has so harmed the United States' reputation for fairness that many believe the national interest requires its closure. Public debate is filled with similar return-to-normalcy demands concerning the detention, interrogation, and trial of suspected terrorists.

"Terrorism has always been less about physical damage than

about fear and the responses fear provokes," says Paul Pillar.[18] The terrorists understand this point well, and exploit it. It is "easy for us to provoke and bait," Osama Bin Laden proclaimed in 2004. "All that we have to do is to send two mujahidin . . . to raise a piece of cloth on which is written al-Qaeda in order to make the generals race there to cause America to suffer human, economic, and political losses."[19] Bin Laden's braggadocio, and the many costs of our response to the terror threat, lead some to urge the government to change course. We would do better against the terrorists, they say, if the government calmed down, stopped being afraid of attacks, stopped assuming the worst, and stopped reacting so aggressively to threats.[20] If the United States were to stop being afraid "and then, despite its best efforts, be attacked, that would be terrible and tragic—just as it is tragic [that] every day in America 100 people die in car crashes and 50 are murdered," argues a leading proponent of the return-to-normalcy view, journalist James Fallows. But "continuing to distort the country's domestic politics and international relations out of excessive fear would be even worse."[21]

The government has calmed down, at least to the outside world, over the last six years: we see fewer colored threat alerts, fewer predictions of doom, and fewer public displays of nervousness and fear. But its internal skittishness is not something we can wish or will away. For generations the Terror Presidency will be characterized by an unremitting fear of devastating attack, an obsession with preventing the attack, and a proclivity to act aggressively and preemptively to do so. The threats have such a firm foundation in possibility, and such a harrowing promise of enormous destruction, that any responsible executive leader aware of the threats—be it the President of the United States, or the Boston police—must assume the worst. Every foreseeable post-9/11 President, Republican or Democrat, will embrace this attitude, just as Lincoln, Roosevelt, and other presidents did in time of war or emergency. If anything, the next Democratic President—having digested a few threat matrices, and acutely aware that he or she alone will be wholly responsible when thousands of Americans are killed in the next attack—will be even more anxious than the current President to thwart the threat, especially if there is no attack in the interim.

The President and everyone else responsible for national security after 9/11 understand that this attitude will lead them to do things that, in hindsight, will seem to be overreactions or errors. National security officials do not have the luxury of hindsight when deciding how to act. But they do understand the potential consequences of not taking threats seriously enough. This is why they obsessively focus on how a genuine threat might look *before the fact*. They know that most of the 9/11 plotters, if arrested in the summer of 2001, would have seemed like unimportant malcontents who lacked the weapons or skills needed to kill three thousand people and cause tens of billions of dollars in damage in a single morning. And so when national security officials learn about groups that seem like al Qaeda cells or copycats, they believe they cannot afford not to act. Nor do they think they can be patient with traditional interrogation techniques when they have in custody someone like Abu Zubaydah, a close associate of Bin Laden who was involved in many prior terrorist attacks on Americans, and who likely had knowledge of future (and possibly near-term) attacks. Counterterrorism officials worry about not profiling when doing so might uncover a plot, or declining to wiretap a slightly suspicious phone number that might lead to the next Zacarias Moussaoui, or releasing a detainee who might come back to kill, or failing to kill a known terrorist when they have him in their sights. They understand that both action and inaction can bring error, and that there are trade-offs between the short-term benefits to safety from acting aggressively and long-term costs to safety from being too aggressive. But their incentives and responsibilities lead them to focus on the short term rather than the long term, and to minimize false negatives that might be the next 9/11 rather than false positives that will invite charges of exaggeration or mistake.

This growing gap between the government's view of the terror threat and what it thinks must be done to stop it, and the public's view of the matter, is an enormous problem for the Terror Presidency and for the country. "[P]ublic sentiment is everything," Abraham Lincoln once said. "With public sentiment nothing can fail; without it, nothing can succeed."[22] When the public does not share a President's assessment of a threat, the President has a hard time garnering the trust and support necessary to meet it. One of the reasons the Clinton administration declined to take risky steps in 1998 to attack and kill Osama Bin Laden was that the public perceived no serious threat from Bin Laden and thus would not understand and support the action against him, especially if (as was possible) it resulted in collateral damage to civilians and civilian property. In other wars, when the public clearly perceived the stakes, it was willing to give the President wide latitude in meeting the threat. Lincoln often invoked public necessity during the

Civil War as a justification to stretch the Constitution and laws to meet the crisis. So did Roosevelt in World War II. In the weeks and months after 9/11, President Bush, too, acted under a generally shared sense of public necessity. But as the years have gone by, the appearance of necessity has faded.

The Terror Presidency's most fundamental challenge is to establish adequate trust with the American people to enable the President to take the steps needed to fight an enemy that the public does not see and in some respects cannot comprehend.[23] This is an enormously difficult task. The Terror President must educate the public about the threat without unduly scaring it. He must persuade the public of the need for appropriate steps to check the threat, explain his inevitable mistakes, and act with good judgment if an attack comes. And he must convince the public that he is acting in good faith to protect us and is not acting at our expense to enhance or protect himself.

FRANKLIN ROOSEVELT FACED a similar set of challenges in the eighteen months prior to the United States' entry into World War II in December 1941.[24] Since World War I a fiercely isolationist United States had been determined never again to waste American resources and lives in a European war that (as many thought of World War I) implicated no American interests. Underlying American isolationism was the conviction that the Atlantic and Pacific oceans provided all the security the United States needed from totalitarian menaces. By 1935, Hitler had consolidated his power in Germany, renounced the Versailles Treaty, and revealed his intentions to rebuild Germany's military strength. The same year, according to historian David Kennedy, "American isolationism hardened from mere indifference to the outside world into studied, active repudiation of anything that smacked of international political or military engagement."[25] Congress in 1935 enacted the first of several neutrality laws that barred the United States from sending arms, munitions, credits, and most other forms of support to any of the belligerents in the growing wars in Europe and Asia. "With stout legal thread," Kennedy explains, "Congress had spun a straightjacket that rendered the United States effectively powerless in the face of the global conflagration that was about to explode."[26]

Through the latter half of the 1930s, as Germany gobbled up countries in central Europe and Japan invaded China, Roosevelt believed (as he said in his 1937 "Quarantine" speech) that there was no escape from the growing global wars "through mere isolation or neutrality," and that only "positive endeavors" could preserve peace.[27] But American isolationism remained steadfast, and Roosevelt's weak attempts to loosen neutrality restrictions to aid countries that opposed Germany and Japan failed. Then in the spring of 1940, Hitler overran the Low Countries and France, chased the British out of Dunkirk, and threatened Great Britain itself with destruction. Roosevelt agreed with British Prime Minister Churchill that if Germany succeeded, "the whole world, including the United States, including all that we have known and cared for, will sink into the abyss of a new Dark Age."[28] And so he finally decided to take forceful steps to educate the American people about the extremity of the threat, to prepare the country militarily, and to break free of neutrality restrictions so that he could aid the British.

Roosevelt's first step in these directions was to reshuffle his cabinet. On June 20, 1940, as France was falling, he announced that he was replacing the Democratic and relatively isolationist Secretaries of War and the Navy with establishment internationalist Republicans who were formerly his political enemies. For the War Department he chose the patrician Henry Stimson, one of the most admired public figures in America. Stimson had served successfully as William Howard Taft's Secretary of War and as Herbert Hoover's Secretary of State, and had voted against Roosevelt in 1932 and 1936. For Secretary of the Navy Roosevelt appointed Frank Knox, the publisher of the *Chicago Daily News*, an avid foe of the New Deal, and his opponent Alf Landon's vice presidential nominee in the 1936 election. Stimson and Knox were well-known supporters of greater military preparedness and support for Great Britain. "The appointments to the Cabinet are in line with the overwhelming sentiment of the nation for national solidarity in a time of world crisis and in behalf of our national defense—and nothing else," Roosevelt told the nation.[29] The "nothing else" part was not quite true. Roosevelt announced the cabinet changes on the eve of the Republican National Convention that would nominate Wendell Willkie as his opponent for the presidential election of 1940. He realized that the appointments would split Republicans on the issues of war preparedness and aid to Great Britain, and weaken Willkie.

Nonetheless, bringing Stimson and Knox into the cabinet served loftier goals as well. "Abroad, the appointments will serve to emphasize the essential unity of America in the rapid development of our military strength which has been rendered imperative by events in Europe," noted an approving *Washington Post* editorial.

"At home," the *Post* added, "this infusion of new blood should help to accelerate the preparedness program" that Stimson and Knox favored, and that as experienced leaders they would be able to see through.[30] Perhaps most fundamentally, the Republican appointments would help Roosevelt during the tough times ahead when he would need to assert extraordinary executive powers to keep the country safe. The *New York Times* observed that the Stimson and Knox appointments "give hostages to the future," for "if the defense program is bogged down by partisanship or incompetence, Mr. Knox and Mr. Stimson will have it in their power to deal the Administration a terrible blow by handing in their resignations."[31] Roosevelt had taken the extraordinary step of tying his hands by giving the keys to the military kingdom to lifelong political opponents. But he understood that tying his hands in this way would significantly strengthen his power as Commander in Chief. He knew that Stimson and Knox shared his goals about military readiness and aid to Britain, and that their support after observing him in private would enhance his credibility and trustworthiness in taking controversial steps to meet the gathering storm.

One of Roosevelt's most controversial actions was his decision in September 1940 to give Great Britain fifty overaged destroyers in exchange for military bases in the Western Hemisphere. Churchill had been begging for the destroyers since May, arguing that they were critical to prevent the Germans from invading Great Britain. Roosevelt hesitated. It was a presidential election year in which isolationism still dominated and any move toward war could bring political harm. Roosevelt and his advisors also worried that the transferred ships would weaken America's defenses and, if Great Britain fell and the Nazis captured the ships, only add to Germany's arsenal. Finally, Roosevelt believed the neutrality laws forbade such a transfer in any event. "[A] step of that kind could not be taken except with the specific authorization of Congress, and I am not certain that it would be wise for that suggestion to be made to the Congress at the moment," Roosevelt wrote a disappointed Churchill in May 1940.[32]

Over the course of the summer, Great Britain's plight became more precarious and her pleas more desperate. Receiving the destroyers was "a matter of life and death," Churchill told Roosevelt in June.[33] A month later he told the President that the "whole fate of the war may be decided by this minor and easily remediable factor," and pleaded that "in the long history of the world this is the thing to do *now.*"[34] Roosevelt convened his cabinet on August 2, 1940, for what Stimson, who had served two other presidents, described as "one of the most serious and important debates that I have ever had in a cabinet meeting."[35] Everyone in the cabinet had become persuaded that Great Britain could survive the German onslaught, especially if it received the destroyers, and that not taking this relatively small step would be much more harmful to United States' interests than doing so. Frank Knox proposed the destroyers-for-bases idea. But how to do the deal legally? For eleven days Roosevelt tried behind the scenes to find a way to get Congress to approve the deal, but this proved politically impossible in a presidential election year. And so on August 13, Roosevelt and his cabinet decided to act unilaterally, without seeking Congress's formal permission, even though three months earlier the President believed such a step would be unlawful.[36] "[E]veryone felt it was a desperate situation and a very serious step to take," Stimson recorded in his diary.[37]

During the month of August 1940 Roosevelt employed a three-prong strategy to legitimate the destroyer deal. The first was to educate the American people on the importance of the transaction. With the crucial help of the "Century Group," a bipartisan organization of prominent public officials who supported aid to Britain, the White House orchestrated a national campaign to convince the country that the destroyers deal was vital to U.S. security. General John J. Pershing, the revered World War I commander, kicked off the effort in a widely covered nationwide radio address. "It is my duty to tell you that in my opinion we face problems of the utmost seriousness and all the things we hold most dear are gravely threatened," he began.[38] Pershing and the other credible figures in the Century Group emphasized that the Germans "despise the American idea and have sworn to destroy it," that "democracy and liberty" were at stake, that the U.S. Navy had no need for the old destroyers but a powerful need for the Western Hemisphere naval bases, and that the destroyer deal was the best way for America to stop the Germans short of American involvement in war.[39]

The second element of Roosevelt's strategy was to consult widely. He pulled out the stops to convince the press to support the deal. And he paid special attention to his political opposition. The President already had the enthusiastic support of Republicans Stimson and Knox. And he agreed with Stimson and Knox, over the objection of the Democrats in his cabinet, that he should reach out to Wendell Willkie, his Republican opponent for President. Willkie declined to endorse the deal, but he publicly gave his "wholehearted support for the president in whatever action he might take to give the opponents of force the material resources of the nation," and added that "the loss of the British fleet would greatly weaken our defense."[40] Roosevelt and his staff also consulted many members of Congress, most notably Charles McNary, the Republican leader in the Senate and Willkie's vice presidential running mate. McNary told the President that he could not publicly support the deal but that he would not oppose it if legitimate grounds could be found for doing it without the Senate's consent.[41]

The final element of the strategy was to secure a legal opinion from Attorney General Robert Jackson. There were two legal obstacles to the deal: neutrality statutes that seemed to ban the transfer, and the fact that the transaction would be done via a unilateral "executive agreement" that seemed to be the Senate's constitutional prerogative to approve (or not) as a treaty. Jackson got around these problems—problems that for months the President and almost everyone else had thought made the transfer impossible—through legal sleights of hand that were criticized at the time as flawed, but that Jackson concluded were reasonable enough as the bombs rained down on London at the height of the Battle of Britain in August 1940. Jackson's opinion was written in a way to minimize the sting of what many viewed as a dangerous assertion of unilateral presidential power. It had a sober tone and was written narrowly so as not to approve one thing more than it needed to. It declined to rely on the President's commander-in-chief powers and focused instead on what Congress had approved and prohibited. It went out of its way to acknowledge that the President's power over foreign relations "is not unlimited." And as if to prove the point, and to assure those made nervous by the unprecedented unilateral transfer of destroyers, Jackson concluded that Congress had in fact banned a related transfer of mosquito boats then under construction, and that the President was bound by this determination.[42]

Armed with Jackson's opinion, Roosevelt on September 3 announced the "epochal" destroyers deal, which he called the most important event in the defense of the United States since the Louisiana Purchase. His strategy in bringing the country around had paid off entirely. The deal quickly proved to be a huge popular success and was seen as bringing the United States important naval bases at little real cost. Willkie and some isolationists quibbled about whether the President should have sought congressional approval. But in the shadow of the deal's obvious benefits to the country, and with Jackson's judicious opinion published in the pages of the *New York Times*, the legitimacy objections of "legalists," as Roosevelt called them, had little public impact.[43]

The relatively modest destroyers-for-bases deal was the most Roosevelt could do for Britain before the election of 1940. But the British needed much more than fifty overaged destroyers, and after the election Roosevelt resolved to give it to them. Many obstacles stood in the way. Britain was broke and had no way to pay for the aid, even if Roosevelt could find a way to provide it. Roosevelt could not provide help of the magnitude required unless he sought and received Congress's express authorization. And getting this support would be difficult, because, as historian Robert Dallek says, "[t]he election and recent opinion polls suggested that the country remained strongly opposed to involvement in the fighting and painfully divided about risking war to save Britain."[44] Mortified about the consequences for America if Great Britain fell, Roosevelt pushed ahead nonetheless. In December 1940, he decided to seek from Congress the power to simply give Great Britain whatever it needed, for free, and ask only that Britain return the materiel when the war was over. When Roosevelt first announced the idea of lend-lease, which it came to be called, he famously analogized it to lending a garden hose to a neighbor whose house is on fire. "I don't say to him before that operation, 'Neighbor, my garden hose cost me fifteen dollars; you have to pay me my fifteen dollars for it.' What is the transaction that goes on? I don't want fifteen dollars—I want my garden hose back after the fire is over."[45]

In December 1940 and January 1941, Roosevelt rallied the country for lend-lease with two of his most famous, successful, and important speeches: the "Arsenal of Democracy" fireside chat on December 29, and the January 6 annual message to Congress, which articulated the idea of a world founded upon "four freedoms." These speeches, and press conferences during the same period, "deepened America's understanding of what was at stake," according to Roosevelt's biographer, Jean Edward Smith.[46] Nonetheless, the country remained divided.[47] The next two months brought "one of the most spirited and important debates in the history of American foreign affairs," noted historian Wayne Cole. "In and out of Congress, Americans argued the need, the merits, and the dangers of the President's proposal."[48] One of the main dangers they debated was the amount of power that would be given to the President. Roosevelt was seeking the authority to give away *any* "defense article" to *any* country whose defense the President deemed vital to the defense of the United States. The House Minority Report was not far off the mark when it said that the "bill gives the President unlimited, unprecedented, and unpredictable powers."[49]

Should Roosevelt be trusted with these powers? The isolationists, of course, did not think so. The *Chicago Tribune* charged that Roosevelt's proposal was a "Dictator Bill" designed "to destroy the Republic."[50] The President is "not asking for a blank check," charged General Robert Wood, the leader of the isolationist America First Committee, "he wants a blank check book with the power to write away your man power, our laws, and our liberties."[51] Similar concerns were expressed in the lengthy hearings on the bill. Can the President simply "give away any part of the Navy he deems satisfactory?" Representative Hamilton Fish of New York asked Secretary of War Stimson.[52] "[T]he thing that worries me in this bill," Representative Charles Eaton of New Jersey said to Stimson, is that "it is apparently adopting the totalitarian method of placing all power in the hands of one man."[53]

Henry Stimson's testimony answering these and similar concerns "attracted a closer and wider attention across the land than did that of any other administration witness," and was "more effective than any other in support of the bill," according to historian Kenneth Davis.[54] Drawing on his experience with several presidents at what he called "close range," Stimson noted in his testimony that he had been "impressed always with the tremendously sobering influence that the terrific responsibility of the Presidency will impose upon any man." He then assured the Congress that it could safely rest the responsibility for the proper implementation of the extraordinarily broad lend-lease authority "with the present President of the United States," whom "I have had ... under close observation for six months."[55] When pressed again and again on whether the President might give away everything in the U.S. arsenal, Stimson replied "with the utmost emphasis" that the "government or law which is so constructed [that is, based on the premise] that you cannot trust anybody will not survive the test of war."[56] The country could not survive without conferring extraordinary authority and discretion on the President in time of crisis. And Stimson the lifelong Republican and man of unquestionable integrity who had worked closely with Roosevelt was there to say that the President could be trusted with this enormous responsibility.

Congress enacted the Lend-Lease legislation by large margins on March 11, 1941. The country had moved from being divided about the bill to being 61 percent in favor of it.[57] "Although actual war was nine months away," noted historian Warren Kimball, "the Lend-Lease Act was a public announcement of the creation of the most productive and co-operative coalition of modern times—the Anglo-American alliance against Nazi Germany."[58] Four days after the Lend-Lease statute passed, Roosevelt spoke about his legislative success at the annual Washington correspondents' dinner. "We have just now engaged in a great debate," he said. "It was not limited to the halls of Congress. It was argued in every newspaper, on every wave length, over every cracker barrel in all the land; and it was finally settled and decided by the American people themselves. Yes, the decisions of our democracy may be slowly arrived at. But when that decision is made, it is proclaimed not with the voice of any one man but with the voice of one hundred and thirty millions. It is binding on us all. And the world is no longer left in doubt."[59]

We can learn a lot from Roosevelt's tactics in responding to a national security threat that he believed the public did not understand and did not take seriously enough. The first lesson is the importance of consultation and consent, even during a crisis. Americans expect presidents to act aggressively to protect the country, especially in an emergency, even if it means skirting the law. Presidential scholar Clinton Rossiter once said that if a president is not "widely and persistently accused in his own time of 'subverting the Constitution,' he may as well forget about being judged a truly eminent man by future generations."[60] One of the marks of a great president is successful leadership in times of crisis. Because the law is not always designed for or up to the task of the crisis, successful leadership sometimes requires bending or breaking the law. But *how* a president does this matters, as Roosevelt's handling of the destroyers deal shows.

Roosevelt the lawyer frequently derided the "legalists" who obsessed about what he viewed as technical legal restrictions during time of crisis, and he was not reluctant to stretch the law when he thought the situation demanded it. But he always worried intensely about larger elements of political legitimation for his actions. When election politics and the press of time made it impossible for Congress to give him formal statutory approval for the destroyers deal, his strategy was to consult widely and to receive consent from important American institutions—the people, the Congress, his cabinet, the parties, the press—on a less formal basis. "Contrary to the latter-day view that a strong President is one who acts without consultation and without notice, Roosevelt [in the destroyers deal] proceeded with careful concern for the process of consent," Schlesinger wrote in 1973, implicitly comparing Roosevelt with Richard Nixon. Though the destroyers-for-bases deal "was unilateral in form," Schlesinger continues, "it was accompanied by extensive and vigilant consultation—within the executive branch, between the executive and legislative branches, among leaders of both parties and with the press."[61]

Roosevelt had learned about the importance of consultation and consent in foreign relations from his days in the Wilson administration. "Remember how Wilson lost the League of Nations, lost the opportunity for the United States to take part in the most important international undertaking ever conceived," he told his Labor Secretary, Frances Perkins, in 1934. "He lost it by not getting Congress to participate. They have a sense of their responsibility, and they can't have sincere convictions unless they are given a chance to examine the situation at close range."[62] Roosevelt was obviously not romantic or naive about congressional relations. He was a manipulative, often secretive, sometimes deceitful, and very skilled politician. He was motivated to consult and garner consent not only because it was the right thing to do but also because it was good politics, even though it was painful and ran the risk of rejection. Consultation and consent allowed him to exercise powers and achieve things that would otherwise have been beyond his grasp. They also served a clarifying and educative function, helping his administration to understand public sentiment, and helping the public to understand what was at stake. And they forced other institutions, especially Congress, to accept partial responsibility for the country's important decisions, thereby ensuring that the President had the country's backing when he took steps that involved the country's fate.

Roosevelt also understood the importance of establishing credibility and trust during times of war or crisis, especially by reaching across the aisle to the opposing political party. In 1940–1941, the public did not know for sure whether he was acting in the national interest or acting in his own interest, and the "dictator" charge was often leveled at him. Having Republicans Stimson and Knox on board for the destroyers deal and the Lend-Lease statute was crucial to rebutting these concerns. "By expanding the circle of those who share the president's privileged access to information, ensuring that policy is partly controlled by officials whose preferences differ from the president's, and inviting a potential whistleblower into the tent, bipartisanship helps to dispel the suspicion that policy decisions rest on partisan motives or extreme preferences, which in turn encourages broader delegations of discretion from the public and Congress," note law professors Eric Posner and Adrian Vermeule.[63] Roosevelt understood these points well.

THE BUSH ADMINISTRATION'S go-it-alone approach to many terrorism-related legal policy issues is the antithesis of Roosevelt's approach in 1940–1941. It is a truism among political scientists and historians who study the American presidency that a president's authority is not measured primarily by his hard power found in the Constitution, statutes, and precedents, but rather by his softer powers to convince the other institutions of our society to come around to his point of view. "The power to manage the vast, whirring machinery of government derives from individual skills as persuader, bargainer, and leader," Schlesinger said, echoing the famous thesis of presidential scholar Richard Neustadt.[64] The Bush administration has operated on an entirely different concept of power that relies on minimal deliberation, unilateral action, and legalistic defense. This approach largely eschews politics: the need to explain, to justify, to convince, to get people on board, to compromise.

Whereas Roosevelt was famous for consulting widely (though not always transparently) within and without his administration before making momentous wartime decisions, the Bush administration is famously secretive and close-looped in its deliberations.

The controversial legal analysis underlying the destroyers-for-bases deal was widely vetted beforehand, both inside the government and to the public in a famous letter to the *New York Times* written by Dean Acheson and Ben Cohen.[65] Many important legal decisions in the Bush administration, by contrast, were made by a very small and largely like-minded group of lawyers, and announced, if it all, without outside consultation. This led to two kinds of problems. The first was that these lawyers made legal and political errors that became very costly to the administration down the road. Many of these errors were unnecessary and could have been avoided with wider consultation. The second problem, perhaps paradoxically, was excessive leaking. "[W]hen everything is classified, then nothing is classified, and the system becomes one to be disregarded by the cynical or the careless and to be manipulated by those intent on self-protection or self-promotion," Justice Potter Stewart said in the *Pentagon Papers* case, anticipating what would happen in the Bush administration three decades later.[66]

The administration also eschewed genuine consultation with Congress, both formal and informal, with members of the President's own party as well as members of the opposition. Political debate is one of the strengths of a democracy in wartime, for it allows the country's leadership to learn about and correct its errors. The Bush administration's failure to engage Congress eliminated the short-term discomforts of public debate, but at the expense of many medium-term mistakes. It also deprived the country of lend-lease-like national debates about the nature of the threat and the proper response that would have served an educative and legitimating function regardless of what emerged from the process. And it hurt the executive branch in dealing with the third branch of government as well. Courts have been much more skeptical of the President's counterterrorism policies than they would have been had the President secured Congress's and the country's express support.

Some will say that presidential-congressional relations are a two-way street, and that in the last six years Congress has dropped the ball in exercising its national security responsibilities. This is largely true but unsurprising. In matters of war and security, Congress's natural posture is to inquire and complain but not make hard decisions. This attitude minimizes congressional responsibility and allows Congress to decide whether to jump on the bandwagon or confer blame, depending on how things turn out. "Decisions on war and peace are tough, and more to the point they are politically risky," says constitutional scholar John Hart Ely, explaining why Congress shies away from real decisionmaking on such issues.[67] "Accountability is pretty frightening stuff."[68] The President cannot avoid accountability for national security decisions. But he can spread the accountability, and thereby minimize the recriminations and other bad effects of the risk-taking that his job demands, by forcing Congress to deliberate, argue, and take a stand. The Bush administration's failure to do this has often left the President alone, holding the bag, as things have gone wrong. Forcing Congress to assume joint responsibility weakens presidential prerogatives to act unilaterally. But it strengthens presidential power overall, as Roosevelt understood.

The administration did finally go to Congress in the fall of 2006, under duress after the Supreme Court said it could not conduct military commissions without Congress's express consent. Congress gave it new rules on commissions similar to what the President had been doing all along, more elaborate but still vague guidelines on interrogation, and various efforts to minimize judicial review. The administration also went to Congress in the summer of 2007 after the secret intelligence court that administers electronic surveillance curtailed the government's power to monitor certain international calls going through American telecommunication switches.[69] Congress gave the President a broad authorization to eavesdrop on international telephone calls and email messages without a warrant.[70] Although the national debate on both bills was truncated, the legislation that emerged in both cases shows that when the President forces Congress to stand up, be counted, and assume responsibility, he can get a lot of what he thinks he needs for national security.

Despite these two important pieces of legislation, the country still lacks the comprehensive, coherent, and durable institutions it needs to surveil, detain, and incapacitate terrorists. "The mission of democratic statecraft," Schlesinger notes, "is to keep institutions and values sufficiently abreast of the accelerating velocity of history to give society a chance of controlling the energies let loose by science and technology."[71] Six years after 9/11, our government has not yet succeeded in this mission. The 2006 military commission legislation remains the subject of extensive litigation and we have not had a single trial by a military commission. Nor do we have a consensus on whether and when terrorists should be tried in military or civilian courts, if at all. Congress and the President also have not acted together to establish a coherent and durable program for detaining the hundreds of dangerous terrorists who probably can never be brought to trial in any forum. As for surveillance, the 2007 surveillance legislation did reflect a consensus in both parties on the need to modernize the United States' ability to monitor terrorists. But the legislation was not comprehensive, and more importantly, it conferred only temporary authorities that expire in six months. Before the bill was even signed, Speaker of the House Pelosi and others were promising to revise the law significantly in the fall.[72] The main concern with the new surveillance law—the issue that stood as the major roadblock to its passage, and the issue that will be front and center during proposed revisions in the months ahead—is that Congress does not trust the Justice Department to oversee the program and ensure that warrantless wiretaps are properly directed to communications overseas.[73]

Until recently, the administration has not worried itself too much with issues of trust and credibility that are so important to political success generally, and especially important when the public the president is trying to lead is divided and unsure about the nature of the threat it faces. The administration lost public trust in the fight against terrorists when it premised a major war on a terror-related threat of weapons of mass destruction that turned out to be wrong. And the war in Iraq has spilled over to and infected everything else that this administration does in the broader war on terrorism. But even if there were no Iraq, or if Iraq were a success, the Bush administration would still suffer credibility problems, for it has taken few steps to enhance trust in its terrorism policies. There are no Henry Stimsons in President Bush's war cabinet.

The best evidence of the administration's indifference to politics in the sense that Roosevelt understood it, the clearest sign of its lack of concern with public credibility, is its open chest-thumping about the importance of maintaining and expanding executive power. The public worries about excessive presidential power in times of war, and a prudent president tries to assuage and meet these concerns. Lincoln and Roosevelt were as powerful as any presidents we have ever had. But they never talked publicly about the need to expand their power as a matter of principle, for doing so would have been self-defeating and politically unwise. When they exercised extraordinary authorities, they did so with a grudging public face, with expressions of respect for constitutional values, and with explanations about why the steps were an unfortunate but necessary means to an important national security end.

A good example of the administration's antithetical approach is the signing statement that President Bush attached to a 2005 law prohibiting "cruel, inhuman, or degrading" treatment in interrogation that placed modest new limits on the President.[74] The law was sponsored by Senator John McCain of Arizona and initially opposed by the White House. After weeks of negotiation, President Bush invited Senator McCain to the White House for what the *Washington Post* described as "a public reconciliation" and a declaration of a "common objective" to make it clear to the world, as President Bush said, "that this government does not torture and that we adhere to the international convention of torture."[75] And yet as soon as the bill became law, President Bush issued a statement saying that it might violate his commander-in-chief powers and he might not always act in compliance with it.[76]

Presidents have issued "signing statements" for many purposes, including to announce their belief that all or part of the statute in question may be inconsistent with the Constitution. But a signing statement serves no formal legal purpose. If President Bush later felt he needed to act in a way contrary to the McCain law, he could have made and acted upon and published the decision at that time without any prior signing statement. The only thing achieved by the statement at the time the President signed the bill was to spoil the tentative consensus and goodwill that had been reached with Capitol Hill on the issue, and further enflame mistrust of the President.

Roosevelt faced a similar issue in connection with the Lend-Lease statute. The statute contained a provision that allowed two Houses of Congress, without the consent of the President, to veto particular decisions that the President made under the law. Roosevelt thought this arrangement violated the separation of powers.[77] He signed the law nonetheless because of its obvious importance. But he worried about the precedential effect of the legislative veto in the statute. So he told Attorney General Robert Jackson to draft a formal memorandum explaining why the act's veto provision was, in Roosevelt's words, "clearly unconstitutional." Roosevelt decided, however, that he should not immediately make public the "signing statement" that contained his constitutional objections. He worried, Jackson later explained, that doing so "might seriously alienate some of his congressional support at a time when he would need to call on it frequently." He also worried that immediate public disclosure of his objection might "strengthen fear in the country that he was seeking to increase his personal power."[78]

The contrast between the two Presidents' approaches raises one of the great puzzles of the Bush administration: Why did the administration so often assert presidential power in ways that seemed unnecessary and politically self-defeating? The answer, I believe, is that the administration's conception of presidential power had a kind of theological significance that often trumped political consequences. The interrogation signing statement was motivated by the same impulse that produced the unsuccessful unitary executive defense of the U.S. Attorney firings, the speeches about the administration wanting to leave the presidency stronger than it found it, the interrogation opinions' overbroad commander-in-chief claims, the go-it-alone strategy with Congress, the resistance to judicial review, and many other politically damaging public assertions of executive power that have characterized the Bush administration. Roosevelt's approach, by contrast, might be seen as an example of his famous duplicity. But it was also less ideological, more pragmatic, and more sensitive to political consequences than the Bush administration's approach. And it was premised on the notion that presidential power is primarily about persuasion and consent rather than unilateral executive action.

The tactics of democratic leadership that Roosevelt employed in 1940–1941 will not invariably succeed. Sometimes the attempt to convince the country or the Congress about a threat will fail, sometimes bipartisanship will backfire, sometimes being pragmatic rather than principled will seem opportunistic and induce distrust. But the Bush administration's strategy is guaranteed not to work, and is certain to destroy trust altogether. When an administration makes little attempt to work with the other institutions of our government and makes it a public priority to emphasize that its aim is to expand its power, Congress, the courts, and the public listen carefully, and worry.

AN IMPORTANT CHARACTER has been missing from this book about the first Terror Presidency: President George W. Bush himself. I met President Bush only twice. We didn't speak either time. But for me and many other officials outside of his intimate circle, the President was an invisible presence whose first priority and command after 9/11 was to do everything possible to stop the next attack. As I write these words, the President has succeeded in this goal. Whatever one thinks about the means he has employed and the mistakes he has made, this is an accomplishment that seemed impossible on September 12, 2001.

I have compared President Bush with prior crisis presidents, Lincoln and Roosevelt. The comparison, I realize, is premature and misleading. Today Lincoln and Roosevelt are considered great wartime presidents and great defenders of the Constitution. We tend to forget about their mistakes and excesses, for which they were roundly criticized as incompetents or dictators in their day, especially early on in their respective wars. We forget these things because we know how great their crises were, and because we view the great presidents benignly against the glow of their epic victories over the slaveholding South and the Nazi and Japanese threats. President Bush, by contrast, is still in the midst of his war on terrorism, a war that many do not believe exists, a war that rightly or wrongly, and in large part because of Iraq, he is not perceived to be winning.[79] For Lincoln and Roosevelt, success in war was its own justification for the means they employed. For Bush, failure in the ongoing war of uncertain menace colors everything.

Future historians may come to view President Bush as we now view Lincoln and Roosevelt. Presidential reputations "rise and fall like stocks on Wall Street, determined by supply and demand equations of a later age," Schlesinger said.[80] Historians might come to think of the interrogation controversies, like Lincoln's suspension of habeas corpus and Roosevelt's Japanese internment, as deeply regrettable but relatively unimportant episodes in the larger arc of the war. These historians might emphasize the novel challenges that President Bush has faced, the novel challenges of the Terror Presidency: The enemy in this war is harder to find but potentially as lethal as any we have ever fought. The existential stakes in this war are less obvious than in prior analogously threatening contexts, thus making it hard to educate and prepare the public for the threat, and thus hard to win its trust. This war has an endless and diffuse character that challenges a democracy's vigilance. The establishment culture is more hostile to and suspicious of this war than it was of World War II or the Civil War. In this war international cooperation is harder to achieve because our enemies are on the territory of our allies, and our allies, whose citizens we are imprisoning as enemy combatants, do not believe we are in a war. This war is fought in an unprecedentedly constrictive legal culture. And the errors in this war are instantly published globally on the Internet, for all to see and criticize.

History may judge President Bush benignly in light of these unusually difficult challenges, especially if the way he has prosecuted the war that began on 9/11 bears greater fruit in the future. But even if President Bush's accomplishments are viewed more charitably by future historians than they are viewed today, the accomplishments will likely always be dimmed by our knowledge of his administration's strange and unattractive views of presidential power. The American people know better today than during the Civil War and World War II that Lincoln and Roosevelt, in Schlesinger's words, regarded "executive aggrandizement as but a means to a greater end, the survival of liberty and law, of government by, for, and of the people," and that "they used emergency power, on the whole, with discrimination and restraint."[81] Lincoln and Roosevelt understood that, as Schlesinger said, the "truly strong President is not the one who relies on his power to command but the one who recognizes his responsibility, and opportunity, to enlighten and persuade."[82]

We are unlikely to come to think of President Bush in this way, for he has not embraced Lincoln's and Roosevelt's tenets of democratic leadership in crisis. He has been almost entirely inattentive to the soft factors of legitimation—consultation, deliberation, the appearance of deference, and credible expressions of public concern for constitutional and international values—in his dealings with Congress, the courts, and allies. He has instead relied on the hard power of prerogative. And he has seen his hard power diminished in many ways because he has failed to take the softer aspects of power seriously. This irony will likely be the Bush presidency's legacy for executive power.

The Islamist terrorist threat will not end when the Bush administration does. Nor will its challenges to our constitutional system. The endless threat of increasingly powerful and dispersed terrorist groups, like the long and frightening Cold War threat that preceded it, will result in the presidency assuming more and more responsibility and power. We must try to build sensible and durable institutions that allow the Terror Presidency to meet this threat within a scheme of democratic accountability. Ultimately, however, our constitutional democracy will not be preserved by better laws and institutional structures, but rather, as Schlesinger taught, by leaders with a commitment to the consent of the governed who have checks and balances stitched into their breasts.[83] In the permanent emergency we face, the best hope for preserving both our security and our liberty is to select leaders who will be beholden to constitutional values even when they are forced to depart from constitutional traditions.

AFTERWORD:
ASSESSING THE FIRST
TERROR PRESIDENCY

After I resigned from the Justice Department in July 2004, I resolved to lead a more normal family life, to spend time on scholarship, and to avoid Washington, D.C., for a while. But soon after I moved to Boston, I started getting phone calls from investigators around the government—not just from the prosecutor investigating the leak of the Terrorist Surveillance Program but also from the congressional intelligence, judiciary, and armed services committees, inspectors general in the CIA and the Justice Department, the Justice Department ethics office, and most recently, the special prosecutor looking into the destruction of the CIA interrogation tapes. The phone calls were invitations to discuss the Bush administration's interrogation and surveillance programs that I had worked on in government.

As the number of trips to Washington to meet with the investigators grew, so too did my worries about our national security system.

Although the investigations were politically necessary responses to stories and allegations of malfeasance in the Bush administration, they swept far beyond those who might have broken laws. The investigators were professionals acting in good faith, but they also acted with a bureaucratic imperative to assess blame and an implicit threat to bring or recommend criminal charges or ethics violations. They reviewed government actions not from the perspective of danger and responsibility and uncertainty as to consequences of those who acted, but rather from the too-clear perspective of calm hindsight. And the investigations occurred in an atmosphere of growing recrimination marked by loud calls from Congress and elsewhere for war crimes prosecutions and truth commissions. I worried that these investigations would cause national security lawyers and counterterrorism officials to return to the dangerous attitude of risk aversion and timidity that was so debilitating before 9/11. So too did Attorney General Michael Mukasey, who was in a better position to know. In several remarkable speeches in 2008, he warned that the climate of recrimination in which Bush administration policies were being criticized and investigated were "chill[ing] the intelligence community and deter[ring] national security lawyers from making the decisions necessary to protect us."[1]

My concerns about a growing risk aversion in government led me to worry too about the presidency, which for our safety's sake must be strong and effective. In chapter 5 I speculated that the Bush administration had "borrowed against the power of future presidencies—presidencies that, at least until the next attack, and probably even following one, will be viewed by Congress and the courts, whose assistance they need, with a harmful suspicion and mistrust because of the unnecessary unilateralism of the Bush years."[2]

As I reflect on these words eighteen months later, I am more convinced that the presidency has become damaged in ways that will be hard to reverse. The novel challenges of the Terror Presidency—a lethal, hard-to-find enemy; growing public doubts about the reality of the threat because of the absence of new attacks; the need for preemptive action that invariably brings mistakes and recriminations; and a suspicious and constrictive legal culture—would have burdened any president. The Clinton administration struggled with these challenges in its more discrete, embryonic, and largely secret war with al Qaeda in the late 1990s.[3] But they were much more daunting for the Bush administration after 9/11. And its reaction to them—aggressive unilateral assertions of presidential power, often in secret, and seemingly in defiance of Congress—led to mistakes, national humiliations, mistrust, and blowback that exacerbated the problem in ways that will burden the presidency beyond 2009.

These concerns about the presidency are far from the mainstream. Most reviewers of the hardback edition of this book focused on my criticisms of the Bush administration's go-it-alone approach and ignored my arguments about the novel challenges of the Terror Presidency and the dangers of our excessively legalistic and retributive national security culture.[4] Over seven years without a homeland attack have led most Americans to downplay the terror threat and the difficulties of meeting it, and to focus instead on Bush administration mistakes. Elite and popular opinions are more worried about an out-of-control presidency than an enfeebled one. A cottage industry (and celebrity) has built up around people and institutions that reveal the latest wicked national security secret; many people cherish these revelations as eagerly as Harry Potter fans cherish J. K. Rowling's latest installment. Each new Supreme

Court defeat for the presidency brings celebration in the press; each new investigation is met with approving cries of justice served.

Very little effort has been spent reflecting on the debilitating effects of these attitudes, and the actions they have spawned, on the presidency and our security. To the contrary, conventional wisdom at the dawn of the Obama administration is that George W. Bush created an unprecedentedly potent presidency. The "power of the president soared to new heights under Bush," Jonathan Mahler wrote in the *New York Times* in November 2008.[5] After the inauguration of the new President, "the mistrust engendered by Bush-Cheney officials would fade away, but their legal and political precedents would remain," said Charlie Savage in the afterword of his book *Takeover: The Return of the Imperial Presidency and the Subversion of American Democracy.*[6] President Barack Obama "enter[s] office as the most powerful president who has ever sat in the White House," echoed Yale law professor Jack Balkin in agreement.[7] The element of truth in these assessments is that President Bush began his presidency the most powerful person on earth and left it having accumulated more formal power. But by itself this is unremarkable. Presidential power always expands during war, and however unfortunate that label might be rhetorically (I increasingly think it is), the struggle with Islamist terrorism is, as a legal matter, a war that has been authorized by Congress and recognized by the Supreme Court.[8]

The natural accumulation of formal presidential war powers during the last eight years, combined with the deep distaste that many feel toward Bush administration policies and failings, has blinded us to how hard it is for the President to meet his responsibilities to keep us safe, and how much the institution of the presidency has weakened in the last eight years of trying to do so. This blindness carries serious consequences, for an underappreciated and weakened presidency is one less capable of thwarting the terrorists who would do us enormous harm.

TO UNDERSTAND WHAT has happened to the presidency, we must begin with Congress, the institution the framers envisioned as the chief constraint on the President but one that has seemed largely compliant during the last eight years. This compliance reached its apex last summer when Congress amended the Foreign Intelligence Surveillance Act, the law that requires the government to get a warrant before electronically surveilling certain suspected terrorists. Beginning in 2001, the Bush administration had sidestepped this law in secret and wiretapped suspected terrorists without a warrant in what came to be known as the Terrorist Surveillance Program. The revelation of this program in December 2005 generated enormous controversy and pushed the administration to finally get Congress on board. Congress assented in July 2008, when 20 Democrats in the Senate and 128 Democrats in the House joined Republicans to expand the historically unpopular President's warrantless wiretapping powers and grant telecommunications firms that had cooperated with the President's unilateral surveillance program immunity from lawsuit.[9]

The 2008 surveillance law was the latest in a string of congressional capitulations during 2001–2008. Here and in other cases, Congress complained loudly about President Bush's unilateralism but supported broad executive power when asked. The contrast with the 1970s Congress, which enacted many laws to curb the imperial presidency, could not be starker, and is one reason why so many people believe that Bush has garnered so much new power. But we should not let this difference with the past overshadow another one: when Congress has said "yes" to President Bush's requests, it has done so in ways that are more restrictive of presidential power than during previous wars.

The 2006 law that gave congressional approval to military commissions, for example, contained scores of unprecedented procedural guarantees for suspected terrorists and related legalistic restrictions that never burdened the many past presidents who used military commissions without special dispensation from Congress and with extremely informal procedures.[10] Similarly, Congress eliminated habeas corpus review of GTMO detentions in 2006, but at the same time it established a different and unprecedented form of judicial review of the President's detention determinations.[11] It's the same story on surveillance. Despite the new powers that Congress gave the President in 2008, he is still much more constrained in his ability to monitor suspected enemy forces than presidents in the past. One area where Congress did push back against the President (but not as much as people think) is interrogation. Today the military and the CIA are barred from using techniques that were thought to be consistent with the Geneva Conventions and available to the President as recently as the 1960s.[12] The President's interrogation powers, like most of his other military powers, are much more constrained by law than at any time in American history.

The courts have been much more aggressive than Congress in pushing back against presidential prerogative. "Never in American history had the [Supreme] Court tried in any significant way to interfere with a war in progress," wrote Arthur Schlesinger Jr. in his

1973 book *The Imperial Presidency*.[13] But this changed after 9/11. Commanders in chief before President Bush detained enemy forces without charge or trial and without judicial scrutiny. Since 9/11, courts have taken ownership of the issue. The Supreme Court for the first time ruled that the Constitution's guarantee of "due process of law"—a fount of judicial creativity—applies to the President's military detention powers. It reversed a decades-long U.S. government position when it ruled that terrorists warrant Geneva Convention protections.[14] Also for the first time, the Court gave constitutional habeas corpus rights to alleged enemy combatants captured and detained outside the United States.[15] It did so after invalidating, again for the first time, a military measure—the 2006 statute that stripped habeas corpus review of GTMO detainees—that had the support of Congress and the President. And the Court suggested that alleged terrorists deserve unprecedented access to lawyers, witnesses, and classified information, adding that "more may be required."[16] As I write these words courts are busy crafting U.S. terrorist detention policies out of whole judicial cloth, deciding as a matter of constitutional law which suspected terrorists can be detained, how much and what kind of evidence and procedures are necessary to detain them, how long they can be detained, and who must be released.

Justice Antonin Scalia has warned that these judge-made counterterrorism policies will result in the release of dangerous terrorists and "almost certainly cause more Americans to be killed."[17] This prediction is controversial but contains what should be an uncontroversial element of truth. Any system of justice that raises its standards to ensure that the innocent remain free does so at the cost of making it harder for the government to detain the non-innocent. The criminal law system's demanding "beyond a reasonable doubt" standard is premised on the idea that it is better for ten guilty people to go free than for one innocent to be convicted. Similarly, the higher hurdles that judges have imposed on the government's military detention powers make it less likely that innocents will be detained but more likely that the dangerous will be released and return to kill. This trade-off is inevitable, and finding the right balance is hard. The bad guys do not wear dog tags, so the chance of mistaken detention is higher than in a traditional war, as is the cost of those mistakes, which is potentially indefinite detention. On the other hand, the average terrorist today is much more dangerous than the average soldier in World War II or the average criminal. So mistakes in either direction are really bad. The political branches have traditionally been responsible for making these hard liberty/security trade-offs because they have more information about the risks in both directions and they face the electorate if they get the trade-off wrong. But now for the first time judges who are neither expert in national security nor politically accountable are making these choices.

This is not an easily reversible trend. Even if President Obama seeks and receives statutory answers to the legal policy questions surrounding terrorist trial and detention, an active judicial role is likely here to stay. Because the Constitution is now relevant to so many of these issues, courts must review whatever Congress produces for constitutional compliance. These precedents will be around for a while and will exert an influence on executive branch lawyers and thus on executive branch decisionmaking even when courts are not involved. Beyond these precedents, judicial attitudes have changed. In recent history the Supreme Court has asserted judicial authority in ever more areas of political life. War and national security cases have largely been exempt from this trend. In these areas, courts have trod lightly, with great deference to executive branch authority and with great self-doubt about the legitimacy of judicial action.[18] But in scores of terrorism-related cases since 9/11, courts have overcome self-doubt, watered down executive deference, made intrusive demands for information, and insisted that judges have the last say. The attitudinal change inherent in these decisions marks a shift of war power from the president to courts.

The press also diminished presidential war power during this period. The Robb-Silberman Commission on the Intelligence Capabilities of the United States Regarding Weapons of Mass Destruction reported in March 2005 that "hundreds of serious press leaks" about our collection capabilities "have significantly impaired U.S. capabilities against our hardest targets" and done "grave harm to our national security."[19] But the problem reached new heights after this report was issued, especially concerning U.S. surveillance capabilities. For terrorists to do anything really bad to us, they must be able to communicate and to coordinate their plans. Modern communications technologies (the Internet, encrypted email, disposable cell phones, and the like) help terrorists do this but also make it easier for the government to discover and preempt terrorist plots. However, the government's advantages work best, and often only, in secret. When terrorists learn how we monitor them, they adapt to prevent detection. Unfortunately, they have learned a lot since 9/11. When I was in government I was "read in" to several top secret intelligence programs related to terrorist surveillance. Beginning with the December 2005 revelation about the Terrorist Surveillance Program in the *New York Times*, every one of these programs, and another one I knew nothing about, was disclosed by the nation's leading newspapers.

These stories have been terrible for our security. They reported details of how the U.S. government monitors international bank transfers that are the key to terrorist financing; mines data and does pattern analysis of telephone and email information; intercepts international communications that "transit" through the United States; analyzes ATM transactions, credit card purchases, and wire payments; and works with private telecommunications firms in these efforts. I am not permitted to say which of these stories are true, but I can say that the true ones involved matters unknown to our enemies and gave the government a big advantage in tracking them. The disclosure of these operational details about U.S. surveillance capabilities helped terrorists to avoid forms of communication that we were good at monitoring, and instead to switch to communication channels in which we lack comparative advantage. The leaks also revealed private industry's secret cooperation with the government—an essential element of our surveillance capability, the disclosure of which has dimmed the willingness of corporations to help. And it is well known that foreign intelligence services are ever more wary about sharing information and engaging in joint intelligence operations because American secrets tend to end up on the front pages of American newspapers. This problem has grown a lot in the last eight years.

There have been harmful leaks in past wars, but the leaks of the past few years mark a change in presidential-press relations, for it is now clearer than ever that the government cannot effectively sanction leaks. The Bush administration tried to punish the leakers but had a hard time identifying them—a difficulty that will only grow

if, as seems likely, Congress enacts a shield law to protect journalists from disclosing their sources. It also tried to punish journalists
who, in publishing operational details about classified surveillance
capabilities, violated a 1950 criminal law.[20] In the end the administration prosecuted neither leakers nor journalists, probably because
doing so would be enormously controversial and would invariably
reveal yet more classified information. The danger is that the regu-
larity and seriousness of these and many other leaks, and the failure
of the government to punish those involved, will legitimize leaking
and lead to more.

Of course, the main cause of leaks was not the absence of sanc-
tions but rather the perception within the government of illegitimate activity. Classified surveillance activities that began in 2001
did not leak until after a legitimacy crisis had developed, beginning
in June 2004, around the time of the Abu Ghraib scandal and the
leaked interrogation memos. Eric Lichtblau, coauthor of the *Times'*
surveillance stories, explained that anxiety about the Terrorist Surveillance Program's circumvention of normal checks and balances
was what led government officials to tell him about it.[21] But once
that story broke, so too did the norm discouraging revelation of
surveillance secrets, and what followed was a rush of new stories
about programs that were unquestionably legal and unquestionably
more damaging to national security. A future government that acts
more openly and with greater care for a right process can diminish the problem of leaks. But after the experience of the last eight
years, the worry is that people inside the government will judge
for themselves whether an action is legitimate or not, and not defer
to authorities whose responsibility it is to make that call. When
combined with the press's more casual attitude toward publishing

classified information, the result is more leaks of secret activities against terrorists.

Director of National Intelligence Michael McConnell concluded last year that these leaks "mean[ ] that some Americans are going to die, because we do this mission unknown to the bad guys because they're using a process that we can exploit and the more we talk about it, the more they will go with an alternative means."[22] McConnell exaggerates a bit here for we cannot know for sure that we will be hit again, or that the surveillance stories will be a contributing cause. But it is accurate to say that the stories made it easier for terrorists to plan and to execute attacks, and in that sense diminished the president's effectiveness and endangered the physical safety of Americans.

A final way in which the presidency has diminished over the last eight years concerns the Office of Legal Counsel, where I used to work. My withdrawal of some of the flawed opinions, the related backing away from OLC positions by many throughout the Bush administration, and the promised housecleaning of OLC opinions by the new Obama administration have weakened the currency of OLC opinions. Many people in the CIA have told me that the agency will never again view OLC opinions as a "golden shield" from legal scrutiny. In the future the CIA will seek opinions from OLC less often and will invariably supplement legal advice from OLC with a political risk assessment. This may seem like a good development in light of the sometimes-poor performance of OLC after 9/11. But it carries a significant downside. Controversial but perfectly legal counterterrorism actions approved by OLC will be resisted because lawyers elsewhere in the national security bureaucracy hold a different legal view or inform their legal conclusions with concerns about desirability of the proposed action. If this happens, the president's room for legitimate maneuver, and our security, will be diminished.

The unreliability of the OLC opinions also has harmful effects on the lawyers' clients in the CIA. In response to the many investigations mentioned earlier, CIA officials are "lawyered up" and are drawing down their legal liability insurance. The ordeal of answering subpoenas, consulting lawyers, digging up and explaining old documents, and racking one's memory to avoid inadvertent perjury is draining, not to mention distracting, for those we ask to keep the country safe. And worse, it has spooked the intelligence community. When the CIA was asked to engage in aggressive tactics early in the Bush administration, it knew from bitter experience that the political winds would change and that it might be subject to "retroactive discipline." And so it sought approval from the president and his cabinet, informed congressional leadership many times about what it was doing, and got what it thought were airtight legal opinions from OLC. But these safeguards failed, and the CIA is once again mired in investigation and controversy. The lesson learned by many is that politically sensitive counterterrorism actions should be avoided, even if they are deemed legal by OLC. We are going to be living with this skittishness for a long time, to the detriment of our security.

OLC will also, I fear, become more politicized. At my confirmation hearing to lead OLC, one senator showed up, and he asked me only a few softballs. That inadequate scrutiny was typical of congressional oversight during the first Bush term. But the worry now is that future confirmation hearings for the head of OLC will become like those for top federal judicial candidates, with senators trying to extract one concession after another from the nominee in ways that will invariably cause even the most scrupulous OLC leader—and especially one with further government ambition— to consider the political consequences of his or her legal analysis. Another worry is that OLC, operating in a culture that has grown deeply suspicious of the presidency, will to try to restore its credibility by issuing excessively cautious opinions that are unduly restrictive of presidential power. This caution will likely be exacerbated by the practice that has developed under the Bush administration of inspectors generals and ethics monitors second-guessing the validity of OLC's legal reasoning. The reaction to the excesses of the Bush-era OLC, in short, will make it hard for the office to return to its tradition of relative independence, including its independence from Congress in protecting presidential prerogative.

"Decision, secrecy, and dispatch"—these were the qualities of the singular and hierarchical presidency that Alexander Hamilton invoked in the *Federalist Papers* in arguing that foreign relations and national security should be the primary responsibility of the president and not Congress.[23] And these are precisely the presidential qualities that—because of the unusual challenges of the Terror Presidency, and some unfortunate responses to these challenges by the Bush administration—have corroded over the last eight years. I am not suggesting that all of the developments outlined here are bad. As I argued in earlier chapters, bringing law to bear on presidential action can legitimate such action, prevent self-defeating abuses, and leave the president in a stronger position. Fear of leaks can cause officials to think twice about what they do, and can deter them from doing things they should not do. Sunshine on and scrutiny of OLC can help to prevent egregious and unnecessary mistakes. The problem is that all of these checks can go too far and do more harm than good. It is impossible to know for sure if they have gone too far unless and until we suffer a second attack and the next investigating commission winds back the clock to discover its causes. But I fear that if and when this happens, the commission will view the institutional reactions to President Bush's counterterrorism policies as a cure worse than the disease, a cure that made it harder for the next president to keep us safe.

SINCE THIS BOOK was published in September 2007, some people have suggested that the Terror Presidency is a myth. They agree with law professor Peter Spiro that Barack Obama's election means that "the war on terror is over" and that "terrorism's no longer likely to pose the peremptory threat that it has since 9/11."[24] There is no way to disprove this claim before the next attack, but I seriously doubt it is true. The Bush administration has disrupted al Qaeda, and the United States is better defended and prepared than it was on 9/11. But the broader threat of Islamist terrorism and the danger of smaller and more powerful weapons have grown, not abated. In December 2008, the bipartisan Commission on the Prevention of Weapons of Mass Destruction Proliferation and Terrorism, led by former Democratic Senator Bob Graham, warned darkly that terrorists would likely carry out a WMD attack in the next five years.[25] "America's margin of safety is shrinking, not growing," the commission concluded.

And so the Terror Presidency that began on September 11, 2001, will not end when George W. Bush leaves office on January 20, 2009. Barack Obama will read the same threat reports. And he will inherit the same challenge of stopping Islamist terrorists who hide among civilians and who want to use ever-smaller and more deadly weapons to disrupt our way of life. President Obama will no doubt change tactics in responding to this threat and will wrap his counterterrorism policies in softer and more attractive packaging than his predecessor. (It would be hard not to.) But his responsibility to keep Americans safe—a responsibility Harry Truman described as "so personal as to be without parallel"[26]—will induce him, like President Bush and all terror presidencies for the foreseeable future, to meet the frightening and difficult-to-detect threat aggressively and preemptively.

To discharge this responsibility successfully, one of President Obama's least appreciated but most important tasks will be to repair the damage done to the presidency during the last eight years. From the day he enters office, the new president, who was a critic of the Iraq invasion and a skeptic about a war framework for counterterrorism, will speak with considerably more credibility than President Bush when he warns, as he invariably will, about the harrowing threat the terrorists pose. The credibility with which he speaks will help narrow the public's hazardous skepticism about the reality of the threat and will make clearer than President Bush ever could the difficulties that any president faces in keeping us safe. As I write these words in December 2008, there is every sign that President Obama will enhance trust in the presidency, and thus presidential effectiveness, by embracing the Lincoln-Roosevelt tenets of democratic leadership outlined in chapter 6: a bipartisan and pragmatic national security team, genuine consultation with and consent from Congress, a less secretive executive branch, an open public embrace of constitutional values, and a greater commitment to educate the nation regularly about the security threat. Let us hope that these efforts will strengthen the second Terror Presidency such that if it exercises good judgment and is lucky, it can prevent the second and more devastating attack that many believe is inevitable, one that will change our nation in ways that will make George W. Bush seem like a civil libertarian.

ACKNOWLEDGMENTS

I have many people to thank for helping me with this book.

I first want to express gratitude to the political appointees and career civil servants who were colleagues in government, and from whom I learned a lot. I want to thank in particular Jim Baker, Jim Comey, Jim Haynes, David Leitch, Dan Levin, Scott Muller, Pat Philbin, and Ed Whelan for their friendship, good advice, and integrity.

I interviewed over two-dozen current and former government officials in preparation for this book. Most of them asked not to be acknowledged or quoted on the record, but I thank them as a group for their time and valuable insights. The quotations in this book from conversations during which I was present are drawn from my memory, but in each case I checked them for accuracy with at least one participant in the conversation, or with someone to whom I recounted the conversation soon after it happened, or both. I thank current and former officials, and others, for their assistance in this regard.

The two people who helped me most in writing the book were Ben Wittes and Andrew Woods. Ben is not a lawyer, but he has a great legal mind and is a great writer. He helped me work out the narrative arc of the book and gave me many very good suggestions. Andrew also helped with the narrative and was a relentless critic of my writing. He helped me work out my ideas in scores of conversations and emails, and was particularly good at picking out decent arguments and illustrations from the many bad ones that I offered. I couldn't have written the book without Ben's and Andrew's help.

I am grateful as well for the excellent comments from, and fruitful conversations with, John Barrett, David Barron, Chris Demuth, Dan Drezner, Charles Fried, Ryan Goodman, Elena Kagan, Frederick Kagan, Phil Heymann, Marty Lederman, Daryl Levinson, Sebastian Mallaby, John Michaels, Richard Posner, Gary Schmitt, Jessica Stern, Bill Stuntz, Cass Sunstein, Elisabeth Theodore, and Leslie Williams. In addition to his helpful comments, Charles Fried also gave me lots of good advice. And in addition to her helpful comments and good advice, Elena Kagan, my dean, gave me extraordinary support and encouragement. Elena also stood by me when many others in her shoes wouldn't have, for which I am very grateful.

I should give a word of acknowledgment to the late Arthur M. Schlesinger, Jr. When I returned to academia from government, I read hundreds of books and articles about the presidency and the executive branch. The person whose work I kept coming back to, the person who seemed to have the most insightful things to say about the presidency by far, was Schlesinger. I never met Schlesinger, but his influence is apparent throughout this book, especially in chapter 6.

A number of talented Harvard Law students did great research and checked citations: Jon Berkon, Douglas Callahan, Candice Chiu, Tijana Dvornic, Bill Gordon, Chaim Kagedan, Neil Shah, Gregory Shill, Jennifer Shkabatur, J. B. Tarter, and Elisabeth Theodore. Candice, Tijana, and Elisabeth worked with me longer than the others. They had a knack for understanding my not-always-clear-or-coherent queries and quickly finding me just what I needed, at all hours of the day and night.

My assistant, Liane Speroni, helped me with many tasks, kept me organized and on time, and made sure everything got done the way it was supposed to be. The Harvard Law Library speedily tracked down a stream of "rush" requests for books and helped me in many other ways as well.

I was deeply fortunate to have the pro bono legal representation of two law firms in connection with this book. Jeffrey Smith, Robert Weiner, and Jon Michaels of Arnold & Porter helped me to marshal the book through the process of pre-clearance review for classified information. Don Ayer, Peter Romatowski, and Marc Ricchiute of Jones Day represented me in connection with the grand jury matter discussed in chapter 6. These lawyers provided me with outstanding legal and other advice. They were also fun to work with. It was a genuine honor to have them represent me.

My agent, Andrew Wylie, took this project on faith, for when we first met I really didn't know what I wanted to write about or how to write a book of this kind. When I sent Andrew the first version of my book proposal last summer, I got back the most brutal and helpful set of criticisms I have ever received. I am grateful for that and for Andrew's other help throughout the process. I am also grateful to Starling Lawrence, my editor at Norton, for agreeing to publish this book, for his patience during the unexpected delays in getting the manuscript into his hands, and for his helpful suggestions. And I am also grateful to the many people at Norton who helped get the manuscript in shape for publication, and to Mary Babcock for her extraordinary edits and other help.

My greatest thanks go to my wife, Leslie Williams, and my two sons, Jack IV and Will, for their love and patience. Leslie is the joy of my life whom I do not deserve; I dedicate the book to her.

I wrote this book quickly, and I worry that despite all of the help I received, it will contain mistakes, for which I alone, of course, am responsible.

NOTES

Preface

1. ELLIOT RICHARDSON, THE CREATIVE BALANCE: GOVERNMENT, POLITICS, AND THE INDIVIDUAL IN AMERICA'S THIRD CENTURY 43–44 (1976).

2. Here is a nonexclusive list:

Attorneys General: JOHN ASHCROFT, NEVER AGAIN: SECURING AMERICA AND RESTORING JUSTICE (2006); FRANCIS BIDDLE, IN BRIEF AUTHORITY (1962); HERBERT BROWNELL, ADVISING IKE: THE MEMOIRS OF ATTORNEY GENERAL HERBERT BROWNELL (1993); HOMER CUMMINGS, SELECTED PAPERS OF HOMER CUMMINGS, ATTORNEY GENERAL OF THE UNITED STATES, 1933–1939 (Carl Brent Swisher ed., 1939); ROBERT H. JACKSON, THAT MAN: AN INSIDER'S PORTRAIT OF FRANKLIN D. ROOSEVELT (JOHN Q. BARRETT ED., 2004); ROBERT F. KENNEDY, THIRTEEN DAYS: A MEMOIR OF THE CUBAN MISSILE CRISIS (1973); RICHARD KLEINDIENST, JUSTICE: THE MEMOIRS OF ATTORNEY GENERAL RICHARD KLEINDIENST (1985); EDWIN MEESE, WITH REAGAN: THE INSIDE STORY (1992); GRIFFIN B. BELL & RONALD J. OSTROW, TAKING CARE OF THE LAW (1986); RICHARDSON, *supra* note 1; ELLIOT L. RICHARDSON, REFLECTIONS OF A RADICAL MODERATE (2000); WILLIAM FRENCH SMITH, LAW AND JUSTICE IN THE REAGAN ADMINISTRATION: THE MEMOIRS OF AN

ATTORNEY GENERAL (1991); DICK THORNBURGH, WHERE THE EVIDENCE LEADS: AN AUTOBIOGRAPHY (2003).

Deputy Attorneys General: WARREN CHRISTOPHER, CHANCES OF A LIFETIME (2001); James Comey, Testimony before the Senate Judiciary Committee (May 15, 2007), *available at* http://gulcfac.typepad.com/georgetown_university_law/files/comey.transcript.pdf.

Solicitors General: *Legends in the Law: A Conversation with Robert H. Bork*, BAR REPORT, Dec.–Jan. 1998, *available at* http://www.dcbar.org/for_lawyers/resources/legends_in_the_law/bork.cfm; Drew S. Days III, *When the President Says 'No': A Few Thoughts on Executive Power and the Tradition of Solicitor General Independence*, 3 J. APP. PRAC. & PROCESS 509 (2001); Drew S. Days III, *Executive Branch Advocate v. Officer of the Court: The Solicitor General's Ethical Dilemma*, 22 NOVA L. REV. 679 (1998); Drew S. Days III, *In Search of the Solicitor General's Clients: A Drama with Many Characters*, 83 KY. L.J. 485 (1994); CHARLES FRIED, ORDER AND LAW: ARGUING THE REAGAN REVOLUTION: A FIRSTHAND ACCOUNT (1992); ERWIN N. GRISWOLD, OULD FIELDS, NEW CORNE: THE PERSONAL MEMOIRS OF A TWENTIETH CENTURY LAWYER (1992); Rex E. Lee, *The Advocate's Role in First Amendment Jurisprudence*, 31 GONZ. L. REV. 265 (1995); Rex E. Lee, *Lawyering for the Government: Politics, Polemics & Principle*, 47 OHIO ST. L.J. 595 (1986); *Rex E. Lee Conference on the Office of the Solicitor General of the United States*, 2003 BYU L. REV. 1 (2003) (reflections of Theodore B. Olson, Charles Fried, Thomas Merrill, Donald Ayer, Drew Days, Walter Dellinger, Michael Dreeben, Seth Waxman, Barbara Underwood, Kenneth Starr, Daniel M. Friedman, Frank Easterbrook, Keith Jones, Andrew Frey).

Office of Legal Counsel: DOUGLAS W. KMIEC, THE ATTORNEY GENERAL'S LAWYER: INSIDE THE MEESE JUSTICE DEPARTMENT (1992); JOHN YOO, WAR BY OTHER MEANS: AN INSIDER'S ACCOUNT OF THE WAR ON TERROR (2006).

Prosecutors: RICHARD BEN-VENISTE & GEORGE FRAMPTON JR., STONEWALL: THE REAL STORY OF THE WATERGATE PROSECUTION (1977); LEON JAWORSKI, THE RIGHT AND THE POWER: THE PROSECUTION OF WATERGATE (1979); WHITNEY NORTH SEYMOUR, UNITED STATES ATTORNEY: AN INSIDE VIEW OF "JUSTICE" IN AMERICA UNDER THE NIXON ADMINISTRATION (1975); JEFFREY TOOBIN, OPENING ARGUMENTS: A

YOUNG LAWYER'S FIRST CASE: UNITED STATES V. OLIVER NORTH (1992); LAWRENCE E. WALSH, FIREWALL: THE IRAN-CONTRA CONSPIRACY AND COVER-UP (1998).

State Department Lawyers: ABRAM CHAYES, THE CUBAN MISSILE CRISIS: INTER-NATIONAL CRISES AND THE ROLE OF LAW (1974); Abraham D. Sofaer, *Iran-Contra: Ethical Conduct and Public Policy*, 40 Hous. L. Rev. 1081 (2003); *cf.* Philip Zelikow, Annual Lecture at the Houston Journal of International Law: Legal Policy for a Twilight War (Apr. 26, 2007), *available at* http://www.hjil.org/lecture/2007/lecture.pdf.

White House Counsel's Office: JOHN W. DEAN, BLIND AMBITION: THE WHITE HOUSE YEARS (1976); LEONARD GARMENT, CRAZY RHYTHM: FROM BROOKLYN AND JAZZ TO NIXON'S WHITE HOUSE, WATERGATE, AND BEYOND (2001); SAMUEL ROSENMAN, WORKING WITH ROOSEVELT (1952); THEODORE C. SORENSEN, DECISION-MAKING IN THE WHITE HOUSE: THE OLIVE BRANCH OR THE ARROWS (1963); THEODORE C. SORENSEN, KENNEDY (1965); Miller Center Conference on the Role of White House Counsels in Presidential Politics and American Governance (Nov. 10, 2006), *available at* http://millercenter.virginia.edu/scripps/digitalarchive/conferenceDetail/11 (statements by Theodore Sorensen, Kennedy White House Counsel; Harry McPherson, Johnson White House Counsel; Judge Abner J. Mikva, Clinton White House Counsel; Peter Wallison, Reagan White House Counsel; Michael H. Cardozo, Carter Deputy White House Counsel; C. Boyden Gray, Bush (41) White House Counsel; Joseph Onek, Carter Deputy White House Counsel; Jane Sherburne, Clinton Special Counsel; Robert Lipshutz, Carter White House Counsel; David G. Leitch, Bush (43) Deputy White House Counsel; Michael J. Egan, Carter Associate Attorney General).

CHAPTER 1. The New Job

1. My description of the building's architectural facts is drawn from the General Services Administration, U.S. Department of Justice, Washington, D.C., *available at* www.gsa.gov (search for "Department of Justice").

2. *See* Theodore B. Olson, *Politicizing the Justice Department, in* THE RULE OF LAW IN THE WAKE OF CLINTON 151 (Roger Pilon ed., 2000).

3. *See* Vanessa Blum, *Curtains Raised for Change at DOJ?* LEGAL TIMES, Mar. 8, 2005; Vanessa Blum, *Ashcroft's Inner Sanctum,* LEGAL TIMES, Oct. 13, 2003.

4. DOUGLAS W. KMIEC, THE ATTORNEY GENERAL'S LAWYER: INSIDE THE MEESE JUSTICE DEPARTMENT (1992).

5. I have been told that Alberto Gonzales moved OLC back to its traditional spot when he became Attorney General.

6. Peter J. Spiro, *The New Sovereigntists: American Exceptionalism and Its False Prophets,* FOREIGN AFFAIRS, Nov./Dec. 2000, at 9.

7. Judiciary Act of 1789, ch. 20, §35, 1 Stat. 73, 93.

8. MASS. CONST. OF 1780. pt. I, art. XXX.

9. *See* Principles to Guide the Office of Legal Counsel (Dec. 21, 2004), *available at* http://www.acslaw.org/files/2004%20programs_OLC%20principles_white%20paper.pdf.

10. William P. Barr, *Attorney General's Remarks, Benjamin N. Cardozo School of Law, November 15, 1992,* 15 CARDOZO L. REV. 31, 35 (1993).

11. Confirmation Hearing on the Nomination of Jack Landman Goldsmith III to be Assistant Attorney General, Office of Legal Counsel, Department of Justice: Hearing before the Senate Committee on the Judiciary, 108th Cong. (2003) (testimony of Jack L. Goldsmith), *available at* http://frwebgate.access.gpo.gov/cgi-bin/getdoc.cgi?dbname=108_senate_hearings&docid=f:91347.wais.

12. William H. Rehnquist, *The Old Order Changeth: The Department of Justice under John Mitchell,* 12 ARIZ. L. REV. 251, 252 (1970).

13. *See* Principles to Guide the Office of Legal Counsel, *supra* note 9.

14. *Quoted in* NANCY V. BAKER, CONFLICTING LOYALTIES: LAW AND POLITICS IN THE ATTORNEY GENERAL'S OFFICE, 1789–1990, at 27 (1992).

15. EUGENE C. GERHART, AMERICA'S ADVOCATE: ROBERT H. JACKSON 221–22 (1958).

16. MAEVA MARCUS, TRUMAN AND THE STEEL SEIZURE CASE: THE LIMITS OF PRESIDENTIAL POWER 187 (1994).

17. *See* David Barron, *Constitutionalism in the Shadow of Doctrine: The President's Non-Enforcement Power,* 63 LAW & CONTEMP. PROBS. 61, 92–95 (Winter/Spring 2000); Frank H. Easterbrook, *Presidential Review,* 40 CASE W. RES. L. REV. 905, 919 (1990).

18. Youngstown Sheet & Tube Co. v. Sawyer, 343 U.S. 579, 634 (1952) (Jackson, J., concurring).

19. *See, e.g.*, Memorandum from Walter Dellinger, Assistant Attorney General, to the General Counsels of the Federal Government, The Constitutional Separation of Powers between the President and Congress (May 7, 1996), *available at* http://www.usdoj.gov/olc/delly.htm; Memorandum from Walter Dellinger, Assistant Attorney General, to John Schmidt, Associate Attorney General, Constitutional Limitations on Federal Government Participation in Binding Arbitration (Sept. 7, 1995), *available at* http://www.usdoj.gov/olc/arbitn.fin.htm.

20. David Gray Adler, *Clinton, the Constitution, and the War Power*, in THE PRESIDENCY AND THE LAW: THE CLINTON LEGACY 46 (David Gray Adler & Michael A. Genovese eds., 2002).

21. *See, e.g.*, Memorandum from Walter Dellinger, Assistant Attorney General, to Abner J. Mikva, Counsel to the President, Presidential Authority to Decline to Execute Unconstitutional Statutes (Nov. 2, 1994), *available at* http://www.usdoj.gov/olc/nonexcut.htm; Memorandum from Walter Dellinger, Assistant Attorney General, to Alan J. Kreczko, Special Assistant to the President and Legal Advisor to the National Security Council, Placing of United States Armed Forces under United Nations Operational or Tactical Control (May 8, 1996), *available at* http://www.usdoj.gov/olc/hr3308.htm.

22. *See* sources in note 17, chapter 4.

23. Adler, *supra* note 20, at 19.

24. OLC concluded otherwise, arguing that Congress had authorized the bombings via its appropriations for the bombings. Memorandum from Randolph D. Moss, Assistant Attorney General, Office of Legal Counsel, to the Attorney General, Authorization for Continuing Hostilities in Kosovo (Dec. 19, 2000), *available at* http://www.usdoj.gov/olc/final.htm. This conclusion flew in the face of the War Powers Resolution's insistence that authorization for war "shall not be inferred . . . from any provision contained in an appropriations act," but OLC argued that this provision from the 1973 War Powers Act was not binding on the 1999 Congress that appropriated for Kosovo. *Id.*

25. GRIFFIN B. BELL & RONALD J. OSTROW, TAKING CARE OF THE LAW 185 (1982) (emphasis added).

26. *See* Douglas Jehl, *The Conflict in Iraq: Prisoners; U.S. Action Bars Rights of Some Captured in Iraq*, N.Y. TIMES, Oct. 26, 2004, at A1.

CHAPTER 2. The Commander in Chief Ensnared by Law

1. GEOFFREY PERRETT, DAYS OF SADNESS, YEARS OF TRIUMPH: THE AMERICAN PEOPLE, 1939–1945, at 358 (1973).

2. FRANCIS BIDDLE, IN BRIEF AUTHORITY 210–11 (1962). The quoted text is Biddle's paraphrase of Baldwin.

3. *Id.* at 213.

4. *Id.* at 213, 218.

5. *Id.* at 219.

6. *Id.* at 219, 226.

7. *Id.* at 219.

8. *See* KENNETH S. DAVIS, FDR: THE WAR PRESIDENT, 1940–1943, at 426 (2000). *See also* PETER IRONS, JUSTICE AT WAR: THE STORY OF THE JAPANESE-AMERICAN INTERNMENT CASES 61–62 (1993).

9. GEOFFREY C. WARD, A FIRST-CLASS TEMPERAMENT: THE EMERGENCE OF FRANKLIN ROOSEVELT 455–56 (1989); *see also* JEAN EDWARD SMITH, FDR 171–73 (2007); JOSEPH E. PERSICO, ROOSEVELT'S SECRET WAR: FDR AND WORLD WAR II ESPIONAGE 32 (2001).

10. WARD, *supra* note 9, at 456.

11. GEOFFREY R. STONE, PERILOUS TIMES: FREE SPEECH IN WARTIME FROM THE SEDITION ACT OF 1798 TO THE WAR ON TERRORISM 222–23 (2004).

12. *See* PERSICO, *supra* note 9, at 7–8; CHRISTOPHER ANDREW, FOR THE PRESIDENT'S EYES ONLY: SECRET INTELLIGENCE AND THE AMERICAN PRESIDENCY FROM WASHINGTON TO BUSH 77–78 (1995).

13. *See* ANDREW, *supra* note 12, at 91; *see also* CURT GENTRY, J. EDGAR HOOVER: THE MAN AND THE SECRETS 210–11 (2001).

14. *See* ROBERT DALLEK, FRANKLIN D. ROOSEVELT AND AMERICAN FOREIGN POLICY, 1932–1945, at 225–26 (1995).

15. Franklin D. Roosevelt, Fireside Chat (May 26, 1940), *quoted in* DALLEK, *supra* note 14, at 225.

16. PERSICO, *supra* note 9, at 167.

17. *See* COMMISSION APPOINTED BY THE PRESIDENT OF THE UNITED STATES TO INVESTIGATE AND REPORT THE FACTS RELATING TO THE ATTACK MADE BY JAPANESE ARMED FORCES UPON PEARL HARBOR IN THE TERRITORY OF HAWAII ON DECEMBER 7, 1941, ATTACK UPON PEARL HARBOR BY JAPANESE ARMED FORCES, S. DOC. No. 159, 77th Cong., 2d Sess. 1–21 (1942), *available at* http://www.ibiblio.org/pha/pha/roberts/roberts.html.

18. *See* DAVIS, *supra* note 8, at 419–24; GREG ROBINSON, BY ORDER OF THE PRESIDENT: FDR AND THE INTERNMENT OF JAPANESE AMERICANS 64–65 (2001).

19. ANDREW, *supra* note 12, at 128; *see also* PERSICO, *supra* note 9, at 167–68.

20. BIDDLE, *supra* note 2, at 225.

21. I am grateful to Professor John Barrett for convincing me of this point.

22. ROBERT H. JACKSON, THAT MAN: AN INSIDER'S PORTRAIT OF FRANKLIN D. ROOSEVELT 59, 74 (2003). For a famous Roosevelt speech deriding "legalisms," see Franklin D. Roosevelt, Speech on Constitution Day, Sept. 17, 1937, *available at* http://teachingamericanhistory.org/library/index.asp?document=1100 ("I ask that [the American people] give their fealty to the Constitution *itself* and . . . exalt the glorious simplicity of its purposes rather than a century of complicated legalism").

23. Michal Belknap, *The Supreme Court Goes to War: The Meaning and Implications of the Nazi Saboteur Case*, 89 MIL. L. REV. 59, 89 (1980).

24. EUGENE RACHLIS, THEY CAME TO KILL: THE STORY OF EIGHT NAZI SABOTEURS IN AMERICA 22, 57 (1961).

25. Felix Cotton, *Death Penalty Asked for Eight Captured Spies*, WASH. POST, June 29, 1942, at 2.

26. *See* Week in Review, N.Y. TIMES, Aug. 2, 1942, § 4, at 2 (reporting contemporary polls by American Institute of Public Opinion).

27. Memorandum from Franklin D. Roosevelt to Francis Biddle (June 30, 1942), *cited in* David J. Danelski, *The Saboteurs' Case*, 1 J. S. CT. HIST. 61, 65 (1996).

28. Lewis Wood, *Army Court to Try 8 Nazi Saboteurs*, N.Y. TIMES, July 3, 1942, at 1, 3.

29. *The Shape of Things*, NATION, July 18, 1942, at 41.

30. Arthur Krock, *In the Nation: Civil Rights in the Saboteurs' Trial*, N.Y. TIMES, July 21, 1942, at 18.

31. Lewis Wood, *Supreme Court Is Called in Unprecedented Session to Hear Plea of Nazi Spies*, N.Y. TIMES, July 28, 1942, at 1, 10.

32. As quoted in RACHLIS, *supra* note 24, at 249.

33. BIDDLE, *supra* note 2, at 331.

34. *Id.*

35. Danelski, *supra* note 27, at 69.

36. Editorial, *Saboteur Case*, WASH. POST, Aug. 1, 1942.

37. Editorial, *The Saboteurs and the Court*, NEW REPUBLIC, Aug. 10, 1942.

38. U.S. DEPARTMENT OF DEFENSE, NATIONAL DEFENSE STRATEGY OF THE UNITED STATES (2005), *available at* http://www.defenselink.mil/news/Mar2005/d20050318nds2.pdf.

39. *See* Homer Bigart, *Berrigan Case a Mistrial on Main Plotting Charge; But Jury Finds the Antiwar Priest and Sister Elizabeth McAlister Guilty of Smuggling Letters at U.S. Prison*, N.Y. TIMES, Apr. 6, 1972, at 1; Linda Charlton, *Philip Berrigan Granted Parole*, N.Y. TIMES, Nov. 30, 1972, at 89.

40. James Ridgeway, *Manhattan's Milosevic: How You Can Do What the Government Won't: Arrest Henry Kissinger*, VILLAGE VOICE, Aug. 21, 2001, at 34; CHRISTOPHER HITCHENS, THE TRIAL OF HENRY KISSINGER (2001).

41. Harold Hongju Koh, *Transnational Public Law Litigation*, 100 YALE L.J. 2347, 2366 (1991).

42. Warren Hoge, *Pinochet Arrest Upheld, but Most Charges Are Discarded*, N.Y. TIMES, Mar. 25, 1999, at A6.

43. Warren Hoge, *After 16 Months of House Arrest, Pinochet Quits England*, N.Y. TIMES, Mar. 3, 2000, at A6.

44. Henry A. Kissinger, *The Pitfalls of Universal Jurisdiction: Risking Judicial Tyranny*, FOREIGN AFF., July/Aug. 2001, at 86, 92.

45. *See* Patrick Bishop, *Kissinger Shuns Summons*, DAILY TELEGRAPH, May 31, 2001, at 18.

46. *See* Larry Rohter, *As Door Opens for Legal Actions in Chilean Coup, Kissinger Is Numbered Among the Hunted*, N.Y. TIMES, Mar. 28, 2002, at A1.

47. *See* Steve Boggan, *'War Crimes' Claims: Kissinger Begins to Stoop under the Weight of Legal Scrutiny; Opinion Bears Down Pinochet; Judge Leaves the Way Open for Charge against Kissinger; Court Rejects Application to Arrest Nixon's Right-Hand Man over Covert CIA Activities in the 1970's,* INDEPENDENT, Apr. 25, 2002, at 5; Leslie Crawford, *Plea to Question Kissinger in UK Refused,* FIN. TIMES, Apr. 23, 2002, at 2.

48. Boggan, *supra* note 47, at 5.

49. Al Webb, *Ex-Aide to Nixon Rejects Criticism; Kissinger Sees No Rights Violations,* WASH. TIMES, May 2, 2002, at A12.

50. Charles J. Dunlap, Jr., Air Combat Command Staff Judge Advocate, Address at the Air and Space Conference and Technology Exposition: The Law of Armed Conflict (Sept. 13, 2005), *available at* http://www.afa.org/Media/scripts/Dunlap_conf2005.asp.

51. Glenn Frankel, *Belgian War Crimes Law Undone by Its Global Reach; Cases against Political Figures Sparked Crises,* WASH. POST, Sept. 30, 2003.

52. Amnesty International, "Collateral Damage" or Unlawful Killings?: Violations of the Laws of War by NATO during Operation Allied Force, June 6, 2000, *available at* http://news.amnesty.org/library/Index/ENGEUR700182000?open&of=ENG-332.

53. Neil A. Lewis, *U.S. Rejects All Support for New Court on Atrocities,* N.Y. TIMES, May 7, 2002, at A11.

54. *See* American Servicemembers' Protection Act of 2002, 22 U.S.C. §§ 7421–7433 (2002).

55. *The Shape of Things,* NATION, Aug. 8, 1942, at 103.

56. Memorandum from Jay S. Bybee, Assistant Attorney General, Department of Justice, to William J. Haynes II, General Counsel, Department of Defense, Potential Legal Constraints Applicable to Interrogations of Persons Captured by U.S. Armed Forces in Afghanistan (Feb. 26, 2002), *reprinted in* THE TORTURE PAPERS: THE ROAD TO ABU GHRAIB 144 (Karen J. Greenberg & Joshua L. Dratel eds., 2005) [hereinafter TORTURE PAPERS].

57. Memorandum from Alberto R. Gonzales, Counsel to the President, to President George W. Bush (Jan. 25, 2002), *reprinted in* TORTURE PAPERS 118.

58. Memorandum from Alberto R. Gonzales, *id.,* at 119–20.

59. *Id.* at 119.

60. *Id.* at 120.

61. *Id.*

62. *Id.*

CHAPTER 3. Fear and OLC

1. Curt Anderson, *Every Threat, Including Hoaxes, Appears in Daily Report for Bush*, STAR-LEDGER (Newark, N.J.), May 25, 2003, at 17; *see also* GEORGE TENET, AT THE CENTER OF THE STORM: MY YEARS AT THE CIA 231–36 (2007).

2. For the information in these last few sentences, see sources cited *supra* note 1.

3. TENET, *supra* note 1, at 99, 232.

4. Interview with James A. Baker.

5. Interview with James B. Comey.

6. *See* NATIONAL COMMISSION ON TERRORIST ATTACKS UPON THE U.S., THE 9/11 COMMISSION REPORT (2004) [hereinafter 9/11 COMMISSION REPORT].

7. DORIS KEARNS GOODWIN, NO ORDINARY TIME: FRANKLIN AND ELEANOR ROOSEVELT: THE HOME FRONT IN WORLD WAR II 310–11 (1995). For further descriptions of the map room, see ERIC LARRABEE, COMMANDER IN CHIEF: FRANKLIN DELANO ROOSEVELT, HIS LIEUTENANTS, AND THEIR WAR 21–23 (1988); JOSEPH PERSICO, ROOSEVELT'S SECRET WAR: FDR AND WORLD WAR II ESPIONAGE 161–62 (2001).

8. GEORGE C. MARSHALL, INFANTRY IN BATTLE 16 (2d ed. 1939). The book was actually published by the Military History and Publications Section of the Infantry School under the direction of then-Colonel Marshall, but it is customary to attribute the quote to Marshall himself. *See, e.g.,* ARTHUR M. SCHLESINGER, JR., THE CYCLES OF AMERICAN HISTORY 423 (1999).

9. Interview with Baker, *supra* note 4. Baker emphasized to me that he was not the first to use the "goalie" metaphor in describing the role of counterterrorism officials.

10. TENET, *supra* note 1, at 245–46.

11. Philip Shenon, *Threats and Responses: The Commission; Panel Plans to Document the Breadth of Lost Opportunities*, N.Y. TIMES, Apr. 11, 2004, §1, at 16.

12. JOHN ASHCROFT, NEVER AGAIN: SECURING AMERICA AND RESTORING JUSTICE 130 (2006).

13. Ron Suskind, The One Percent Doctrine: Deep inside America's Pursuit of Its Enemies Since 9/11 (2006).

14. Chitra Ragavan, *Cheney's Guy*, U.S. News & World Rep., May 29, 2006, at 32.

15. Dana Priest, *Covert CIA Program Withstands New Furor*, Wash. Post, Dec. 30, 2005, at A1.

16. Letter from Thomas Jefferson to John B. Colvin (Sept. 20, 1810), *in* 12 The Writings of Thomas Jefferson 418 (Andrew A. Lipscomb ed., 1903).

17. *Id.* at 422.

18. *See* Declaration of National Emergency by Reason Of Certain Terrorist Attacks by the President of the United States of America, *available at* http://www.whitehouse.gov/news/releases/2001/09/20010914-4.html. President Bush made his original emergency declaration retroactive to September 11. *Id.* In addition, on September 23, 2001, President Bush declared that the United States is in "a national emergency in response to the unusual and extraordinary threat posed to the national security, foreign policy, and economy of the United States by grave acts of terrorism and threats of terrorism committed by foreign terrorists." *See* Message from the President of the United States, Blocking Property and Prohibiting Transactions with Persons Who Commit, Threaten to Commit, or Support Terrorism, 147 Cong. Rec. H5964, *available at* http://www.whitehouse.gov/news/releases/2001/09/20010924.html. This emergency declaration has been renewed each year since, most recently in September 2006. *See* Continuation of the National Emergency with Respect to Persons Who Commit, Threaten to Commit, or Support Terrorism, 71 Fed. Reg. 55,725 (Sept. 22, 2006).

19. *See* Daniel A. Farber, Lincoln's Constitution (2003).

20. Harry V. Jaffa, A New Birth of Freedom: Abraham Lincoln and the Coming of the Civil War 362 (2000).

21. Letter from Abraham Lincoln to Albert Hodges (Apr. 4, 1864), *in* 7 The Collected Works of Abraham Lincoln 281 (Roy P. Basler ed., 1953).

22. Arthur M. Schlesinger, Jr., The Imperial Presidency 60 (1973).

23. Kenneth S. Davis, FDR: The War President, 1940–1943, at 600 (2000).

24. 88 Cong. Rec. 7044 (1942).

25. Davis, *supra* note 23, at 601.

26. Dana Milbank, *In Cheney's Shadow, Counsel Pushes the Conservative Cause*, WASH. POST, Oct. 11, 2004, at A21.

27. *See* President's statement on Signing of H.R. 2863, *available at* http://www .whitehouse.gov/news/releases/2005/12/20051230-8.html.

28. Kenneth T. Walsh et al., *The Cheney Factor: How the Scars of Public Life Shaped the Vice President's Unyielding View of Executive Power*, U.S. NEWS & WORLD REP., Jan. 23, 2006, at 40.

29. Jane Mayer, *The Hidden Power; The Legal Mind behind the White House's War on Terror*, NEW YORKER, July 3, 2006, at 44.

30. HOUSE SELECT COMMITTEE TO INVESTIGATE COVERT ARMS TRANSACTIONS WITH IRAN AND SENATE SELECT COMMITTEE ON SECRET MILITARY ASSISTANCE TO IRAN AND THE NICARAGUAN OPPOSITION, REPORT OF THE CONGRESSIONAL COMMITTEES INVESTIGATING THE IRAN-CONTRA AFFAIR, S. Rep. No. 216, H. Rep. No. 433, 100th Cong., 1st Sess. 11 (1987).

31. *Id.* at 11, 19.

32. *Id.* at 437.

33. *Id.* at 457.

34. *Id.* at 474.

35. Charlie Savage, *Cheney Aide Is Screening Legislation; Adviser Seeks to Protect Bush Power*, BOSTON GLOBE, May 28, 2006, at A1.

36. LOUIS FISHER, THE POLITICS OF SHARED POWER: CONGRESS AND THE EXECUTIVE 166 (3d ed. 1993).

37. Oral History: Richard Cheney, *Frontline* (PBS), http://www.pbs.org/ wgbh/pages/frontline/gulf/oral/cheney/1.html.

38. Mayer, *supra* note 29, at 44.

39. *Cf.* Interview with Vice President Richard B. Cheney, *This Week* (ABC television broadcast, Jan. 27, 2002) ("One of the things that I feel an obligation on, and I know the president does, too, because we talked about it, is to pass on our offices in better shape than we found them to our successors").

40. Council on Foreign Relations, *Making Intelligence Smarter: The Future of U.S. Intelligence, available at* http://www.fas.org/irp/cfr.html.

41. MELISSA BOYLE MAHLE, DENIAL AND DECEPTION: AN INSIDER'S VIEW OF THE CIA FROM IRAN-CONTRA TO 9/11, at 40 (2004).

42. *See* Nomination of Scott W. Muller to be General Counsel of the Central Intelligence Agency: Hearing before the Select Committee on Intelligence, 107th Cong. (2002) (opening statement of Sen. Bob Graham), *available at* http://www.fas.org/irp/congress/2002_hr/100902muller.html.

43. *See generally* ROBERT BAER, SEE NO EVIL: THE TRUE STORY OF A GROUND SOLDIER IN THE CIA'S WAR ON TERRORISM (2002).

44. STEVE COLL, GHOST WARS: THE SECRET HISTORY OF THE CIA, AFGHANISTAN, AND BIN LADEN, FROM THE SOVIET INVASION TO SEPTEMBER 10, 2001, at 425 (2004).

45. *See id.* at 425; 9/11 COMMISSION REPORT, at 132 & n. 123.

46. COLL, *supra* note 44, at 425.

47. *See* COLL, *supra* note 44, at 424–30; 9/11 COMMISSION REPORT, at 132–33.

48. 9/11 COMMISSION REPORT, at 93.

49. R. Jeffrey Smith, *Worried CIA Officers Buy Legal Insurance; Plans Fund Defense in Anti-Terror Cases,* WASH. POST, Sept. 11, 2006, at A01.

50. For CIA Agents, Insurance Sometimes Necessary, *Morning Edition* (NPR radio broadcast, Dec. 14, 2005).

51. *Id.*

52. Memorandum from John Yoo, Deputy Assistant Attorney General, Office of Legal Counsel, to Timothy Flanigan, Deputy Counsel to the President, The President's Constitutional Authority to Conduct Military Operations Against Terrorists and Nations Supporting Them (Sept. 25, 2001), *reprinted in* TORTURE PAPERS.

53. *Id.*

54. *Id.* at 24.

CHAPTER 4. When Lawyers Make Terrorism Policy

1. James Risen & Philip Shenon, *Traces of Terror: The Investigation; U.S. Says It Halted Qaeda Plot to Use Radioactive Bomb,* N.Y. TIMES, June 11, 2002, at A1.

2. Padilla v. Hanft, 423 F.3d 386, 388 (4th Cir. 2005).

3. A copy of Hamdi's birth certificate can be found at http://fl1.findlaw.com/news.findlaw.com/hdocs/docs/hamdi/hamdi92680birthc.pdf.

4. See sources cited in Curtis A. Bradley & Jack L. Goldsmith, *Congressional Authorization and the War on Terrorism,* 118 HARV. L. REV. 2047, 2106 n. 271 (2005).

5. Bob Woodward, Bush at War 15 (2002).

6. President George W. Bush, Address to a Joint Session of Congress and the American People (Sept. 20, 2001), *available at* http://www.whitehouse.gov/news/releases/2001/09/20010920-8.html. *See also* White House, The National Security Strategy of the United States of America 5 (2002), *available at* http://www.whitehouse.gov/nsc/nss.pdf ("The United States of America is fighting a war against terrorists of global reach. The enemy is not a single political regime or person or religion or ideology. The enemy is terrorism—premeditated, politically motivated violence perpetrated against innocents.").

7. Bruce Ackerman, *The Emergency Constitution*, 113 Yale L.J. 1029, 1032 (2004).

8. Bruce Ackerman, *Talk of 'War' Is Misleading and Dangerous*, Philadelphia Inquirer, Sept. 12, 2006.

9. *See* Bradley & Goldsmith, *supra* note 4, at 2068–70.

10. *See* National Commission on Terrorist Attacks upon the U.S., The 9/11 Commission Report 132, 485 n.123 (2004).

11. Authorization for Use of Military Force, Pub. L. No. 107-40, 115 Stat. 224 (2001).

12. *Id.*

13. *For Rumsfeld, 'War on Terror' Is Misleading Label*, Chicago Tribune, Dec. 12, 2006, at 23; Jane Perlez, *Briton Criticizes U.S.'s Use of 'War on Terror,'* N.Y. Times, Apr. 17, 2007, at A10.

14. Hamdan v. Rumsfeld, 126 S. Ct. 2749, 2775 (2006); *see also* Hamdi v. Rumsfeld, 542 U.S. 507 (2004) (plurality opinion).

15. *See* Andrew C. McCarthy & Alykhan Velshi, *We Need a National Security Court*, *in* Outsourcing American Law (forthcoming 2007).

16. *See* sources cited *supra* note 10.

17. I base this conclusion in part on a guess about what such a legal opinion might look like, in part on OLC's 1998 rationale for capturing and, if necessary, killing Bin Laden, see *supra* note 10, and in part on the assertion by Mike Scheuer, the head of Alec Station (the CIA unit tracking Bin Laden) and the founder of the rendition program, that lawyers (including Justice Department lawyers)

required a showing that each rendition target was a "threat to the United States and/or its allies." *See* Extraordinary Rendition in U.S. Counterterrorism Policy: The Impact on Transatlantic Relations: Hearing before the International Organizations, Human Rights and Oversight Subcomm. and the Europe Subcommittee of the House Foreign Affairs Committee 110th Cong. (2007) (statement of Michael Scheuer). *See also* Michael Scheuer, *A Fine Rendition*, N.Y. TIMES, Mar. 11, 2005, at A23.

18. *Hamdi*, 542 U.S. at 518.

19. Carlotta Gall, *A Nation Challenged: Taliban; Prison Sealed Off as U.S. Picks Inmates to Interrogate*, N.Y. TIMES, Dec. 30, 2001, at B1.

20. *See* Carlotta Gall, *Traces of Terror: Prisoners; Video Vividly Captures Prelude to Fortress Revolt*, N.Y. TIMES, July 16, 2002, at A15; Katharine Q. Seelye, *A Nation Challenged: The Detention Camp; U.S. to Hold Taliban Detainees in 'the Least Worst Place,'* N.Y. TIMES, Dec. 28, 2001, at B6; Christopher Marquis, *A Nation Challenged: The Fighting; U.S. Troops Reinforcing Safety of Base in Kandahar*, N.Y. TIMES, Feb. 16, 2002, at A9.

21. Interviews with current senior Defense Department official and former senior Defense Department official.

22. *See* Press Release, Office of the Press Secretary, President Discusses Creation of Military Commissions to Try Suspected Terrorists (Sept. 6, 2006), *available at* http://www.whitehouse.gov/news/releases/2006/09/20060906-3.html.

23. *See* Ann Devroy, *U.S. to Double Refugee Capacity at Guantanamo; Officials Make Plea to Cubans*, WASH. POST, Aug. 25, 1994, at A1.

24. Memorandum from Patrick F. Philbin, Deputy Assistant Attorney General, and John Yoo, Deputy Assistant Attorney General, Office of Legal Counsel, to William J. Haynes II, General Counsel, Department of Defense, Possible Habeas Jurisdiction over Aliens Held in Guantanamo Bay, Cuba (Dec. 28, 2001), *reprinted in* THE TORTURE PAPERS: THE ROAD TO ABU GHRAIB 29, 37 (Karen J. Greenberg & Joshua L. Dratel eds., 2005) [hereinafter TORTURE PAPERS].

25. Esther Schrader, *Response to Terror: POWs Will Go to Base in Cuba*, L.A. TIMES, Dec. 28, 2001.

26. Several public documents have referred to Philbin's memo on this matter:

Memorandum from Patrick F. Philbin, Deputy Assistant Attorney General, Office of Legal Counsel, to Alberto Gonzales, Counsel to the President, Re: Legality of the Use of Military Commissions to Try Terrorists (Nov. 6, 2001). *See,* e.g., http://leahy.senate.gov/press/200406/062204c.html.

27. Interview with Bradford Berenson.

28. These quotations are actually taken from a document under the signature of Fred Ikle, for whom Feith worked. *See* Memorandum from Fred Ikle, Undersecretary of Defense for Policy, to Alan Gerson, Acting Legal Counsel, USUN Mission, Re: UNGA Sixth Committee—Item 122—Status of the Protocols Additional to the Geneva Convention of 1949 and Relating to the Protection of Victims of Armed Conflicts 7 (Oct. 24, 1984). But Feith wrote the draft for Ikle (which made similar arguments to his essay on the subject, *see* Douglas J. Feith, *Law in the Service of Terror: The Strange Case of the Additional Protocol*, 1 NATIONAL INTEREST 36 (1985)) and was the person responsible for identifying and pushing Protocol I issue to a successful conclusion. In a memorandum sent to the Secretary of Defense through Ikle's office, Richard Perle, Feith's direct boss, gave Feith the credit, arguing that he "argued publicly and within the government that such action would be morally correct and a blow against attempts to weaken the laws of war as they pertain to the protection of civilian populations and against those who would legitimate terrorist groups." Memorandum for the Secretary of Defense through the Undersecretary of Defense for Policy from Richard Perle, Assistant Secretary of Defense for International Security Policy, Geneva Protocols Ratification Package—Information Memorandum (Feb. 26, 1987). And Ikle scribbled a handwritten note on the memo agreeing with Perle. *Id.*

29. Memorandum from George P. Shultz, Secretary of State, to the President, 1977 Protocols Additional to the Geneva Conventions of 1949 on Protection of War Victims (Mar. 21, 1986).

30. Message from the President of the United States, Protocol II Additional to the 1949 Conventions, and Relating to the Protection of Victims of Noninternational Armed Conflicts, Jan. 29, 1987, S. Treaty Doc. No. 2, 100th Cong., 1st Sess. (1987).

31. Editorial, *Denied: A Shield for Terrorists*, N.Y. TIMES, Feb. 18, 1987, at A22.

32. Editorial, *Hijacking the Geneva Conventions*, WASH. POST, Feb. 18, 1987, at A18.

33. Memorandum from William H. Taft IV, Legal Advisor, Department of State, to Alberto Gonzales, Counsel to the President, Comments on Your Paper on the Geneva Convention (Feb. 2, 2002), *reprinted in* TORTURE PAPERS 129, 133.

34. Memorandum from John Yoo, Deputy Assistant Attorney General, Office of Legal Counsel, and Robert J. Delahunty, Special Counsel, Department of Justice, to William J. Haynes II, General Counsel, Department of Defense, Application of Treaties and Laws to al Qaeda and Taliban Detainees (Jan. 9, 2002), *reprinted in* TORTURE PAPERS 38, 53–62.

35. Douglas J. Feith, *Conventional Warfare*, WALL ST. J., May 24, 2004.

36. Interview with Douglas Feith.

37. Feith, *supra* note 35.

38. Memorandum from Colin L. Powell, Department of State, to Alberto Gonzales, Counsel to the President, Draft Decision Memorandum for the President on the Applicability of the Geneva Convention to the Conflict in Afghanistan (Jan. 26, 2002), *reprinted in* TORTURE PAPERS 122, 122.

39. *Id.* at 123.

40. *See* Memorandum from George W. Bush, President of the United States, to the Vice President, Secretary of State, Secretary of Defense, Attorney General, Chief of Staff to the President, Director of CIA, Assistant to the President for National Security Affairs, Chairman of the Joint Chiefs of Staff, Humane Treatment of al Qaeda and Taliban Detainees (Feb. 7, 2002), *reprinted in* TORTURE PAPERS 134, 134–35.

41. U.S. Department of the Army, Field Manual No. 27-10, The Law of Land Warfare ¶ 71(a) (1956).

42. *See* Memorandum from William H. Taft IV, Legal Advisor, Department of State, to William J. Haynes II, General Counsel, Department of Defense, Memo Re: President's Decision About Applicability of Geneva Conventions to al Qaeda and Taliban (Mar. 22, 2002), *reprinted* in THE TORTURE DEBATE IN AMERICA 283, 307 (Karen J. Greenberg ed., 2005).

43. *See* Memorandum from George W. Bush, *supra* note 40.

44. Katharine Q. Seelye & Steven Erlanger, *A Nation Challenged: Captives; U.S. Suspends the Transport of Terror Suspects to Cuba*, N.Y. TIMES, Jan. 24, 2002, at A1.

45. Youngstown Sheet & Tube Co. v. Sawyer, 343 U.S. 579, 635 (1952) (Jackson, J., concurring).

46. Robert Kagan, *Power and Weakness*, 113 POLICY REV. 3 (2002), *available at* http://www.hoover.org/publications/policyreview/3460246.html.

47. Craig Whitlock, *U.S. Faces Obstacles to Freeing Detainees*, WASH. POST, Oct. 17, 2006, at A1.

48. Jeffrey Goldberg, *A Little Learning: What Douglas Feith Knew, and When He Knew It*, NEW YORKER, May 9, 2005, at 36.

49. *See* sources cited *supra* note 17.

50. *Cf.* Address by Philip Zelikow, Annual Lecture to Houston Journal of International Law: Legal Policy for a Twilight War (Apr. 26, 2007), *available at* http://www.hjil.org/lecture/2007/lecture.pdf.

51. Interviews with a current and a former senior government official.

52. Address by Philip Zelikow, *supra* note 50.

53. *See* Hamdi v. Rumsfeld, 542 U.S. 507 (2004).

54. *See* Rasul v. Bush, 542 U.S. 466 (2004).

55. *See* Hamdan v. Rumsfeld, 126 S. Ct. 2749 (2006).

56. *See, e.g.*, Scott Shane, *The Question of Liability Stirs Concern at the C.I.A.*, N.Y. TIMES, Sept. 16, 2006, at A12.

57. Linda Greenhouse, *Justices, 5-3, Broadly Reject Bush Plan to Try Detainees*, N.Y. TIMES, June 30, 2006, at A1.

58. Adam Liptak, *The Court Enters the War, Loudly*, N.Y. TIMES, July 2, 2006.

59. Press Release, *supra* note 22.

60. Scott Shane & Adam Liptak, *Shifting Power to a President*, N.Y. TIMES, Sept. 30, 2006, at A1.

CHAPTER 5. Torture and the Dilemmas of Presidential Lawyering

1. *See* Memorandum from Jay S. Bybee, Assistant Attorney General, to White House Counsel Alberto Gonzales, Standards of Conduct for Interrogation under 18 U.S.C. §§ 2340–2340A, (Aug. 1, 2002) [hereinafter Bybee Memorandum],

reprinted in THE TORTURE PAPERS: THE ROAD TO ABU GHRAIB 172 (Karen J. Greenberg & Joshua L. Dratel eds., 2005) [hereinafter TORTURE PAPERS].

2. *See* Press Release, The White House, President Discusses Creation of Military Commissions to Try Suspected Terrorists, *available at* http://www.white house.gov/news/releases/2006/09/20060906-3.html.

3. *See* Sen. Carl Levin, Senate Floor Speech on the Amendment to Establish an Independent Commission on Detainee Treatment (Nov. 4, 2005), *available at* http://www.senate.gov/~levin/newsroom/release.cfm?id=248311.

4. *See* 18 U.S.C. §§ 2340, 2340A.

5. *Id.*

6. JOHN YOO, WAR BY OTHER MEANS ix (2006).

7. Bybee Memorandum, *supra* note 1, at 176.

8. *Id.* at 207.

9. Interview with CIA lawyer.

10. Bybee Memorandum, *supra* note 1, at 172.

11. *See, e.g.*, 8 U.S.C. § 1369 (2000); 42 U.S.C. §§ 1395w–22(d)(3)(B); 1395dd(e) (2000).

12. Burnet v. Coronado Oil & Gas Co., 285 U.S. 393, 406 (1932) (Brandeis, J., dissenting).

13. *See, e.g.*, Memorandum from Walter Dellinger, Assistant Attorney General, to Alan J. Kreczko, Special Assistant to the President and Legal Advisor to the National Security Council (May 8, 1996), *available at* http://www.usdoj.gov/olc/hr3308.htm.

14. Bybee Memorandum, *supra* note 1, at 207 (emphasis added).

15. Interview with CIA lawyer.

16. Memorandum from Daniel Levin, Acting Assistant Attorney General, Office of Legal Counsel, to James B. Comey, Deputy Attorney General, Legal Standards Applicable under 18 U.S.C. §§ 2340–2340A (Dec. 30, 2004), at n.8, *available at* http://www.usdoj.gov/olc/18usc23402340a2.htm. Letter from Michael J. Garcia, U.S. Attorney, to Lawrence S. Lustberg et al., Re: ACLU et al. v. Department of Defense et al., No. 04 Civ. 4151 (Nov. 9, 2006), *available at* http://www.aclu .org/images/torture/asset_upload_file825_27365.pdf (enclosing CIA administrative

response with respect to items on plaintiff's August 16, 2004 list). *See also* ACLU, Responsive Records Specifically Identified in Plaintiff's May 25, 2004 Torture FOIA Request (Aug. 16, 2004), *available at* http://www.aclu.org/images/torture /asset_upload_file272_27380.pdf; Nomination of John Rizzo to be CIA General Counsel: Hearing before the Senate Select Committee on Intelligence, 110th Cong. (2007).

17. Interview with George Tenet, *60 Minutes* (CBS television broadcast, Apr. 29, 2007), *available at* http://www.cbsnews.com/stories/2007/04/25/60minutes/main2728375.shtml.

18. *See* GEORGE TENET, AT THE CENTER OF THE STORM 241–42 (2007).

19. *See* Memorandum from Donald Rumsfeld, Secretary of Defense, to James T. Hill, Commander, U.S. Southern Command, Counter-Resistance Techniques in the War on Terrorism (Apr. 16, 2003), *reprinted in* TORTURE PAPERS 360.

20. *See* U.S. Department of the Army, Field Manual No. 34-52, Intelligence Interrogation, *available at* http://www.fas.org/irp/doddir/army/fm34-52.pdf

21. Philbin explained our reasoning in testimony the following summer. Treatment of Detainees in the Global War against Terrorism: Hearing before the House Permanent Select Committee on Intelligence, 108th Cong. (2004) (statement of Patrick F. Philbin, Deputy Associate Attorney General).

22. Memorandum from William J. Haynes II, General Counsel, Department of Defense, to Donald Rumseld, Secretary of Defense, Counter-Resistance Techniques (Nov. 27, 2002), *reprinted in* TORTURE PAPERS 237.

23. *See* Nomination of William Haynes II to be U.S. Circuit Judge for the Fourth Circuit: Hearing before the Senate Judiciary Committee, 109th Cong. (2006) (statement of William Haynes). *See also* Press Briefing by White House Counsel Alberto Gonzales, Department of Defense General Counsel William Haynes, Department of Defense Deputy General Counsel Daniel Dell'Orto and Army Deputy Chief of Staff for Intelligence General Keith Alexander, June 22, 2004, *available at* http://www.whitehouse.gov/news/releases/2004/06/2004062 2-14.html; Department of Defense, Working Group Report on Detainee Interrogations in the Global War on Terrorism: Assessment of Legal, Historical, Policy, and Operational Considerations (Apr. 4, 2003), *reprinted in* TORTURE PAPERS 286.

24. *See* Military Justice and Detention Policy in the Global War on Terrorism: Hearing before the Subcommittee on Personnel of the Senate Armed Services Committee, 109th Cong. (2005) (testimony of Daniel J. Dell'Orto, Principal Deputy General Counsel, Department of Defense).

25. Letter from Daniel Levin, Acting Assistant Attorney General, to William J. Haynes II, General Counsel of the Department of Defense, *available at* http://balkin.blogspot.com/Levin.Haynes.205.pdf.

26. Jess Bravin, *Pentagon Report Set Framework for Use of Torture—Security or Legal Factors Could Trump Restrictions, Memo to Rumsfeld Argued*, WALL ST. J., June 7, 2004, at A1.

27. Dana Priest & R. Jeffrey Smith, *Memo Offered Justification for Use of Torture; Justice Dept. Gave Advice in 2002*, WASH. POST, June 8, 2004, at A01.

28. YOO, *supra* note 6, at 185, viii, 182.

29. Interview with former senior government official.

30. TENET, *supra* note 18, at 245–46.

31. David Johnston, *Uncertainty about Interrogation Rules Seen as Slowing the Hunt for Information on Terrorists*, N.Y. TIMES, June 28, 2004, at A8.

32. Memorandum from Daniel Levin, *supra* note 16.

33. *Id.* at n.8.

34. Press Release, Office of the Press Secretary, President Discusses Creation of Military Commissions to Try Suspected Terrorists, Sept. 6, 2006, *available at* http://www.whitehouse.gov/news/releases/2006/09/20060906-3.html.

35. *Id.*

36. Interview with Tenet, *supra* note 17.

37. NANCY BAKER, CONFLICTING LOYALTIES: LAW AND POLITICS IN THE ATTORNEY GENERAL'S OFFICE, 1789–1990, at 3 (1992).

38. Arthur M. Schlesinger, Jr., *War and the Constitution: Abraham Lincoln and Franklin D. Roosevelt*, in LINCOLN: THE WAR PRESIDENT (Gabor S. Boritt ed., 1992), 145, 157.

39. Letter to the Editor, Edward S. Corwin, *Executive Authority Held Exceeded in Destroyer Deal*, N.Y. TIMES, Oct. 13, 1940.

40. DANIEL PATRICK MOYNIHAN, ON THE LAW OF NATIONS 72 (1990).

41. Brown v. Allen, 344 U.S. 443, 540 (1953) (Jackson, J., concurring in the result).

42. Marcella Bombardieri, *Harvard Hire's Detainee Memo Stirs Debate*, BOSTON GLOBE, Dec. 9, 2004, at A1.

43. *See* Draft Memorandum from Jack Goldsmith III, Assistant Attorney General, to William H. Taft IV, General Counsel, Department of State, et al., Draft of an Opinion concerning the Meaning of Article 49 of the Fourth Geneva Convention as It Applies in Occupied Iraq (Mar. 19, 2004), *reprinted in* TORTURE PAPERS 366.

44. Dana Priest, *Memo Lets CIA Take Detainees Out of Iraq*, WASH. POST, Oct. 24, 2004, at A01.

45. Article 49 of the Convention prohibits "transfers" and "deportations" of protected persons to places outside of occupied territory for any reason. It also says that the "occupying power"—in Iraq, the United States—"shall not deport or transfer parts of its own civilian population into the territory it occupies." If the prohibition on deportation and transfer barred even temporary relocations of Iraqis to places outside Iraq, then the same terms in the same article seemed to bar the temporary relocation of American civilians into Iraq. But there were thousands of U.S. civilians working for the Coalitional Provisional Authority and in other capacities in Iraq, and no one thought their nonpermanent presence in Iraq was illegal. This conclusion was consistent with additional research suggesting that the purposes of Article 49 were to prohibit permanent relocations in and out of occupied territory. And so the draft memorandum concluded that the United States could relocate "protected persons" from Iraq "to another country to facilitate interrogation, for a brief but not indefinite period." It qualified this advice in two ways. First, the draft memorandum noted that the relevant sources of law did not indicate "exactly how long" a protected person could be taken from Iraq. It cautioned that a violation of Article 49 was a "grave breach" of the Geneva Conventions that would be a crime under the War Crimes Act, and recommended that any proposed relocations "be carefully evaluated for compliance with Article 49 on a case-by-case basis," and offered to provide additional advice as needed. Second, the draft noted that protected

persons temporarily relocated outside of Iraq would "retain the benefits" of the Geneva Conventions. Iraqis could be relocated for purposes of questioning, but the Convention's prohibitions on torture and on physical and moral coercion precluded anything rough. *See* Draft Memorandum from Jack Goldsmith, *supra* note 43.

46. *See* Confirmation Hearing on the Nomination of Alberto R. Gonzales to Be Attorney General of the United States before the Senate Committee on the Judiciary, 109th Cong. (2005) (response of Alberto R. Gonzales to questions submitted by Senator Edward Kennedy); Confirmation Hearing on the Nomination of Alberto R. Gonzales to Be Attorney General of the United States before the Senate Committee on the Judiciary, 109th Cong. (2005) (response of Alberto R. Gonzales to supplemental questions submitted by Senator Edward Kennedy); Confirmation Hearing on the Nomination of Alberto R. Gonzales to Be Attorney General of the United States before the Senate Committee on the Judiciary, 109th Cong. (2005) (response of Alberto R. Gonzales to questions submitted by Senator Patrick Leahy, submitted on behalf of Senator Carl Levin).

47. *See* Draft Memorandum from Jack Goldsmith, *supra* note 43.

48. Bombardieri, *supra* note 42, at A1.

49. *Id.*

50. Daniel Klaidman, Stuart Taylor Jr. & Evan Thomas, *Palace Revolt*, NEWSWEEK, Feb. 6, 2006, at 34.

51. James Comey, Intelligence under the Law, Remarks at NSA Law Day, Ft. Meade, Maryland (May 20, 2005), *in* 10 GREEN BAG (forthcoming 2007).

CHAPTER 6. The Terror Presidency

1. *See* JAMES RISEN, STATE OF WAR: THE SECRET HISTORY OF THE CIA AND THE BUSH ADMINISTRATION (2006); James Risen & Eric Lichtblau, *Bush Lets U.S. Spy on Callers without Courts*, N.Y. TIMES, Dec. 16, 2005, at A1. For the government's description of the program, see FISA for the 21st Century: Hearing before the Senate Committee on the Judiciary, 109th Cong. (2006) (statement of General Michael V. Hayden, CIA Director; statement of Steven G. Bradbury, Acting Assistant Attorney General, Office of Legal Counsel, Department of Justice);

Responses to Questionnaire on FISA for the 21st Century, Senate Committee on the Judiciary, 109th Cong. (2006) (answer of Lieutenant General Keith B. Alexander). *See also* FISA for the 21st Century: Hearing before the Senate Committee on the Judiciary (C-SPAN television broadcast, July 26, 2006), *available at* http://www.cspan.org.

2. I was very fortunate that three outstanding attorneys from the law firm of Jones Day—Donald Ayer, Peter Romatowski, and Marc Ricchiute—agreed to represent me before the grand jury pro bono.

3. Peter Baker, *Surveillance Disclosure Denounced; 'Disgraceful,' Says Bush of Reports,* WASH. POST, June 27, 2006, at A1.

4. *See* sources cited *supra* note 1.

5. Eric Lichtblau & David Johnston, *Court to Oversee U.S. Wiretapping in Terror Cases,* N.Y. TIMES, Jan. 18, 2007, at A1.

6. WILLIAM HOWARD TAFT, THE PRESIDENCY 47–50 (1916).

7. Letter from James Madison to Thomas Jefferson (May 13, 1798), *in* THE COMPLETE MADISON: HIS BASIC WRITINGS, at 257–58 (Saul K. Padover ed., 1953).

8. ARTHUR M. SCHLESINGER, JR., THE IMPERIAL PRESIDENCY x (1973).

9. John R. Ellement & Andrew Ryan, *Bomb Squad Removes Suspicious Object That Closed I-93 North,* BOSTON GLOBE, Jan. 31, 2007, *available at* http://www.boston.com/news/globe/city_region/breaking_news/2007/01/bomb_squad_remo.html; John R. Ellement, Mac Daniel & Andrew Ryan, *Suspicious Objects Found throughout Boston after Morning Bomb Scare,* BOSTON GLOBE, Jan. 31, 2007, *available at* http://www.boston.com/news/globe/city_region/breaking_news/2007/01/suspicious_obje.html.

10. Michael Levenson & Raja Mishra, *Turner Broadcasting Accepts Blame, Promises Restitution,* BOSTON GLOBE, Feb. 2, 2007, at A1.

11. Suzanne Smalley & Raja Mishra, *Froth, Fear, and Fury: Cartoon Devices Spur Antiterror Sweeps; Two Men Are Arrested,* BOSTON GLOBE, Feb. 1, 2007, at A1.

12. Message from Ed Davis, Boston Police Commissioner, to the Boston Police Department (Feb. 1, 2007), *available at* http://www.bpdnews.com/2007/02/message_from_the_police_commis_2.html.

13. Joseph Carroll, *Only 29% of Americans Say U.S. Is Winning War on Terrorism: Lowest Percentage Recorded to Date*, GALLUP NEWS SERVICE, June 22, 2007, *available at* http://www.galluppoll.com/content/?ci=27955.

14. Lydia Saad, *Public: Iraq War Far and Away Top Problem for U.S.*, GALLUP NEWS SERVICE, Mar. 22, 2007, *available at* http://www.galluppoll.com/content/?ci=26944&pg=1; Lydia Saad, *Americans View of 'Most Important Problem' Continues to be Iraq*, GALLUP NEWS SERVICE, June 22, 2007, http://www.galluppoll.com/content/default.aspx?ci=27949&pg=2.

15. Interview by Dr. Sidney Mathews, Major Roy Lamson, and Major David Hamilton with General George C. Marshall (July 25, 1949), *quoted in* Maurice Matloff, *Allied Strategy in Europe, 1939–1945, in* MAKERS OF MODERN STRATEGY FROM MACHIAVELLI TO THE NUCLEAR AGE 677, 681 (Peter Paret ed., 1986).

16. Paul R. Pillar, *Counterterrorism Gives, Iraq Takes Away: Responses to "Is There Still a Terrorist Threat?" Round 2*, FOREIGN AFF., Sept. 11, 2006, *available at* http://www.foreignaffairs.org/special/9-11_roundtable/9-11_roundtable_pillar-2.

17. The best treatment is JOHN MUELLER, OVERBLOWN: HOW POLITICIANS AND THE TERRORISM INDUSTRY INFLATE NATIONAL SECURITY THREATS, AND WHY WE BELIEVE THEM (2006).

18. Paul R. Pillar, *Even Hyped Threats Can Be Real: Responses to 'Is There Still a Terrorist Threat?' Round 1*, FOREIGN AFF., Sept. 7, 2006, *available at* http://www.foreignaffairs.org/special/9-11_roundtable/9-11_roundtable_pillar.

19. MUELLER, *supra* note 17, at 3.

20. *Id.*; James Fallows, *Declaring Victory*, ATLANTIC MONTHLY, Sept. 2006.

21. James Fallows, *Act as if Mueller Is Right: Responses to "Is There Still a Terrorist Threat?" Round 1*, FOREIGN AFF., Sept. 7, 2006, *available at* http://www.foreignaffairs.org/special/9-11_roundtable/9-11_roundtable_fallows.

22. Abraham Lincoln, First Lincoln Douglas Debate, Ottawa, Ill. (Aug. 21, 1858), *in* 1 ABRAHAM LINCOLN: COMPLETE WORKS, COMPRISING HIS SPEECHES, LETTERS, STATE PAPERS, AND MISCELLANEOUS WRITINGS 298 (John G. Nicolay & John Hay eds., 1907).

23. The best academic treatment of this issue, from which I have learned

much, is Eric A. Posner & Adrian Vermeule, *The Credible Executive*, 74 U. Chi. L. Rev. 865 (2007).

24. My account of Roosevelt's prewar efforts draws on Wayne S. Cole, Roosevelt and the Isolationists, 1932–1945 (1983); Robert Dallek, Franklin D. Roosevelt and American Foreign Policy, 1932–1945 (1995); Kenneth S. Davis, FDR: Into the Storm, 1937–1940 (1993); Kenneth S. Davis, FDR: The War President, 1940–1943 (2000); Doris Kearns Goodwin, No Ordinary Time: Franklin and Eleanor Roosevelt: The Home Front in World War II (1995); David M. Kennedy, Freedom from Fear: The American People in Depression and War, 1929–1945 (2005); Jean Edward Smith, FDR (2007).

25. Kennedy, *supra* note 24, at 384, 393; *see also* Robert Shogan, Hard Bargain: How FDR Twisted Churchill's Arm, Evaded the Law, and Changed the Role of the American Presidency (1999).

26. Kennedy, *supra* note 24, at 394, 401.

27. President Franklin D. Roosevelt, Quarantine the Aggressors (Oct. 5, 1937), *available at* http://sagehistory.net/worldwar2/docs/FDRQuar.htm.

28. Kennedy, *supra* note 24, at 440.

29. *Two Appointments*, Time, July 1, 1940; Arthur Krock, *Roosevelt Move Fails to Satisfy His Critics; Appointment of Knox and Stimson to the Cabinet, They Insist, Hampers rather than Helps Solidarity*, N.Y. Times, June 23, 1940, at E3.

30. Editorial, *The Cabinet Changes*, Wash. Post, June 21, 1940, at 10.

31. Editorial, *Two Appointments*, N.Y. Times, June 21, 1940, at 18.

32. Cited in Schlesinger, *supra* note 8, at 105.

33. Dallek, *supra* note 24, at 243.

34. *Id.* at 244 (emphasis added).

35. Smith, *supra* note 24, at 469.

36. *Id.*; Dallek, *supra* note 24, at 245.

37. Goodwin, *supra* note 24, at 142.

38. John H. Crider, *Pershing Would Let Britain Have 50 Old U.S Destroyers to Guard Our Own Liberty*, N.Y. Times, Aug. 5, 1940, at 1.

39. The quotations come from General Pershing's speech, in *id.*

40. Smith, *supra* note 24, at 471.

41. Shogan, *supra* note 25, at 178; *see also* Schlesinger, *supra* note 8.

42. Robert H. Jackson, U.S. Attorney General, to the President, Opinion on Exchange of Over-Age Destroyers for Naval and Air Bases (Aug. 27, 1940), *reprinted in* 34 AM. J. INT'L L. 728 (1940).

43. SMITH, *supra* note 24, at 472; SHOGAN, *supra* note 25, at 242–45, 259.

44. DALLEK, *supra* note 24, at 253.

45. DAVIS, FDR: THE WAR PRESIDENT, *supra* note 24, at 75.

46. SMITH, *supra* note 24, at 487.

47. GOODWIN, *supra* note 24, at 215.

48. COLE, *supra* note 24, at 414.

49. WARREN F. KIMBALL, THE MOST UNSORDID ACT: LEND-LEASE, 1931–1941, at 176 (1969).

50. KENNEDY, *supra* note 24, at 472.

51. COLE, *supra* note 24, at 414.

52. Lend-Lease Bill: Hearing on H.R. 1776 before the Senate Committee on Foreign Affairs, 77th Cong. 92 (1941).

53. *Id.* at 102.

54. DAVIS, FDR: THE WAR PRESIDENT, *supra* note 24, at 106.

55. Lend-Lease Bill, *supra* note 52, at 110.

56. *Id.* at 148. My interpretation of this sentence follows DAVIS, FDR: THE WAR PRESIDENT, *supra* note 24, at 106.

57. GOODWIN, *supra* note 24, at 215.

58. KIMBALL, *supra* note 49, at 241.

59. President Franklin D. Roosevelt, Speech on Lend-Lease at the White House Correspondents' Association Dinner (Mar. 15, 1941), *available at* http://www.miller center.virginia.edu/scripps/digitalarchive/speeches/spe_1941_0315_roosevelt.

60. CLINTON ROSSITER, THE AMERICAN PRESIDENCY 130 (1987).

61. SCHLESINGER, *supra* note 8, at 106, 109.

62. FRANCES PERKINS, THE ROOSEVELT I KNEW 340 (1946).

63. Posner & Vermeule, *supra* note 23, at 901.

64. ARTHUR M. SCHLESINGER, JR., THE CYCLES OF AMERICAN HISTORY 284 (1999); *see generally* RICHARD E. NEUSTADT, PRESIDENTIAL POWER AND THE MODERN PRESIDENTS: THE POLITICS OF LEADERSHIP FROM ROOSEVELT TO REAGAN (1991).

65. SHOGAN, *supra* note 25, at 190.

66. New York Times Co. v. United States, 403 U.S. 713, 729 (1971) (Stewart, J., concurring).

67. JOHN HART ELY, WAR AND RESPONSIBILITY: CONSTITUTIONAL LESSONS OF VIETNAM AND ITS AFTERMATH 52 (1995).

68. *Id.* at ix.

69. James Risen, *Bush Signs Law to Widen Legal Reach for Wiretapping*, N.Y. TIMES, Aug. 6, 2007, at A1.

70. *Id.*

71. SCHLESINGER, *supra* note 64, at 422.

72. *See* Tim Starks, *Pelosi Seeks to Change FISA Bill*, Cong. Q., Aug. 5, 2007, *available at* http://public.cq.com/docs/cqt/news110-000002567347.html; Press Release, Speaker Nancy Pelosi, Pelosi Requests Conyers and Reyes Offer Legalizations to Amend FISA 'As Soon as Possible' (Aug. 4, 2007), *available at* http://speaker.house.gov/0278pr/?id=0278.

73. *See* Lara Jakes Jordan, *Gonzales Issue Snarls Surveillance Law*, ASSOCIATED PRESS, Aug. 3, 2007, *available at* http://www.guardian.co.uk/worldlatest/story/0,,-6824136,00.html.

74. Detainee Treatment Act of 2005, Pub. L. No. 109-148, div. A, tit. X, 119 Stat. 2739 (to be codified at 42 U.S.C. § 2000dd to 2000dd-1).

75. Editorial, *Unchecked Abuse*, WASH. POST, Jan. 11, 2006, at A20.

76. President's Statement on Signing of H.R. 2863, the "Department of Defense, Emergency Supplemental Appropriations to Address Hurricanes in the Gulf of Mexico, and Pandemic Influenza Act, 2006" (Dec. 30, 2005), *available at* http://www.whitehouse.gov/news/releases/2005/12/20051230-8.html.

77. The Supreme Court agreed with Roosevelt when it struck down similar "legislative vetoes" as unconstitutional forty years later. INS v. Chadha, 462 U.S. 919 (1983).

78. Robert H. Jackson, *A Presidential Legal Opinion*, 66 HARV. L. REV. 1353, 1357 (1953). Roosevelt told Jackson that he believed his views on the legislative veto provision should be published in the future, but left the time and manner of doing so to Jackson's discretion. Jackson opted to reprint Roosevelt's memorandum in the *Harvard Law Review* twelve years later. *Id.*

79. In June of 2007, only 29 percent of Americans said the United States and its allies are winning the "war on terrorism." This was "the lowest percentage holding this view since the 9/11 terrorist attacks." Carroll, *supra* note 13.

80. SCHLESINGER, *supra* note 64, at 373.

81. Arthur M. Schlesinger, Jr., *War and the Constitution: Abraham Lincoln and Franklin D. Roosevelt, in* LINCOLN, THE WAR PRESIDENT: THE GETTYSBURG LECTURES 145, 174 (Gabor S. Boritt ed., 1992).

82. SCHLESINGER, *supra* note 8, at 326.

83. *Id.* at 418.

Afterword: Assessing the First Terror Presidency

1. *See* Remarks Prepared for Delivery by Attorney General Michael B. Mukasey at the 2008 Annual Meeting of the Federalist Society, Washington, D.C., Thursday, Nov. 20, 2008, *available at* http://www.usdoj.gov/ag/speeches/2008/ag-speech-081120.html; *see also* Remarks Prepared for Delivery by Attorney General Michael B. Mukasey at the Boston College Law School Commencement Ceremony, Newton, Massachusetts, May 23, 2008, *available at* http://www.usdoj.gov/ag/speeches/2008/ag-speech-0805236.html.

2. *See* 140, *supra.*

3. *See* ANDREW MCCARTHY, MEMORIES OF THE JIHAD (2008); STEVE COLL, GHOST WARS: THE SECRET HISTORY OF THE CIA, AFGHANISTAN, AND BIN LADEN, FROM THE SOVIET INVASION TO SEPTEMBER 10, 2001 (2004); 9/11 COMMISSION REPORT (2004).

4. At least three reviewers did not skirt these issues. *See* Benjamin Wittes, *The Proper Use of Power*, HOOVER DIGEST, *available at* http://www.hoover.org/publications/digest/13848117.html; Gabriel Schoenfeld, *In the Matter of George W. Bush v. The Constitution*, COMMENTARY (June 2008), *available at* http://www.commentarymagazine.com/printarticle.cfm/in-the-matter-of-george-w--bush-v--the-constitution-11388; Michael Barone, *The Overlawyered War*, U.S. NEWS & WORLD REPORT, Sept. 16, 2007, *available at* http://www.usnews.com/articles/opinion/mbarone/2007/09/16/the-criminalizing-of-warfare-has-brought-the-overlawyered-war.html.

5. Jonathan Mahler, *After the Imperial Presidency*, NEW YORK TIMES, Nov. 9, 2008, *available at* http://www.nytimes.com/2008/11/09/magazine/09power-t.html.

6. CHARLIE SAVAGE, TAKEOVER: THE RETURN OF THE IMPERIAL PRESIDENCY AND THE SUBVERSION OF AMERICAN DEMOCRACY 349 (paperback ed. 2008).

7. Quoted in MAHLER, *supra* note 5.

8. For Congress's actions, *see, e.g.*, the Authorization to Use Military Force, Pub. L. No. 107-40, 115 Stat. 224 (2001); Military Commissions Act of 2006, Pub. L. No. 109-366, 120 Stat. 2600. For Supreme Court cases, *see, e.g.*, Boumediene v. Bush, 128 S.Ct. 2229 (2008); Hamdan v. Rumsfeld, 548 U.S. 557 (2006); Hamdi v. Rumsfeld, 542 U.S. 507 (2004).

9. FISA Amendments Act of 2008, Pub.L. No.110-261 (July 10, 2008).

10. Military Commissions Act of 2006, Pub. L. No. 109-366, 120 Stat. 2600.

11. *Id.*

12. *See* William Ranney Levi, *Interrogation's Law*, YALE L. J. (forthcoming).

13. ARTHUR SCHLESINGER JR., THE IMPERIAL PRESIDENCY 287 (1973).

14. Hamdan v. Rumsfeld, 548 U.S. 557 (2006); Hamdi v. Rumsfeld, 542 U.S. 507 (2004).

15. Boumediene v. Bush, 128 S.Ct. 2229 (2008).

16. *Id.*

17. *Id.* (Scalia, J., dissenting).

18. There are nominal exceptions to this point, most notably Ex Parte Milligan, 71 U.S. 2 (1866), Ex Parte Endo, 323 U.S. 283 (1944), and New York Times Co. v. United States, 403 U.S. 713 (1971) (the Pentagon Papers case). But these cases did not have an impact on their respective wars (for they all came after or late in the wars), and they did not entail a change in judicial attitudes toward the president and national security.

19. THE COMMISSION ON THE INTELLIGENCE CAPABILITIES OF THE UNITED STATES REGARDING WEAPONS OF MASS DESTRUCTION 381, *available at* http://www.wmd.gov/report/wmd_report.pdf.

20. For the details in support of this claim, *see* Jack Goldsmith, *Secrecy and Safety*, THE NEW REPUBLIC, Aug. 13, 2008 (reviewing ERIC LICHTBLAU, BUSH'S LAW: THE REMAKING OF AMERICAN JUSTICE (2008)).

21. ERIC LICHTBLAU, BUSH'S LAW: THE REMAKING OF AMERICAN JUSTICE (2008).

22. Chris Roberts, Transcript: Debate on the Foreign Intelligence Surveillance Act, *available at* http://www.elpasotimes.com/news/ci_6685679 (Aug. 22, 2007).

23. Federalist No. 75; *see also* Federalist No. 70.

24. *See* http://opiniojuris.org/2008/11/05/president-for-the-world.

25. *See* http://www.preventwmd.org.

26. HARRY S. TRUMAN, YEARS OF TRIAL AND HOPE, 1946–1952 ix (1955).

INDEX